AF352423

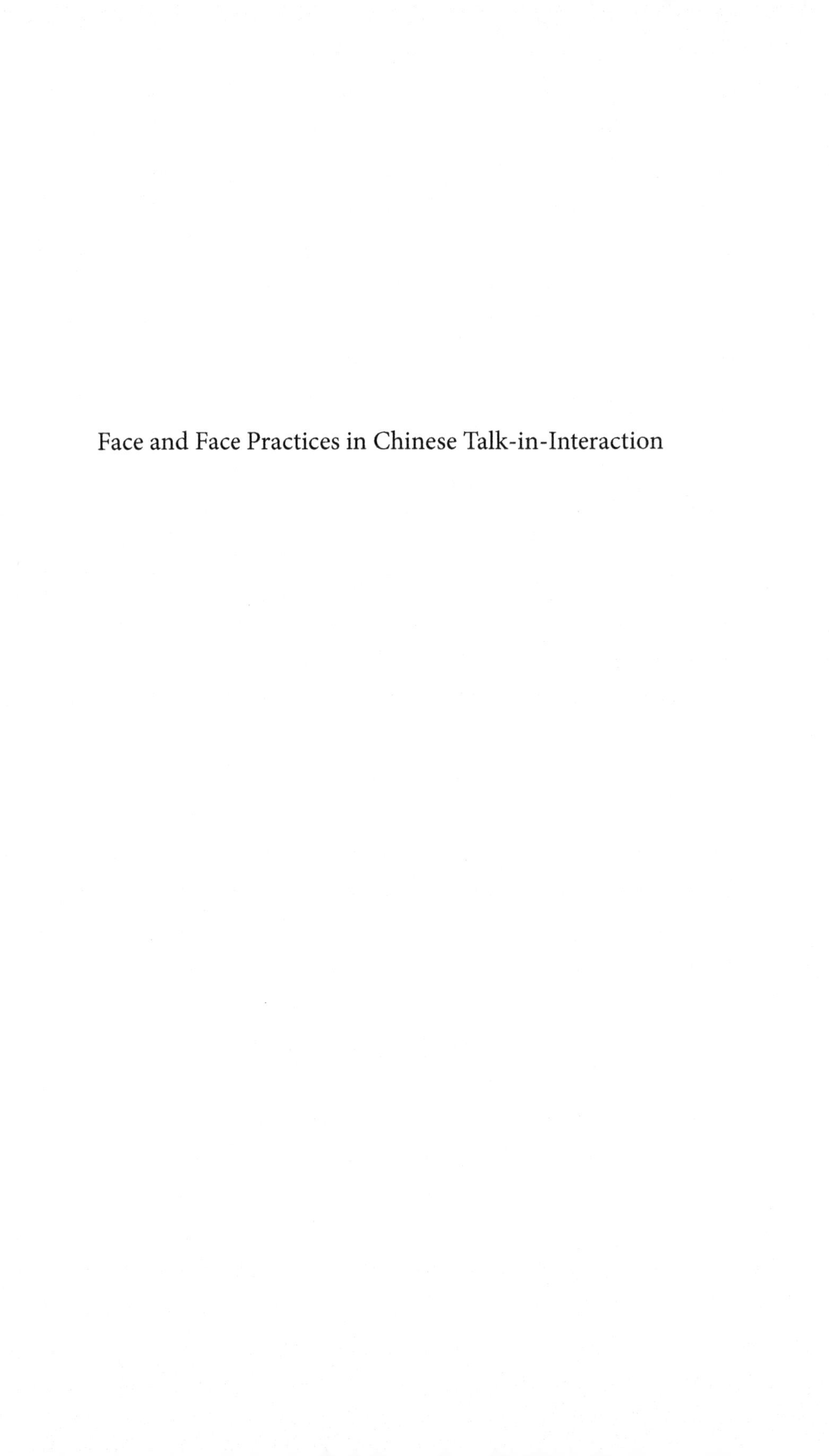

Face and Face Practices in Chinese Talk-in-Interaction

Pragmatic Interfaces

Series Editors:
Németh T. Enikő, University of Szeged
Dániel Z. Kádár, Hungarian Academy of Sciences
Károly Bibok, University of Szeged

In the last two decades it has become increasingly clear that language and language use cannot be studied separately and independently of each other. This new approach assumes an interaction between grammar (phonology, morphology, lexicon, syntax and semantics) and pragmatics. An analysis of the interfaces between each component of grammar and pragmatics (the 'interface view') can also be applied to hard-pragmatics and soft-pragmatics research. Hard-pragmatics studies the field of language use from philosophical, linguistic and logical points of view, while soft-pragmatics explores phenomena of language use from a social and socio-cultural perspective.

The definitions hard- and soft-pragmatics, adopted around the 1980s, have become somewhat dated since pragmatics has become a field of its own, and so these two trends have merged to some extent. Also, various pragmaticians made important attempts to blend these approaches. Nevertheless, a border between these areas continues to exist: hard-pragmaticians rarely venture into socio-pragmatic issues, and, vice versa, soft-pragmatic studies rarely make use of formal tools of hard-pragmatics.

Pragmatic Interfaces fills an important knowledge gap in the field of pragmatics as the first major publication project devoted to studying grammar–pragmatics interfaces and merging of soft-pragmatics with hard-pragmatics. Through this merging many pragmatic phenomena could be essentially revisited. *Pragmatic Interfaces* follows an interdisciplinary approach, allowing scholars from different areas of grammar and pragmatics to collaborate.

Published:
Impoliteness in Corpora: A Comparative Analysis of British English and Spoken Turkish
Hatice Çelebi

Forthcoming:
Politeness Phenomena across Chinese Genres
Xinren Chen

Face and Face Practices in Chinese Talk-in-Interaction
A Study in Interactional Pragmatics

Wei-Lin Melody Chang

SHEFFIELD UK   BRISTOL CT

Published by Equinox Publishing Ltd.

UK: Office 415, The Workstation, 15 Paternoster Row, Sheffield, South Yorkshire S1 2BX

USA: ISD, 70 Enterprise Drive, Bristol, CT 06010

www.equinoxpub.com

First published 2015

© Wei-Lin Melody Chang 2015

British Library Cataloguing-in-Publication Data

A catalogue record for this book is available from the British Library.

ISBN-13 978 1 78179 134 9 (hardback)

Library of Congress Cataloging-in-Publication Data

Chang, Wei-Lin Melody.

Face and face practices in Chinese talk-in-interaction : a study in interactional pragmatics / Wei-Lin Melody Chang.

pages cm. -- (Pragmatic Interfaces)

Includes bibliographical references and index.

ISBN 978-1-78179-134-9 (hb)

1. Chinese language--Discourse analysis. 2. Intercultural communication. 3. Pragmatics--Psychological aspects. 4. Nonverbal communication. 5. Facial expression. 6. Gesture. I. Title.

P302.15.C4C35 2015

495.101'45--dc23

2015010607

Typeset by Steve Barganski

Printed and bound in Great Britain by

Printed and bound by Lightning Source Inc. (La Vergne, TN), Lightning Source UK Ltd. (Milton Keynes), Lightning Source AU Pty. (Scoresby, Victoria)

Contents

Acknowledgements

There are many people who have contributed to my academic journey of writing this book, which started out as my PhD thesis at Griffith University. It would never have been accomplished without their generous support, priceless encouragement and valuable advice. Here I would like to acknowledge my indebtedness and gratitude to them all.

First and foremost, I would like to give my heartfelt thanks to Michael Haugh for his continuing encouragement and for generously giving his time and advice. I thank Michael for introducing me to interactional pragmatics and for sharing with me his insights into the field. Without his valuable suggestions and patient guidance from my original PhD project to the reading of the drafts, this book would not have been completed so smoothly. He has also been a great mentor and given kind support along the journey, especially during difficult and frustrating periods.

My special thanks go to Robert Arundale, whose extensive knowledge in interactional pragmatics made this book possible, from the earliest stage until the last phase of the book. I thank Robert for his valuable comments and discussions through reading earlier versions of this work. His continuous patience, encouragement and inspiration will always remain with me.

Further gratitude goes to Daniel Kádár, for his generous and kind support through giving me opportunities for research collaboration with him in the course of my PhD. His continuing support and kindness have had a profound influence upon my journey of learning how to be a researcher and to communicate with the scholarly community. I also thank Sue Trevaskes, for her perceptive advice on my research and an earlier revision of my typescript and for giving her time to comment on my work.

During the fieldwork, I also benefited from the assistance given by employees of Company H who kindly granted me access to their workplace and to the local government mediation sessions. Here I would like to show my appreciation to the employees and my personal contacts for their generous time and help, taking time to be interviewed and providing me with their insights.

My appreciation is also due to the Griffith Graduate Research School and School of Languages and Linguistics for their financial support. I would not have been able to complete my research without their generous assistance. I would also like to extend my gratitude to my colleagues at the School of Languages and Linguistics in Griffith University and many good friends in both Taiwan and in Australia for their continuous encouragement and support over the years.

Lastly, I would also like to express deep appreciation to my family, particularly to my father, who has been supportive of my research, and to whom I can hardly express my thanks in words. Without his help in employing his connections in Taiwan and being with me every step along the way, it would not have been possible to complete this book. I gratefully dedicate this book to them, and, of course, all the shortcomings of this book remain mine.

Transcription symbols and abbreviations used in morphological glosses

Transcription symbols (Jefferson 2004)

(.)	micro-pause
(0.2)	timed pause
( )	uncertainty about transcription
-	cut-off of prior sound in a word
hhh	hearable aspiration or laugh particles
CAPITALS	higher pitch volume
°	markedly soft speech
<u>underlining</u>	stressed word or part of word
↑↓	marked rises or falls in pitch
[ ]	overlapping talk
=	talk 'latched' onto previous speaker's talk
:	stretching of sound
?	rising intonation
(( ))	transcribers' description of non-verbal activity
><	rushed or compressed talk
%	code-switch (between Taiwanese and Mandarin Chinese)

Abbreviations used in morphological glosses (Wu 2004)

ASSC	Associative (-de)
CP	Complement
C	Classifier
INT	Interjection
N	Negation
PRT	Particle
Q	Question marker

CHAPTER 1

Introduction

1.1 Why this book?

Face, in a figurative sense, is associated with our social image, about which we can have feelings of pride, satisfaction, embarrassment or humiliation, and is thus something which every individual in society is concerned about. The earliest recorded use of the term 'face' is actually found in Chinese discourse, at that time being called *mian*, and was only borrowed by English in the nineteenth century in the form of the calques 'save face' or 'lose face' (Hinze 2002). Concern about face or *mianzi* has thus long been seen as an integral part of Chinese culture, through which every individual enacts their role, which is exercised through interpersonal relationships, as well as being exploited in various communication strategies. Anyone who has grown up in a Chinese community is invariably familiar with the expressions *mei mianzi* (without *mianzi*) or *diu mianzi/lian* (losing *mianzi/lian*), as they are deeply embedded in discourse about Chinese language and culture. The concept of *mianzi/lian* is regarded as an extremely important notion in Chinese society, and so is generally assumed to lie at the core of social practice and communication in Chinese.

As the term *mianzi* is prominent for the Chinese, a large number of studies on face have been produced with an emphasis on the conceptualisation of *mianzi* and *lian*, and theories of face specific to Chinese discourse. However, not many studies have focused on interactional aspects of face. In mainly focusing on discourse *about* face (*mianzi/lian*) researchers have not accounted for how face actually arises in Chinese communication. It is thus important to investigate face in actual conversations in order to gain an understanding of how face is interactionally managed and achieved in Chinese social interactions, and thereby achieve greater insight into Chinese culture. As a native speaker of Chinese myself, I have frequently observed or encountered face-sensitive interactions, both in intracultural and intercultural settings. Yet many current explanations for the Chinese collocations related to face issues, particularly for English speakers, can hardly grasp the whole picture, and what actually occurs often remains a mystery beyond what can be described by using Chinese folk notions. This has motivated me to investigate the underpinnings of face and discussion of its salience in Chinese communication. My purpose in this book is to unravel the complexity of sources which construct face and drive face practices in Chinese from emic perspectives with a specific focus on business settings. This book, I hope, will provide a more explanatory account for how face and face practices arise and for people's interpretations of face in talk-in-interactions that will help us gain a better understanding of face dynamics in social practice.

1.2 Outline of this book

Chapter 2 discusses previous research on face and the research on face to date, which highlights the importance of an interactional perspective on face. A number of studies that have explored face in the context of Chinese society are then discussed, focusing in particular on issues that have arisen from neglecting the interactional aspect of face. Based on this review it is argued that face should be constructed as interactional, relational and emotively invested, and as such is systematically addressed in current studies of face in Chinese. My goal in Chapter 2 is to demonstrate the significance of the inclusion of interactional and relational perspectives as well as the emotivities in investigating face in Chinese. The dynamics of these three perspectives play a key role in social practices in Chinese culture.

Chapter 3 describes the data sets, the theoretical framework and the contextual background of this project. The participants in the data are insurance company agents, their related clients and people involved in department store industry. Since business people in the insurance industry in Taiwan have considerable opportunities to negotiate insurance or business cases with their clients, they provide useful data to be examined in relation to face practices in business contexts. Therefore, this book seeks to provide insight through an interactional analysis of Taiwanese face, drawing from emic conceptualisations of *mianzi* and *lian* elicited through ethnographic analysis and post-recording interviews. These were employed in order to justify the analysis of the projecting and interpreting of face by the participants in interactions, and thereby gain an understanding of how face is interactionally achieved in business contexts. With the data from ethnographic and post-recording interviews, it is also hoped that those methodologies can support the emic conceptualisations of face elicited from Chinese speakers, elaborating the interplay between cognitive and relational dimensions of face. Following up the weaknesses in the field discussed in Chapter 2, I further argue that the unsolved issues can be addressed by drawing on Face Constituting Theory (FCT) (Arundale 2006, 2009, 2013) to explore the interactional achievement of face, focusing in particular on business negotiations conducted in a mixture of Taiwanese and Mandarin Chinese. In such contexts, business people and clients frequently encounter situations associated with face, and thus it is very salient in doing business, due largely in part to the importance of achieving a balance between profits and a good reputation in the business world (Chang & Haugh 2013). Drawing from both etic and emic perspectives, this book demonstrates that the dialectic of connection and separateness proposed in FCT is an integral part of interpersonal communication. The interconnection and interplay of cognitive and relational aspects of face is investigated through an interactional analysis employing FCT. The contextual background of business settings is also presented in this chapter. The data sets mainly involve both dyadic and multiparty business interactions in which insurance agents' visits to their clients and mediations of financial compensation are examined. Further details and conventions of business practices in the selected business industry of this research are therefore explained in this chapter.

Chapter 4 focuses on the analysis of ethnographic interviews with the native informants about emic concepts of face in Taiwanese business interactions. This provides an overview of native perspectives on the emic concepts of *mianzi* that are relevant to communication in business settings. Through the analysis four key themes emerged: (1) *mianzi* is a socially constructed image of persons or groups; (2) a close interrelationship holds between *mianzi, guanxi* ('relationship') and *ganqing* ('emotive quality'); (3) a dynamic tension exists between *mianzi* and pursuing *lizi* ('profit' or 'gain') which is likely to be specific to business negotiations; and (4) upholding *mianzi* and avoiding damage to it in business interactions is claimed to be crucial. This analysis hopes to contribute to our understanding of what business people *say* about face by drawing from the native informants' knowledge and experiences in relation to face.

The analysis of the interactional data is then presented in Chapter 5. A number of excerpts of the interactions from the dyadic insurance business negotiation and the multiparty mediation session are used to show how face is interactionally achieved in these institutional settings. In particular, there are five main face practices identified, and it is argued that they are employed to achieve the ultimate interactional goal, that is, in an insurance case, to increase or reduce the amount of compensation for the injured party involved in the car accident at the end of each interaction. Then the discussion in Chapter 6 comes subsequently to discuss and summarise the emerging themes in the business interactions. This chapter ends with a proposed alternative theoretical model for analysing face in

Chinese or even across cultural contexts. It is therefore suggested that face should be theorised by both taking a cognitive as well as interactional perspective into account, since face is not only conjointly co-constituted in interaction, but also constitutive of the interaction.

Finally, the conclusion in Chapter 7 reviews and summarises the face and face practices in Taiwanese business contexts. Implications for theorising face and the prospects for future research are also discussed. It is hoped that this book will shed light on theorising face from a more dynamic perspective and also contribute to the field of pragmatics in face research.

CHAPTER 2

Emic and etic perspectives on face

2.1 Theorising face to date

Studies focusing on face have been widely discussed in various academic fields, including psychology, sociology, social anthropology, intercultural communication, politeness and so on, since Goffman's pioneering works (1955, 1967) on face. His work inspired a series of examinations and analyses, as well as invoking numerous disputes and challenges in debates about theorising and conceptualising face over the past few decades. The foci of Goffman's concept of face have remained a significant force in theorising human communication, particularly in the field of linguistics. Goffman (1955) appears to have drawn from English calques of Chinese emic face evaluative terms in developing his theory of face, in other words, folk descriptions of face-related events based on the rich metalanguage of Chinese interpersonal interaction. He discussed, for example, how face can be *maintained, lost, saved* and *given* (pp. 213–215). These can be traced directly back to the Chinese expressions *you/gu mianzi, diu mianzi, liu mianzi* and *gei mianzi*, respectively (Hu 1944), as Table 1 shows.

Table 1. Chinese collocations of *face* vs English calques of *face*

Chinese collocations	Goffman (1955)
gu mianzi (顧面子)	maintain face
liu mianzi (留面子)	save face
diu mianzi (丟面子)	lose face
gei mianzi (給面子)	give/gain face

Goffman (1955, 1967) proposed an ethnographic approach for investigating face-to-face encounters where people make claims to face in social environments.

He defined face as follows: 'the positive social value a person effectively claims for himself by the line others assume he has taken during a particular contact' (Goffman 1967: 5). This definition of face describes human beings' interactional behaviour in terms of how participants continually position themselves in the contingent flow of their social environments. The *line*, according to Goffman, is explicated as patterns of verbal and non-verbal acts by which the participants express themselves during interaction. Thus, face is portrayed as an individual construction of self-image, or personal possession, which is created by the participant him/herself, and assessed or evaluated by others during the face-to-face encounters (Arundale 2006). Furthermore, the *line* is maintained by the participants who expect his/her attributes would be sustained as a particular face, including showing concern for the emotional states of others in contingent situations (Goffman 1967: 17). According to Goffman, face is thus constructed as an individual image with emotions attached to it, being consistently evaluated through one's display of personal attributes in the flow of interactional events. While face is an individual image, it is an impression formed by others through evaluating or assessing the lines of actions taken by one during contacts, rather than an image that one possesses of oneself. Face is specifically conceptualised according to Goffman as one's 'my your me' instead of 'my me' (Arundale 2009: 34; Haugh & Hinze 2003: 1585).

This concept was also later developed as the theory of facework as an interactional ritual where every individual maintains and saves the face of oneself and others through interaction (Goffman 1967: 14). To explain the social activities associated with face in interactional communication, facework is defined as follows: '[t]he actions taken by the person to make whatever he is doing consistent with face' (Goffman 1967: 12).

Based on Goffman's definition of facework, the actions taken that are inconsistent with face encompass both avoidance processes and corrective processes: avoidance processes are employed by participants to avoid threats to one's face, whereas corrective processes are used for saving face when it is threatened (Arundale 2009: 35). That is to say, every individual attempts to show concern for face reciprocally during encounters in order to uphold face, save face or even prevent face threats. One adjusts one's speech or behaviour according to one's face in order to avoid losing face or to save face in face-threatening situations. Goffman (1967) further noted about facework that '[w]hether or not the full consequences of face-saving actions are known to the person who employs them, they often become habitual and standardised' (p. 13). Facework is thus claimed as a ritual where people employ certain face-saving acts in social practices. In other words, individuals are ritualised in how to interact with each other thereby constituting facework within a society while dealing with threats to face, with this facework becoming particularly salient in instances where persons conduct remedial moves in face-to-face interaction.

Goffman's seminal work on the conceptualisation of face and facework has drawn attention from numerous scholars. One of the most famous works is that of Brown and Levinson's (1978, 1987) universal theory of politeness, which has been hugely influential in the area of social communication and interaction. They argue that the concept of face is the 'public self-image that every member wants to claim for himself' (Brown & Levinson 1987: 61). This concept coincides with Goffman's explication of face, which is conceptualised both as a self-image claimed by any individual, as well as being emotionally invested, since it can be maintained, lost, enhanced and so on (Chang 2008: 7). However, the notion of face here is more specifically emphasised as self-oriented and as a personal possession, which one projects to others for oneself. In other words, face as defined by Brown and Levinson is constructed as one's own desired self-image that one puts forward in goal-oriented interactions (O' Driscoll 1996: 9), rather than Goffman's conceptualisation of face, which is formed through others' evaluations or assessments.

Brown and Levinson further presented their theory of face as wants, the notion of negative face, positive face and attendant politeness strategies. Positive face is defined as the desire to be approved of or appreciated by others, whereas negative face is regarded as the want to be unimpeded by others (Brown & Levinson 1978: 63). The dimension of positive and negative face is claimed to be universal as their theory proposes that every individual has these two face wants (Brown & Levinson, 1987: 66). These two face wants are the core determinants underlying politeness theory. Brown and Levinson (1978) contended that there are certain kinds of acts which intrinsically threaten face (face-threatening acts, FTAs) as they may impede the addressee's or speaker's face wants (p.70), one being to create/maintain one's positive self-image (positive face), and the other being to avoid oneself being impeded by others (negative face). Therefore, according to Brown and Levinson's politeness theory derived from their notion of face, the degree of politeness should be considered when carrying out speech acts in order to avoid or even restore threats to these two face wants. Although what is desirable varies across cultures, it is argued that positive and negative face dualism can be applied universally to all language use (Brown & Levinson 1978: 67).

However, over the past few decades, a number of challenges to Brown and Levinson's conceptualisation of face have emerged in the discussion of their notion of negative and positive face. There are three key issues involved in the considerable debates surrounding Brown and Levinson's notion of face. The first is the claim that face is regarded as a self-oriented or autonomous self (negative face), which can be problematic when applied to different cultural contexts. Particularly in those studies which investigate Asian languages, it has been long argued that the notion of face should not necessarily emphasise avoiding imposition from others (Bargiela-Chiappini 2003, 2006; Chang 2008; Gu 1990; Haugh 2005; Mao 1994; Matsumoto 1988; Watts 2003; Yabuuchi 2004; Yu 2003). It is argued that the distinction between negative and positive face should be broadened and further developed in order to accommodate variation across different cultures (Haugh 2009a: 2), specifically with regard to the conceptualisation of negative face. For instance, when compared with Brown and Levinson's face, Chinese face emphasises public image rather than individual wants or desires. In other words, an individual values the community's judgment and perceptions of one's behaviour and character more than one's desires or wants to be unimpeded (Mao 1994: 460, self emphasis). On the other hand, face can be shared across groups of people, and is not merely restricted to being associated only with individuals (Haugh 2005; Ho 1976). For instance, Chinese face is shared by those to whom individuals are closely related, particularly in regard to sharing the honourable achievements of family members in Taiwanese society (Chang 2008: 22). It is apparent that Brown and Levinson's claim does not adequately explain face and facework as a universal concept, and thus the perspectives of cultural-specificity should be taken into account when analysing face and facework.

The second key issue that has emerged as scholars attempt to investigate face has been how to accommodate cross-cultural variation, focusing on how facework strategies are used in human communication in different cultural contexts (Domenici & Littlejohn 2006; Scollon & Wong-Scollon 1994; Ting-Toomey 1999, 2005b). Instead of being constructed by Brown and Levinson as the core of politeness, face is broadened by those North American researchers into a notion of personal identity, which is something people co-constitute with others during negotiations (Domenici & Littlejohn 2006: 13; Ting-Toomey 1999: 3). In this way, the focus of face moves towards a concern for I-identity and we-identity in communication theories, with particular emphasis on the dimensions of collectivism and individualism and the varying cultural value placed on them across different conceptualisations of face. Cultures that have a collectivistic orientation place greater emphasis on relationships in a community, which is 'we-identity', whereas individualistic-oriented communities tend to focus on more individual values or what they term an 'I-identity' (Domenici & Littlejohn 2006: 151–152; Ting-Toomey 2005b: 73–74). This move towards treating face as a form of identity examines cultures and societies at a macro level. However, the dimension of collectivism and individualism is seen as less salient in micro-interaction (Chang 2008: 11).

A third issue has also emerged that relates to the distinction between emic and etic perspectives on theorising face. An emic perspective is based on native participants' folk notions within a society, and aims to 'understand speech practices which make sense to the people concerned, i.e. in terms of indigenous values, beliefs and attitudes, social categories, emotions, and so on' (Goddard 2006: 2), whereas an etic perspective depends upon observations and distinctions judged appropriate by a community of scientific observers (Harris 1968: 571, cited in Harris 1990: 48).[1] For example, Brown and Levinson's argument that negative face is the desire that others do not impede the hearer's freedom is an etic concept. However, Gu (1990: 242) claims that, from an emic perspective of Chinese politeness when examining an invitation to a dinner party, the notion of negative face does not provide a coherent account. A Chinese speaker may insist on inviting the guest to dinner (the speaker also implies he/she will pay for dinner) even if the hearer has explicitly refused this invitation. However, this will not be interpreted by the native speaker of Chinese as a face-threatening act towards the guest's negative face. Instead, he/she thinks the speaker is being intrinsically polite, as the speaker's insistence indicates a genuine sincerity (*chengyi*). By taking an emic perspective on theorising face and politeness, that is, as a native speaker of Chinese, Gu invokes the folk notion in analysing Chinese face to justify his theoretical arguments against Brown and Levinson's face theory. This dispute between emic and etic perspectives thus draws attention to a theoretical tension that needs further work if we are to achieve a more innovative path in research on face.

Haugh (2009a: 4) argues that the debate about cross-cultural validity arising from Brown and Levinson's (1978, 1987) claim about universal face theory turns on a broader dispute about the validity of explanation of social behaviours rooted in the cognition of individuals versus explanation of norms shared across socio-cultural groups. In the development of research on face since Goffman's initial work on face and facework, there has been an underlying tension between a folk conceptualisation of face as a cultural state which constrains social behaviours and a theoretical conceptualisation of face as a cognitive state which motivates social behaviours. An interactional perspective potentially mediates between cognitive and socio-cultural perspectives on face. While there have been

---

1. The emic–etic distinction was first used and coined by the anthropologist Pike in 1954. It underlies the basic contributions of modern anthropology to the working world, which is the ability to understand and interpret other cultures (Headland 1990: 15, 17). It was originally based on the distinction between phon*etic* and phon*emic* approaches to sound in linguistics. A phonetic perspective analyses all the different sound distinctions possible. A phonemic perspective focuses on sound distinctions which are meaningful. For example, in English there is a difference in meaning between 'bed' and 'bet'. However, we make no distinction between aspirated and unaspirated 'k' (e.g. 'car'). Phonetically there is a difference between aspirated and unaspirated 'k', but not phonemically (Pike 1990: 31).

various challenges and debates on face research, Goffman's explication of face and facework has recently been subject to calls for more insightful and detailed analysis, as scholars have argued that his work laid the seeds for an interactional approach to analysing face (Bargiela-Chiappini 2003). Goffman (1967) claims that 'face is much more than just verbal behaviour. At such times [in interpersonal contact] the person's face clearly is something that is not lodged in or on his body, but rather something that is diffusely located in the flows of events in the encounter' (p. 7). As he defined face as 'something diffusely located in the flows of events in the encounter', he emphasised a more interactional approach to face. Bargiela-Chiappini (2003) re-introduced Goffman's concepts of face and facework by arguing that his sophisticated notion of interactional order could be further developed to accommodate a more valid explication of face and politeness theory.

It has been argued that Goffman's notion of facework in terms of 'interactional order' can be drawn on in examining cultural conceptualisations of the social self and its relationship to others, and so provide an alternative approach to analysing the relevance of face and facework in interpersonal interactions (Arundale 2006: 198; Bargiela-Chiappini 2003: 1463). Arundale (2006: 202) argues that face is more equivalent to relationships rather than identity, as relationship is a dyadic phenomenon whereas identity is essentially an individual phenomenon. He goes on to argue that 'framing face as relational rests directly on framing it as interactional' (Arundale 2006: 201) and thus conceptualising face as a relational phenomenon inextricably grounds it as an interactional phenomenon. Moreover, by defining face as 'a meaning or action, or more generally an interpreting, that a participant forms [about him/herself] in verbal and visible communication' (Arundale 2006: 201), face emerges through interactions as a joint accomplishment of interlocutors (Arundale 2006; Chen 1990). In other words, face emerges through perceptions and interpreting of the communicative acts, and thus is co-constituted in interaction (Haugh 2009a). Face is thus interactionally achieved through interactions by the social self as well as through the other participants' evaluations within a relationship. This alternative perspective of analysis on how face is framed on the basis of relational dimensions in the interaction promises a more insightful understanding of face and facework. According to these theories of face, face is thus fundamentally interactional, and yet is also an example of the surfacing of cognising in interaction. It is hypothesised that one's cognitive state of positioning or evaluating oneself in relationship with others might critically impact one's interaction with others.

However, on the other hand, while theories of face from an etic perspective seem to currently predominate in pragmatics (Haugh 2013: 54), this has highlighted the debate on the first-order and second-order theories of face. It is generally argued that face can be a term used 'by scholars from over the world to denote the same concept whatever their origin or specifics of their empirical application of it' (O'Driscoll 2011: 23). Even though the conceptualisation of face was originally derived from the Chinese, it is also assumed that 'the salience of the term "face" ... on the other hand, appears to be very cross-culturally limited. Moreover, even where comparable lexemes *are* salient, they do not appear to capture quite the same phenomenon ...' (O'Driscoll 2011: 22). Nevertheless, there is in fact extensive research on the conceptualisation of face from many different languages bringing in folk notions relating to face, particularly from Asian cultures, where face is highly salient (Chang & Holt 1994; Choi & Lee 2002; Gao 1996, 1998, 2009; Haugh 2005, 2007a; Haugh & Hinze 2003; Haugh & Watanabe 2009; Hinze 2005, 2012; Ho 1976; Hu 1944; Hwang, 1987, 2006; Lin & Yamaguchi 2007; Lim & Choi 1996; Mao 1994; Yabuuchi 2004). These second-order studies on face have essentially provided some important findings which suggest that second-order theories of face should be revived in order to enrich the conceptualisation of face in this field and to avoid under-theorising face by depending on only the etic perspective. Such formulations are theoretical (or second-order) constructs, but should also be informed by emic (first-order) understandings of meanings, actions and evaluations (of persons and relationships). On this view, it is incumbent upon the analyst that the meaning, action or evaluation not only has validity within the theoretical framework being utilised (Haugh 2007b: 310, 2009a: 10–12; Haugh, Chang & Kádár 2015: 77; cf. Arundale 2010a: 2094–2096, 2010b: 155–159), but is also consistent with the first-order understandings of the participants in the interaction being analysed.

In the following section, therefore, the Chinese origin of theories of face are investigated, with a particular focus on Chinese emic perspectives on face and related notions and how they can contribute insights to the theorising of face more generally.

2.2 Face in Chinese society

As mentioned earlier, the Chinese emic notions of *mianzi* and *lian* underlie much of the previous theorising about face. Numerous significant pieces of research on face draw from folk collocations of Chinese in explicating facework (Brown & Levinson 1987; Goffman 1955; Spencer-Oatey 2005), as Table 2 shows. Those Chinese face-related collocations were introduced into English and then re-theorised from an etic perspective. However, it is important to retrace the theories from the perspectives of their original home, rather than merely applying etic theories to explicate face in Chinese. Investigation of those two main emic concepts of face in

Chinese, *mianzi* and *lian*, is thus essential to gain a better understanding of face without neglecting its origin.

Table 2. Folk collocations in Chinese and face-related collocations in English

Chinese collocations	Goffman (1955)	Brown and Levinson (1987)	Spencer-Oatey (2005)
gu mianzi (顧面子)	maintain face	maintain face	in face
liu mianzi (留面子)	save face	enhance face	
diu mianzi (丟面子)	lose face	lose face	lost face
gei mianzi (給面子)	give/gain face	enhance face	gain face
	threaten face	threaten face	threaten face

2.2.1 Mianzi/lian

The use of face in both folk and academic discourse can be traced back to the Chinese term *mian*. While *mian* originally referred to the 'front of the head', being recorded in oracle bone script during the Shang dynasty (sixteenth to eleventh century BC), it was first extended to mean 'surface' and 'appearance', and then later extended to the figurative sense of 'reputation' or 'good name' around the fourth century BC (Hu 1944: 46). It developed various compounds and collocations over the centuries under the influence of Confucianism, serving as the basis for 'strengthening and expressing the harmonization of human relationships among men in society' (Cheng 1986: 340).[2] Some of the earlier compounds involving *mian* in Chinese included *mianmu* and *timian*, which were also borrowed by other Asian languages including Japanese and Korean from as early as the ninth century AD (Haugh 2005: 213–215). The borrowing of face in this figurative sense occurred in English more recently as a calque in the form of 'save face' and 'lose face' in the late nineteenth century (earliest Oxford English Dictionary entry is 1876). In early western/Chinese discussions about face, it was often glossed as 'false social appearance' (Hinze 2002: 20).

The emic concepts of Chinese face are represented by two main lexemes in Chinese: *mianzi* (面子) and *lian* (臉). In Hu's (1944) anthropological analysis of Chinese face, these two concepts are argued to be central social constructs for Chinese speakers. In her seminal paper, she differentiates the terms of *mianzi* and *lian* by linking with *face*, providing the definitions of these two emic notions of Chinese face. *Lian* is related to moral character with respect to others; it is 'both

---

2. *Lian* was first found in the written Chinese lexicon from around the sixth century AD and gained the figurative sense of 'good name' about the time of the Song dynasty (960–1279), and is thus not as old a term as *mian* (Hinze 2002: 85–86).

social sanction for enforcing moral standards and an internalised sanction' (Hu 1944: 45). On the other hand, *mianzi* is related to reputation achieved through success, ostentation and 'getting on in life' (Hu 1944: 45). Hu's (1944) pioneering investigation of those terms has inspired academics to further examine the metapragmatics or conceptualisations of face in Chinese, as the key terms for face, *mianzi* and *lian*, are invariably embedded in discourse about Chinese language, culture and social practice (e.g. Gao 2009; Ho 1976; Hinze 2005; Mao 1994; Yabuuchi 2004; Yu 2003). These studies investigating the folk or emic notion of face differ from Brown and Levinson's conceptualisation of face, as they involve ethnographic research, which entails undertaking emic analyses of 'face' in Chinese contexts. In other words, by explicating the use of Chinese collocations and expressions related to *mianzi* and *lian*, most studies of Chinese face have taken a largely emic perspective on face where they attempt to examine the concepts of *mianzi* and *lian* 'in terms of the conceptual schemes and categories regarded as meaningful and appropriate by native members of the culture whose beliefs and behaviours are being studied' (Lett 1990: 130). These explications of the emic concepts of face are thus ultimately based on how people ordinarily talk about and conceptualise particular interpersonal and social aspects of what they are doing; for example, expressions such as *diu mianzi/diu lian* (losing face), *you mianzi/you lian* (having face), *yao mianzi/yao lian* (wanting face). In the case of Chinese society, these emic concepts have developed over thousands of years into an explicit folk ideology of face (Chang & Haugh 2013: 2).

Mianzi is characterised as the socially constructed image of a person or a group of persons. In other words, *mianzi* is conceptualised as the positive value a person can claim for him/herself (or his/her group) through being acknowledged by others with a positive attitude, deference and approval during the flow of interaction (cf. Goffman 1967: 5). If they receive positive evaluations, such as compliments, respect, expressions of satisfaction, acknowledgments of superiority (including status and professional background) or trustworthiness, they interpret this as *you mianzi* ('having *mianzi*'). This positive attitude and feeling of respect between people has a key impact on *mianzi*, although only if it is mutually understood and acknowledged by both parties. *Mianzi* is thus socially constructed rather than being merely a psychological construct as Ho (1976) argues: 'a person's face is assessed in terms of what others think of him; the assessment does not include what a person thinks of himself, but may include what he thinks others think of him' (Ho 1976: 876).

This emphasis on *mianzi* as relating to feelings of respect and positive attitude expressed through interactions emerged, for instance, in the following excerpt from an ethnographic interview reported in Chang and Haugh's study (2013: 5).

(1) EI-W1: 2: 30

1   I: *Weishenme hui juede you mianzi?*

為什麼會覺得有面子?[3]

Why do you think [people] have *mianzi*?

2   W: *Mianzi…e… zhe zhong wenti, mianzi haoxiang shuo ni jieshou kending de shihou ni jiu juede shuo wo hen you mianzi.*

面子…呃…面子這種問題,面子好像說你接受肯定的時候,你覺得說我很 有面子。

Mianzi, well, it seems that when you are approved of by people, then you will feel 'you have *mianzi*'.

3   I: *mm*

嗯。

hmm

4   W: *Ni bei chengzan de shihou hen you mianzi, bei gua de shihou jiu hen meiyou mianzi, women jiandan xingrong dagai jiushi zhe yangzi de ganjue.*

你被稱讚的時候很有面子,被刮的時候就很沒有面子,我們簡單形容大概就是這樣子的感覺。

You would feel you have *mianzi* when you are praised; you would feel you lose *mianzi* when you are criticised. I think we can simply put it this way.

5   I: dui

對。

yes

((section omitted))

6   W: *… Zai ren gen ren zhijian de duidai limian, ou zunzhong, zhezhong zunzhong de ganjue du, ni jiu* ((Taiwanese)) *lí tō ū tsun-tiōng guá guá tō ū bīn-tsú, ou wo ganjue shi zhe ge yangzi, na haiyou yi zhong shi yi zhong taidu, na zhong suowei taidu zhijian de ganjue, ye hui zhao dao mianzi, ta bujiande jiu shi shuo,* ((Taiwanese)) *guá kā lí*

---

3. Here Chinese characters were provided as the majority of the responses from the interviewees were in Mandarin Chinese, with very minimal code-switching into Taiwanese. However, as the majority of the business interactions and negotiations were spoken in Taiwanese, which has no standardised phonological conventions and characters, only the romanisation of the transcription was presented in the following excerpts of the analysis chapter. This is to avoid misleading interpretations arising from the Mandarin Chinese characters if being used to represent Taiwanese phonologically.

> o-ló, a lí tō tsiok ū bīn-tsú e, *you shihou gua de ye hen you mianzi ye,*
> ((Taiwanese)) guá kā lí *gei ni yi xie ou, er, hen bucuo jianyi,* ((Taiyu))
> hō lí, *chansheng ou, ni keneng hui you zhengmian de yingxiang,*
> *huiyou lingwai yi ge guangming mian*
>
> …在人跟人之間的對待裡面,喔尊重,這種尊重的感覺度,你有
> 尊重我我就有面子(台語),喔我感覺是這個樣子,那還有一種是
> 一種態度…那種所謂態度之間的感覺,也會找到面子,它不見得
> 就是說,我稱讚你(台語),啊你就很有面子(台語),有時候刮的也
> 很有面子耶,我給你一些喔,呃,很不錯建議,給你(台語),產生喔,
> 你可能會有正面的影響,會有另外一個光明面。
>
> [*Mianzi* is generated] from the relationship between people. It's a feeling
> of respect (*zunzhong*). If you respect me, then I have *mianzi*. *Mianzi*
> also refers to an 'attitude'. [You can] also find 'mianzi' from the so-called
> attitude [between people]. It does not necessarily mean you have *mianzi*
> when I praise you; sometimes [you] will have *mianzi* when [you] are
> criticised [by someone]. I give you some good suggestions which may
> bring you some positive influence that is another promising aspect.

Reflecting the way in which face in Chinese is often described in the literature, this informant characterises *mianzi* as involving approval from others (turn 2), and as involving both a feeling and an attitude which are generated in relationships between people (turn 6). Interestingly, while the informant initially says that approval is shown through praise, and disapproval through criticism (turn 4), he later claims that being criticised does not automatically lead to loss of face. Indeed, criticism can also sometimes be recognised as 'having *mianzi*' in business settings (turn 6). In other words, when a person is criticised, he or she would not necessarily interpret it as face-threatening conduct if the criticism is positive or beneficial for him or her.

While Hu (1944) differentiated between *mianzi* and *lian* in terms of their moral import, in practice the two terms appear to point towards a common underlying concept. According to Ho (1976: 868), for instance, 'the concept of *mianzi* is not entirely devoid of moral content'. The meanings of *lian* and *mianzi* vary according to verbal context and in addition are not completely differentiated from each other in that the terms are interchangeable in some contexts. Consequently, although the distinction between the two sets of criteria for judging face – based on judgments of character and, broadly, of the amoral aspects of social performance – is justified, it cannot be anchored to a linguistic distinction between the two terms *lian* and *mianzi*, as proposed by Ho. Furthermore, Hinze (2005: 175) proposes that *mianzi* and *lian* can be distinguished in terms of the degree of face threat involved. *Mianzi* tends to be used for less serious FTAs, while *lian* is used for more serious FTAs. For example, a professor who reveals his/her ignorance at a departmental meeting might 'lose *mianzi*', but might be said to have 'lost *lian*' if he/she displayed ignorance in giving a key-note speech at an international conference.

Numerous studies of face in Chinese mainly focus on explicating the notions of *mianzi* and *lian* and their related collocations, as these are invariably embedded in folk and academic discourse about Chinese language, culture and social practice. This is typically how face-related studies are being studied, that is, through looking into folk discourse in Chinese contexts. More specifically, it has been given relatively little attention on the dimension of interrelationship between participants in regards to *mianzi* and *lian*, and expressions and collocations related to emic notions of *mianzi* and *lian* have been the foci in traditional research. Several scholars have proposed that the collective meanings of *mianzi*, *guanxi* and emotional components (*ganqing* and *renqing*) of Chinese social relations need to be investigated in terms of their interrelationships as these components are inevitably involved in face practices in Chinese social relationships (Chan 2006; Chang & Holt 1994; Gao, Ting-Toomey & Gudykunst 1996; Hwang 1987; Yang 1994), echoing Chang and Holt's (1994) argument that '*mianzi*, human emotion and interpersonal relations must be understood as a whole' (p. 103). Therefore, as *mianzi*/*lian* are situated within a broader network of cultural meanings, Chinese face needs to be understood with reference to relevant folk notions, including *guanxi* (interpersonal relations/social network*)*, *zijiren*/*wairen* (the dimension of inside/outside) and *ganqing* and *renqing* (emotivity), to be able to establish a more insightful analysis of face in Chinese.

2.2.2 Guanxi (interpersonal relations/social network)

Guanxi can be literally translated as relations or relationships between human beings. To say that people have *guanxi* indicates that they are interconnected as a group, which has implications for their relationships with each other (Chang 2008: 6). According to Chang and Holt (1994), *guanxi* is defined as a social source which is invoked by interactants through the functioning of face in order to establish interpersonal relationships or resolve interpersonal issues.

> *Guanxi* refers to the manner in which Chinese strategically employ relations as a social resource. It implies a close connection between people, an interlinkage which brings along with it interactants' special rights and obligations. It is this latter, deeper, more subtle level of meaning which paves the way for *mianzi* to function in solving interpersonal problems. Put simply, to grant *mianzi* is to acknowledge the importance or validity of the *guanxi* of the inter-

actants. *Guanxi* is the token which permits *mianzi* to work (Chang & Holt 1994: 106).

Having good or important relationships is reflexively crucial for one to be able to claim sufficient *mianzi* between interactants in order to achieve a particular goal or solve a particular problem by means of one's *guanxi*. In other words, *mianzi* is constructed in interpersonal relationships in which *guanxi* is implicitly embedded, and thus interactants have rights and obligations to conduct certain communicative acts. The most common circumstance where *guanxi* relates to *mianzi* is the use of such phrases as *kan wo de mianzi* ('to employ my *mianzi*') or *gei mianzi* ('giving *mianzi*'), either directly as appeals to *mianzi* in interactions, or reflexively to describe particular business interactions. Such direct appeals or reflexive uses of *mianzi* are possible only because the parties involved perceive that they have *guanxi*. In other words, *mianzi* is invoked when people ask someone with whom they have *guanxi* to help out or achieve some goals, particularly for achieving business aims. *Guanxi*, which encompasses both rights and obligations, is employed for establishing harmony and strengthening reciprocal relationships through facework, that is, through giving and/or saving face in Chinese contexts.

For instance, the same informant from the previous quote of Chang and Haugh's study (2013: 6) above, went on to explain face practices in terms of *guanxi*:

(2) EI-W1: 4: 07

7   W: *Zhe yeshi hen you mianzi de ou, yinwei renjia yuanyi qingnangxiangshou ma ... na zong shi you yi xie guanxi de ma. er xiang lao qianbei kan de qi wanbei de hua, xiang wo qianbei ou, ta jiu hui zhen de ba ta suoyou yiqian cengjing xue guo de dongxi, ta jingli guo de dongxi, jiao women hen duo.*

這個也是很有面子喔,因爲人家願意傾囊相授嘛...那總是有一些關係的嘛。呃像老前輩看得起晚輩的話,像我的前輩喔,他就會真的把他所有以前曾經學過的東西,他經歷過的東西,教我們很多。

This can be also [interpreted as] 'have *mianzi*' because the person would like to 'empty one's pocket to give' (*qingnangxiangshou*,) ... [it indicates] there's a relationship (*guanxi*) [between people]. It's like a forerunner values a junior. Like [one of] my superiors, he really teaches us a lot about what he has learned and his experiences. [He] teaches us a lot.

The informant uses the idiomatic expression *qingnangxiangshou* (literally 'to empty one's pockets to give') here to show how the person making the criticism is actually giving everything he or she has, whether material things, skills or ideas and so on, without hiding anything from the person being criticised. This means that criticisms made in business contexts, according to the informant, can be interpreted as *you mianzi* ('having *mianzi*'), since criticism illuminates the intimate *guanxi* ('relationship') between those two people. Gao and Ting-Toomey (1998) also suggest that 'in Chinese culture, criticism often is perceived as affectively based and relational in nature' (cited in Gao 2009: 185). 'Having *mianzi*' can thus involve an intimate attitude and positive feelings which are indexed through criticism between people who have *guanxi*. The level of intimacy and interpersonal attitudes that are reflexively indexed through evaluations from others are all crucial factors that impact on *mianzi* in business networks.

From this example, then, it can be seen that *guanxi* ('relationship') is a crucial element involved in the interactional achievement of *mianzi* in business settings. The close link between *guanxi* and *mianzi* thus emerges as an important dimension of the emic conceptualisation of face. *Guanxi* denotes the relationship, network or social capital that circulates in reciprocal business relationships as noted for Chinese interactions more broadly (Hwang 1987). In many circumstances where *guanxi* is involved, it often relates to the concept of *mianzi* or, reflexively, *mianzi* is used in social interactions, particularly in business contexts. Such direct appeals or reflexive uses of *mianzi* are only possible because the parties involved perceive that they have *guanxi* in the first place. In other words, *mianzi* is invoked when people ask someone with whom they have *guanxi* to help out or achieve some particular business aim. *Guanxi*, which encompasses both rights and obligations, is thus employed in establishing harmony and strengthening reciprocal relationships through giving and/or saving *mianzi* (Pan 2000: 68–71). However, the employment of *guanxi* is not limited to those who are already directly acquainted. One can ask a favour of someone whom one does not know, for instance, as long as there is an intermediary who mediates the *guanxi* between oneself and the other party. The person gives the intermediary *mianzi* by agreeing to the request from the third party, thereby also giving the one who asked the favour *mianzi* in passing (Chang & Haugh 2013: 7).

Therefore, *guanxi* can be emphasised in regard to Chinese social life as a vehicle which drives facework in Chinese, as it is originally derived from the philosophical ideal of Chinese relationships. According to Confucian philosophy, harmony and stability of a society are possible when the five basic relationships are maintained: (1) father–son (the relation of closeness), (2) emperor–subject (the relation of righteousness), (3) husband–wife (the relation of distinction), (4) elder–younger (the relation of order) and (5) friend–friend (the relation of faithfulness) (Chang & Holt 1994: 103–104). These role relations indicate that accompanying the positions that one holds are particular responsibilities marked through differentiated status, which highlight a network of role interdependency within Chinese society (Yang 1992; cited in Goodwin & Tang 1996: 295). In other words, through interpersonal *guanxi* built between participants within Chinese society, the notion of face and facework is an important mechanism by which to manifest obligation and reciprocity (Yang 1994: 140). As it is important to acknowledge 'differing orders of relationship (that) provide the context in which *mianzi* is to be played out according to the varying degrees of relationship' (Chang & Holt 1994: 105), *guanxi* thus becomes the motivation for individuals to be concerned about face. Likewise, facework can be a lubricant for Chinese negotiators to develop dynamics in the network, particularly in business contexts, 'if *guanxi* is perceived as an infrastructure of the relationship network' (Leung & Chan 2003: 1593). Having an acquaintance within the network of *guanxi* is therefore believed to make negotiations easier.

It is also worth noting that *mianzi* is found to be more salient in terms of constraining the art of *guanxi* than *lian* (Chang & Haugh 2013; Hinze 2002; Yang 1994). Hinze, for instance, argues that the notion of *mianzi* is crucial to the maintenance and development of interpersonal relationships in Chinese society. There are also more Chinese collocations related to *mianzi* than *lian* used in interpersonal contexts to request assistance from others, reciprocate favours, negotiate resource allocation, mediate disputes, gain compliance, establish solidarity, and manage the image of self and others (2002: 218). Consequently, *mianzi* seems, predominately in the domain of *guanxi*, to be a significant component in maintaining and constructing interpersonal relationships.

2.2.3 Zijiren/wairen (the dimension of inside/outside)

Zijiren and *wairen* are two important emic concepts within Chinese society, encompassing a distinction between in-group and out-group members (Gabrenya and Hwang 1996; Gao, Ting-Toomey & Gudykunst 1996; Goodwin & Tang 1996; Scollon & Wong-Scollon 1991). According to Gu (1990), *zijiren* encompasses two categories: automatic and selected. Automatic insiders include kinship members, colleagues and classmates, whereas selected ones have a special connection or relations which are developed over time through a workplace or elsewhere (cited in Gao 1996: 87). While *zijiren* refers to in-group members who have lasting or kin relationships, *wairen* are out-group members who do not have kinship or connective ties (Gabrenya & Hwang 1996: 311). The connection between the *zijiren–wairen* distinction and *guanxi* is that the distinction between insider and outsider is inevitably constructed in the context of relationship development. Accordingly, the importance placed on the *zijiren–wairen* dimension illustrates that the maintenance of relationships lies at the core of social communication in Chinese society.

This distinction between *zijiren* and *wairen* not only positions people in different relational circles, but also invests their place (*wei*) with particular rules in Chinese interpersonal interactions (Gao 1996: 87). In other words, while the dimension of *zijiren* and *wairen* is embedded in Chinese social interactions, distinctive patterns of communication based on this relational principle varies accordingly. To illustrate, the expectation within Chinese speakers is that *zijiren* and *wairen* are treated in different ways, as *zijiren* shares a sense of unity and interdependency (Gao, Ting-Toomey & Gudykunst 1996: 228; Yang 1992). This dimension thus determines ways of communication which differ based on this dichotomy. For instance, once a person is recognised as *zijiren*, he/she benefits from privileges and special consideration, and subsequently the relationship of *zijiren* tends to stay very solid. More precisely, one can help out a *zijiren* in various ways, while a *wairen* needs to follow the rules (Gao 1996: 87–88). Nevertheless, it is also argued that in intimate relationships, particularly in family relationships, imperative requests are more appropriate, while interrogative requests are expected to be used with others (Wierzbicka 1996). This explains why people within a *zijiren* group have more obligations and are more affection-oriented. With regard to the insider effect in terms of unity and interdependency, the Chinese self tends to bear responsibility and obligation to protect face or favour benefits of in-group members, whereas out-group members can be treated rather differently. On the other hand, the process of the transformation from *wairen* to *zijiren* involves a time-consuming and arduous development process, since it takes a long time to develop a close and intimate interpersonal relationship in Chinese society. In the development of relationships through a period of time, researchers argue that Chinese individuals are more likely to express emotions with intimate friends rather than with strangers or acquaintances, and tend to deal with problems by having 'heart-to-heart' conversations with their co-workers, friends and family (Krone, Garrett & Chen 1992: 288; Schneider 1985). In contrast, as *wairen* are not regarded as lying within the same social circle, they are often excluded from communication contexts, thus Chinese speakers rarely involve strangers in their conversations. For this reason, Chinese individuals are occasionally perceived as distant and cold to outsiders (Bo 1992, cited in Gao, Ting-Toomey & Gudykunst 1996: 228). This *zijiren–wairen* distinction thus arguably highlights that Chinese communication is heavily emotionally invested, and that face practices in Chinese contexts might vary in reflecting this dichotomy. In this discussion, then, it has been argued that the relational aspect of emic notions should be taken into account when analysing face in Chinese contexts.

2.2.4 Emotivity (ganqing and renqing)

While the relational aspect of emic concepts is relevant to face in Chinese as discussed previously, communication in Chinese contexts is also highly emotionally invested. As Chang and Holt argue, a good relationship is built through emotional components as its basis, which also actively and reflexively maintains the relationship (1994: 86). It is thus further claimed that giving life to a relationship is achieved through showing an appropriate amount of human emotion (Chang & Holt 1994: 110). That is to say, showing emotions serves as a fundamental mechanism to maintaining as well as establishing relationships. *Ganqing* and *renqing* are the two key emic notions of emotivity in Chinese. These two emic concepts are both translated as 'emotion' in English, and yet, to some extent, they involve different orientations in Chinese communication. *Ganqing* represents the emotional commitment in a long-standing and intimate relationship, and also involves a great deal of interpersonal effort and care (Chang & Holt 1994; Yang 1994: 121). A relationship with *ganqing* encompasses a sense of mutuality, interdependency, sacrifice in giving, and relational obligation (Chang & Holt 1994; Gao 1996; Yang 1994), which is employed to show emotional commitment. In terms of establishing emotional sentiments, *ganqing* is constructed through constant interactions with others, and it is expected one will make more effort in order to foster and cultivate the relationship (Chang & Holt 1994: 108). It is therefore argued that *ganqing* is more affection oriented, which is more often observed within the family, and amongst close friends and favourite relatives, particularly the ones considered as in-group members. On the other hand, *renqing* involves a lesser degree of affection than *ganqing* as emotional commitment is the core of the notion of *ganqing*. *Renqing* is conceptualised as a proper social form in which behaviours and discourse are expected to articulate 'the moral and decorous character of social conduct' (Yang 1994: 122). Similar to the notion of *ganqing*, *renqing* encompasses the features of obligation, interdependency, yet it also emphasises more a sense of indebtedness, reciprocity and mutual aid which resides in reciprocal relations. This reciprocal relation with *renqing* is constructed through a social relationship where one conducts oneself in proper ways and treats others according to social expectations. As Yang claims, 'the stress is on proper conduct, rather than natural predisposition' (1994: 68). In other words, those features of *renqing* are more based on emotional attachment and a sense of obligation and indebtedness rather than being affection or commitment oriented. For instance, if one is helped by others, one is expected to return the favour with gifts or other means in order to be in line with proper social conduct as well as to avoid a failure of social expectations in terms of the Chinese phrase *qian renqing zhai* (to owe a debt of human emotion). It is thus arguable that, compared to *gan-*

qing, renqing is a more socially oriented concept by which one is expected to abide in order to get along well with others in Chinese society. On the other hand, *renqing* can also be understood according to Gao as 'social investment for personal gains' (1996: 92), at times functioning as an instrument to regulate interpersonal relationships in Chinese interaction. For instance, *renqing* can be expressed or built by doing favours or giving gifts to the interactant, although one will have to return this favour in terms of reciprocation through the established relationship between the parties.

Since emotivity is constructed through interpersonal relationships, and relationships are also emotionally invested, the interrelationship between emotivity (*ganqing/renqing*), relationships (*guanxi, zijiren/wairen*) and face (*mianzi/lian*) practices should be investigated holistically in order to gain a more insightful perspective on Chinese interaction. According to Hsiang (1974), the act of acknowledging a relationship means that one shows one's emotion towards one's relational participant. To show one's emotional concern for the other is to respect the other's *mianzi*. Hsiang then further explains that, 'Giving people *mianzi* makes it easy to gain for oneself "human emotion", whereas hurting other's *mianzi* results in hurting one's human emotions' (1974: 57). Through 'giving' and 'claiming' *mianzi*, relational participants acknowledge the mutual bond between them, thereby showing emotional support (Chang & Holt 1994: 109). In other words, only in the context of acknowledging emotivity (*ganqing/renqing*) entailing mutual obligations within a reciprocal relation (*guanxi*) can face (*mianzi/lian*) be employed as a relational resource in face practices, such as claiming, giving or saving face in Chinese interactions. Due to emotivity being a fundamental notion in building interpersonal relationships in Chinese society, face becomes more salient and sensitive when people interact with each other in terms of emotional expressions, thus reflecting their perceptions of their relationships. In showing emotivity through face practices, the emotive basis of the interpersonal relationship itself is constructed, pointing towards the reflexive nature of the emic concepts underlying interpersonal exchanges. In order to appreciate Chinese communication and cultivate a better social network, the interconnection of face, emotivity and relationship should be taken into consideration as the basis of social interactions in Chinese contexts.

2.3 Face practices

An investigation of emic concepts may provide us with a more insightful perspective when analysing and theorising face. However, if we only rely on emic concepts to inform the analysis of face, we may not be able to grasp the whole picture of what meaning and actions are actually achieved in the interaction. Therefore, an investigation into the dimension of practice should also be supplemented by theorising face in order to avoid being dependent on the conceptualisations of face only. As Arundale (2008) argues, 'talk about how face is created does not itself create face' (2008: 11, n. 1). The actual practice of face also needs to be taken into account when theorising face.

Face practices are a 'recurrent and recognisable way of constructing (sequences of) utterances that afford particular meanings, actions and evaluations' (Haugh, Chang & Kádár 2015: 78). In other words, face practices are usual or regular ways of doing things which can be interactionally acknowledged by others from the same speaking community, and thus those practices do not exist idiosyncratically, but rather are always defined in relation to other discursive practices, drawing upon them in complex ways. It is argued that as interpretations of meanings and actions are interactionally achieved, interpretations and evaluations of persons and/or relationships may also coordinately arise. The emergence of interpretations and evaluations on a particular social action are regularly associated with the face that a person attempts to achieve in the interaction. Through the sequences of interpretations and evaluations of the interactant's face, it is argued that face practices are manifestations of participants' understandings as face arises in the interactions. When such interpretations and evaluations arise in recurrent and recognisable ways, it is suggested that this coordinate set of interpretations and evaluations of the interactant's relational separation and connection constitutes a 'face practice' (cf. Haugh, Chang & Kádár in press). Consistent with Chang and Haugh (2013: 15), emic conceptualisations do *not* always reflect actual emic practices. A theory of face should thus ultimately be informed by emic concepts but not be unduly constrained by them in explicating emic practices. The following section thus draws attention to the importance of examining face practices and concepts which need to be linked together in order to gain a better understanding of actual face practices.

While studies of emic concepts of face have shed considerable light on Chinese culture and social practice, they do not necessarily help us better understand how face actually arises in the first place. In order to further our understanding of face in Chinese, then, we need to make recourse to actual interactional or discourse data. There have been, however, relatively few studies of face in Chinese from a discourse perspective that closely analyse how face is interactionally managed and achieved in actual Chinese social interactions (Chen 1990; Pan 2000; Su 2009; Myers-Scotton 2006; Yang 2010). When emic concepts of face in Chinese have received considerable attention in the literature thus far, emic practices, whereby participants can be observed to be demonstrably orienting to and interactionally achieving face through particular linguistic and non-linguistic behaviour, have been relatively neglected by analysts.

The distinction between emic concepts and emic practices is made here because, while we might expect some level of correspondence between particular emic face practices and their reflexive emic conceptualisations, they are ultimately of a different type or order of analysis. While emic practices are recognisable to cultural insiders, they are only recognisable through their doing in interaction, and so they are not always explicated in folk ideologies of face. As Arundale goes on to argue, '[n]ot all emic practices are necessarily part of a culture's emic conceptualisation of face, and there are likely to be aspects of the emic conceptualisation that have no counterpart in the explanation of emic practices (2008: 3).

Since explicating emic concepts and emic practices involves a different order of analysis, conflating them introduces unnecessary conceptual confusion into our theorising of face. Therefore, it is argued that, although emic concepts of face should inform the theorising of face, they are not in themselves a suitable basis for constructing a more general theory of face (Haugh 2009a: 5). Instead, as Arundale (2006) argues, a theory of face should be framed by analysts as an explanatory set of concepts and principles that are sensitive to culture-specific construals of what is ultimately a culture-general phenomenon.

Moreover, building on Su's (2001, 2009) previous studies, it is also argued that the explication of face practices in Taiwan may need to take code-switching into account. Code-switching has been recently drawn to scholars' attention in the field of face research, particularly in the examination of face practices in interactions. It is commonly argued by those who investigate code-switching in multilingual societies that it is a mode of communication which requires complex sociolinguistic skills (Su 2001: 430–431). As Myers-Scotton (2006) argues that code-switching is 'the use of two language varieties in the same conversation' (p.239), bilingual speakers are commonly found to code-switch during interactions due to either linguistic or social motivations. Speakers who are linguistically motivated may switch to another code of language in order to fill a pragmatic or lexical gap in one language, or to accommodate for the listener's pragmatic or lexical gap in one language (Myers-Scotton 2006: 143–144). In other words, code-switching functions as a linguistic strategy to compensate for the lack of linguistic competence on the part of speakers. On the other hand, in terms of socially motivated code-switching, speakers may choose another code of language to assert an identity as the speaker of the language which carries certain status in a given situation (Auer 2005; O'Driscoll 2001), or to show that one understands associated meanings in communicative situations (Watanabe 2009: 36). With regard to social motivations, Gumperz (1982) also argues that code-switching is a type of *contextualisation cue*, signalling as well as assisting the marking of a speaker's intention and the recipient's interpretation of it. He defines contextualisation as follows:

> Speaker's and listener's use of verbal and nonverbal signs to relate what is
> said at any one time and in any one place to knowledge acquired through
> past experience, in order to retrieve the presupposition they must rely on to
> maintain conversational involvement and assess what is intended (Grumperz
> 1992: 230, cited in Su 2001).

This indicates that when speakers code-switch with each other, they presuppose, infer and interpret the in situ communicative meaning based on social context and knowledge. In line with Grumperz's point of view on social motivation, Myers-Scotton (2006) proposes the Markedness Model (MM), which explains that code-switching is an implicature which marks the speaker's intentionality in the communicative situation (1998: 20). The rights and obligations (RO) set lies at the core of MM in determining whether the speaker is using marked or unmarked choices of language code in communication. By using either marked or unmarked language choices, the speaker is said to imply or convey a particular message to the recipient, for instance, to index a particular interpersonal relationship (cited in Myers-Scotton 2006: 143).

Code-switching, in terms of social motivation, might be useful to explain face practices in a bilingual society. According to Watanabe, the motivation of choice of language code not only relates to smooth communication but also reflects the social alignment of the speaker. More specifically, he claims that code-switching can be used to enhance the solidarity of the group which thus reduces the distance in power relationships, but it can also be used to increase the perceived distance in power relationships between interactants, such as projecting face threats (2009: 40, 256). Su (2001, 2009) also explores how bilingual speakers in Taiwanese society manipulate two codes to perform their communicative tasks, and how they handle face-threatening situations through code-switching. She claims that code-switching is used as a resource for bilingual speakers to avoid commitment to the social implications of either code in handling face-threatening situations (Su 2001: 446).

As the data for this research focuses on examining face practices in business interactions in Taiwan – an examination of code-switching – this study may reveal new perspectives on face. Taiwan has four major ethnic groups: people originally from Southern Min, the Mainlanders, Hakka and Aborigines, with the Aborigines being the original inhabitants of Taiwan who speak Austronesian languages. In the seventeenth and eighteenth centuries, large groups of immigrants from coastal areas of mainland China moved to Taiwan, which was the first wave of immigration. At the same time, they brought with them the dialect of Southern Min, which became the dominant language and is called 'Taiwanese' today. After the civil war in 1949, when the Chinese Nationalist government was defeated, a large number of people retreated to Taiwan and re-established the government, which resulted in the second wave of immigration. The central government advocated Mandarin as the official language and even forbade Taiwanese people from using the Taiwanese dialect in order to exert political power. Over a period of time the status of numerous Taiwan-born politicians who speak the Taiwanese dialect as their L1 has gradually risen, as Taiwanese and other indigenous dialects have become more influential. Most Taiwanese residents are bilingual speakers now, speaking both Taiwanese and Mandarin dialects, although the Taiwanese dialect is used predominately in rural areas. Mandarin, on the other hand, is still considered the most prestigious dialect in Taiwan, and is mostly used in formal settings (Su 2009). While in terms of historical language shift Taiwan's political background is very influential, code-switching is now commonly observed in daily conversations between Taiwanese people.

Since the current study investigates face practices in Taiwan by adopting a conversational analysis (CA) approach involving naturally occurring interactions in business settings, it is believed that the participants may use the linguistic strategy of code-switching to deal with face-related issues, as illustrated in the study by Su (2001, 2009), who argues that code-switching is used to manage face-threatening communicative situations. Su's study is the one of few examples employing a conversation analytic framework to carefully examine how Taiwanese bilingual speakers use code-switching to negotiate interpersonal relationships and achieve specific communicative goals, particularly when face is at risk. Accordingly, the linguistic strategy of code-switching between dialects in terms of face-salient incidents in Taiwan deserves more attention, and this research thus aims to further explore the interconnection of code-switching and face practices.

2.4 Face as interactional, relational and emotively invested

Since problems with the application of Brown and Levinson's (1987) notion of negative face in Chinese have emerged, numerous studies of face in Chinese have subsequently appeared, particularly those which take an emic perspective. Such studies have focused on explicating the emic notions of face, *mianzi* and *lian*, and their related collocations and expressions, as these are invariably embedded in folk and academic discourse about Chinese language, culture and social practice (e.g., Gao 1998, 2009; Hinze 2005; Ho 1976, 1994; Hu 1944; Mao 1994; Yu 2003). These studies have largely drawn from analyses of metapragmatic data where cultural insiders describe *mianzi* and *lian* directly, or use these terms in discourse to describe particular incidents. Most studies of Chinese face have thus taken a largely emic perspective on face where they attempt to explicate the concepts of *mianzi* and *lian* 'in terms of the conceptual schemes and categories regarded as meaningful and appropriate by native members of the culture whose beliefs and behaviours are being studied' (Lett 1990: 130). In other words, these explications of the emic concepts of face are ultimately based on how people ordinarily talk about and conceptualise particular interpersonal and social aspects of what they are doing. In the case of Chinese society, these emic concepts have developed over thousands of years into an explicit folk ideology of face. However, while studies of emic concepts of face have shed considerable light on Chinese culture and social practice, they do not necessarily help us better understand how face actually arises in the first place. In order to further our understanding of face in Chinese, then, we need to make recourse to actual interactional or discourse data. However, there have been relatively few studies of face in Chinese from a discourse perspective that closely analyse how face is interactionally managed and achieved in actual Chinese social interactions (Chang & Haugh 2013; Chen 1990; Pan 2000; Su 2009). While emic concepts of face in Chinese have received considerable attention in the literature thus far, emic practices, whereby participants can be observed to be demonstrably orienting to and interactionally achieving face through particular linguistic and non-linguistic behaviour (Chang & Haugh 2013), have been relatively neglected by analysts.

As previously argued, Goffman's notion of facework in terms of the 'interactional order' provides insightful perspectives into examining face and facework (Arundale 1999, 2006, 2013; Bargiela-Chiappini 2003; Haugh & Watanabe 2009; Spencer-Oatey 2000, 2005, 2007), particularly in regard to Brown and Levinson's notions of negative and positive face, which have been found to be inherently problematic, as they are not sufficiently abstract to encompass relational aspects of face, as well as being framed without reference to how they emerge in interaction (Chang 2008: 12). Face is arguably achieved through interactions, encompassing participants' evaluations within a relationship. How face is framed on the basis of relational dimensions in interactions thus represents a significant re-theorising of face in taking an interactional approach to explore face-related communication. Building on the previous discussion of theories of face and their application to Chinese society, the next section outlines how this research aims to further investigate face in Chinese in terms of its interactional, relational and emotive dimensions.

2.4.1 Face as interactional

Lerner (1996) first defines face as 'the ongoing and ever-changeable level of regard that accrues to persons engaged in interaction' (p. 303), and then argues in relation to threats to face that 'both the possibility and terms of the disregard as well as the resources available to deal with it are part of the sequential organisation of talk-in-interaction' (p. 316). In other words, face (and facework) is defined, in

CA's perspective, as an emerging product accomplished in the sequence of inter-actions. Arundale (2004) also argues that face should be defined as a social con-struct within interactions. The key claims of his conceptualisation of face make it distinct from 'personal social attributes like social identity, public self-image, or social wants'. Instead, face is claimed 'as a conjoint, social accomplishment that is endogenous to using language because it is achieved as an integral part of the interaction among participants' (Arundale 2010a: 2079). Accordingly, Arundale (1999, 2006, 2010a) proposes that 'Face Constituting Theory' (FCT) primarily accounts for face, which is seen 'as participants' understandings of relational connectedness and separateness, conjointly co-constituted in talk/conduct-in-in-teraction' (2010a: 2078), and is interactionally achieved in conjunction with the interactional achievement of meanings and actions. FCT employs a new concep-tualisation of face to explicate the complex of *relational factors* involved in the interactional achievement of face in communication. Arundale goes on to argue as follows:

> [B]ecause humans interact only by means of utterances and/or behaviours, the practices of interaction through which persons achieve connection with others and separation from them must be integral with the practices of inter-action through which they achieve meanings and actions. That is, participants interactionally achieve and conjointly co-constitute interpretings of face in talk as they interactionally achieve and conjointly co-constitute interpretings of meaning and action (2010a: 2087).

In this way, in order to study face achieved through interactions, Arundale (2008) proposes the 'Conjoint Co-Constituting Model of Communication' (CMC) to account for interactional organisation. This contrasts with Brown and Levinson's individualistic perspective, in that an 'interactional achievement' model of com-munication takes the minimum unit of analysis, the relational dyad. Interaction, in a strong sense of interactional achievement, is therefore defined as a 'non-sum-mative phenomenon involving two or more cognitively autonomous persons engaged in affording and constraining one another's designing and interpreting of utterances and/or observable behaviours in sequence' (Arundale 2010a: 2079). In other words, within a conjoint co-constituting model of communication, par-ticipants mutually afford and constrain each other's interpretings, which are thus non-summative emergent, leading to the interactional achieving of meanings and actions. Arundale's (2006, 2010a) FCT thus provides an integrated explanation of face and facework, where actions and meanings dynamically emerge through dyadic communication, explaining how individual interactants produce and interpret sequences of utterances. According to FCT, face and facework, which are dynamic in authentic communication, need to be treated as a conjoint product and so investigated through interactions.

However, face interpretations are not restricted to direct face-to-face interaction, and can also be largely consistent over time and across situations (Arundale 2010a). Since face is arguably interactionally achieved as a non-summative property, the concept of interpretation needs to be extended in a broader sense. One's co-constituting interpretings of the face of others in daily conversations can also take place when one observes others without engaging with them. In other words, an analyst also needs to take into account one's straightforward constituting or contemplating of face interpretings of others apart from engagement in talk-in-interaction (Arundale 2010a: 2090). Face interpretation, on the other hand, is constructed through 'dyadic cognition' (Arundale & Good 2002), which does not solely exist in individual's psychology as opposed to the traditional view of singular cognition developed in social psychology (e.g. Spencer-Oatey 2007, 2009; Langlotz 2010). The concept of 'dyadic cognizing' involves 'how dyads engage one another's attentional processes to produce the phenomena of joint attention that have been seen as central both in the achievement of conversation' (Clark 1996, cited in Arundale & Good 2002: 145). The dyadic cognising refers to the *reformulation* that participants project or anticipate of their own and other's utterances through using all levels of linguistic structure. 'There is a progression through the production of an utterance in what is being anticipated, and the anticipation takes place with the retroactive assessing of interpretations of what has been produced in the utterance or the conversation' (Arundale & Good 2002: 134; Good 1995: 144). In other words, face interpretations are contingent since face-to-face interactions involve the speaker's and the recipient's simultaneous anticipation and retroactive assessment when perceiving and responding to utterances (Haugh 2009b: 98). This is not to overlook the cognitive perspective in interactions as the individual does exercise psychological activities. However, contrary to the traditional view of individual-oriented socio-cognition, individuals generate cognitions dependently of one another; on the other hand, the concept of *reformulation* is to shed light on face interpretations which are not constructed by the singular driver of individual's cognition, but should be examined by taking the interactional perspective into account according to the principle of dyadic cognising.

The concept of dyadic cognition is therefore perforce relevant to the interpreting of face. Constituting face interpreting outside of direct face-to-face interaction appears to be largely consonant with the Chinese concept of face, which is not restricted to only situated contexts. Ho (1994: 274), for instance, argues that face is defined in terms of the enduring, attributes, which are consistent over time and across situations unless there is a significant change in public perception of the person's conduct, performance or social status. A broadly interactional perspective on face thus includes not only synchronous communication, that is face-to-face interaction, but also asynchronous communication. In this sense, FCT points to three levels of complexity involved in constituting face interpretations, which lie in synchronous as well as asynchronous interactions. Interpretations of face formed by individuals encompass three different levels of direct, displaced and reflexive interpretings (Arundale 2010a: 2090). At the first level, direct face interpretation refers to individual's own interpretation of face, that is, 'my interpreting of our-connection-and-separation-at-this-moment'. At the second level, displaced face interpretation indexes an individual's level of another person's direct interpretation of face, which is 'my interpretation of your interpretation of our-connection-and-separation-at-this-moment'. At the third level, a reflexive face interpretation indexes an individual's interpretation of another person's interpretation of the first individual's direct face interpretation, that is, 'my interpreting of your interpreting of my interpreting of our-connection-and-separation-at-this-moment' (Arundale 2010a: 2090, cited in Arundale 2013). The three levels of complexity of face interpretations can therefore be applied in understanding the emic perspective of face in Chinese, in order to tease out the cultural-specific construal at each level of complexity that would be useful for providing a valid account for analysis of face and face practices in Chinese contexts.

From the perspective of a native speaker's intuition, face is invariably and deeply embedded in Chinese psychology, and so it is hypothetically argued that face in Chinese might function as a cognitive construct that is constitutive of native speakers' behaviours in that inferences about face can create social expectations that are consequential for recipient design. Since participants form face interpretings that necessarily involve three levels of complexity arising from dyadic cognition when engaged in recipient design, these direct, displaced and/or reflexive face interpretings may themselves occasion particular social actions (Haugh 2010a: 2112). That is, face interpretings are constituted external or parallel to direct face-to-face interaction. Through social expectations or sanctions, face is not only framed as co-constituted in interaction, but also as a co-constitutive of interactions (Haugh 2009a: 12). In other words, face is arguably not only co-constituted through normative use of language, but also constrains how people use language in interactions. It is thus believed that the co-constituted sense of face and the cognitive-based sense of face reflexively influence each other in the emergence and re-institution of face practices.

2.4.2 Face as relational

Face, as previously argued, is an interactional phenomenon which arises as participants conjointly achieve meanings and actions in interaction. The achieving of relational connection and separation is thus integral to the achieving of meanings and actions. According to Arundale (2006: 200–203), one needs to position the analysis of face at the level of a minimum social system of two interacting individuals in order to conceptualise face in terms of relationships between persons (Arundale, 2010a: 2092–2093). A relationship refers to a non-summative system of two or more persons. It broadly involves the 'establishing and maintaining of connection between two otherwise separate individuals' (Arundale 2010b: 138), in systems ranging from dyads to relatively closed social groupings and through to large, diffuse social networks. In characterising relationships as non-summative systems, following Arundale (2010b: 140), the 'reciprocal conditionality or systemic interdependence' of the persons as a social system constitute the relationship. This means that relationships cannot be fully explicated in terms of the identities of persons in interaction (cf. Locher 2008, 2011; Spencer-Oatey 2007, 2009). Haugh (2013), for instance, critiques He and Zhang's (2011) study of face as relational identity in a reception occasion. He argues that face is 'not only a socially attributed aspect of self that is derived through one's relational identity within a group, but also with reference to the relationships between those persons' (pp. 56–57). In other words, face cannot only involve awareness of one's position or image within a network of relationships with others, but also relationships in themselves (Chang & Haugh 2011b, 2013; see also O'Driscoll 2011). Thus, while the move to analysing identities and relationships in CMC in a coordinated, systematic way is a welcome one, particular care needs to be taken not to conflate the two (Haugh, Chang & Kádár 2015: 77–78).

This thereby appears to contrast with Spencer-Oatey's claim about the inter-relationship between identity and face, where face is conceptualised as belonging to individuals and to collectives, and yet it also applies to interpersonal relations (2007: 654). In this way, we can see that face conceptualised as belonging to individuals as a kind of public self-image of self-identity only exists through virtue of the social, that is, the relationship between those people in front of whom this so-called identity face is maintained, threatened, enhanced and so on. In other words, there can be no individual identity face without there being a relationship in which it is relevant. Rather than separating them, then, analysing face holistically within relationships is needed. In order to show key differences between an identity-based vs relational-based approach to face, two examples are given: one example applying Rapport Management Theory, and the other applying FCT.

Drawing from the identity-based research on face from Spencer-Oatey (2005: 111, 113–114), the following example primarily focuses on the interpreting of rapport management in Chinese–British interactions. A British company designs, manufactures and sells an engineering product that is used in industrial plants throughout the world. In every contract signed in China, they agree to host a delegation of up to six people who are involved in the deal in some way. The cost of hosting the delegation is added to the contract price, and there is an unofficial understanding that any balance remaining at the end of the visit is given to the visitors as 'pocket money'. On the last day of the delegation visit, a few hours before the Chinese visitors are due to leave, the British company gives each of the visitors an envelope containing 'pocket money', the cash left over after the costs of the visit has been deducted from the figure in the contract allocated to the visit. The visitors open their envelopes, count the money, and then claim that the amount was too little.

(4)

Phil:	I'd just like to say it's a great pleasure to have you come here. Thank you very much for coming. I'd just like to make a presentation to each of you for *[company name]*.
Int:	*[interprets into Chinese]*
Phil:	*[Phil stands up and presents an envelope to Sun. Sun stands up, takes it, and shakes hands with him. Phil hands one to Ma, who also stands up. They shake hands.]*
Chen:	Take them all together.
Phil:	*[Phil gives an envelope to each of the others: Chen, Lin, Shen and Xu.]*
	[Visitors open their envelopes and count the money inside. Sun takes a pen and sheet of paper from Sajid, and prepares to sign the receipt.]
Sun:	How much?
Xu:	*[Counts the money carefully and openly.]*
Xu:	570, 570, this doesn't seem enough.
	[Heated discussion in Chinese among the visitors. They agree to ask for a list of the costs.]
Xu:	We must definitely have a list of the costs.
Int:	How much money did you give them altogether?
Xu:	US$4000. US$4000 per person.
Int:	*[interprets into English]*
Sajid:	The contract, the contract doesn't say we have to give them money.
Int:	*[interprets into English]*
Shen:	It does, it does.
Int:	*[interprets into English]*

Xu: How much is the airfare? Ask them to show us the list of costs.

Int: *[no interpretation]*

Sajid: To get a rough idea (???) we (???) that we have to pay you (???)

Sun: All we want is a list.

Int: *[no interpretation]*

[Note: (???) = unintelligible speech]

(Spencer-Oatey 2005: 115)

In this interaction, the management of rapport is argued by Spencer-Oatey to revolve around three elements: behavioural expectations, interactional wants and face sensitivities. The Chinese visitors believed they were entitled to more 'pocket money' because of the contractual agreement between the companies, and they were thus expecting to receive it. When they did not receive as much money as they were expecting, this triggered a transactional goal (to obtain this extra money) that they then pursued. However, some of the visitors felt that the ruthless pursuit of this goal could be damaging to their face, and so they tried to balance their interactional wants with their claims to face (Spencer-Oatey 2005: 115).

However, it appears that the argument in this analysis is not sufficient to fully account for this face-sensitive incident. The request for more 'pocket money' from the Chinese delegation, at first, is derived from the contractual relationship which may have been perceived differently by the two parties during the negotiation. This may be part of the reason causing the divergence of expectations about this act of 'pocket money' giving. This intercultural difference also has a critical influence on the perceived relationships, yet the analysis merely emphasises the concerns of representing Chinese identity, being powerful, benevolent and harmonious (Spencer-Oatey 2005: 115). Yet, these expectations would not have arisen in the negotiations if there were no (contractual) relationship between the two parties in the first place. The analysis stops at the point where the identity face of the Chinese delegation was damaged, which resulted in an emotional response of 'feeling bad' towards the British company. However, this not only damages the Chinese delegations' identity face, but it also damages their relationship with the British company. The behaviour of the British company has apparently threatened their connective face, which influences the ongoing development of their relationship, particularly their business relationship. In other words, this incident also involves damage to their 'relational face'. Therefore, overemphasising concerns about protecting the identity face of the Chinese leads to an underdeveloped or incomplete analysis of face. The expectations arising in this relationship thus need to be further explained through further analysis.

By considering face as relational, FCT arguably yields a more comprehensive analysis of face in interactions. Taking relationships as a significant aspect of social practices, in FCT Arundale (2010a) claims that relationality arises through the dialectical interplay of *connection* and *separateness* in interaction (p. 2086). The dialectic of connectedness and separateness is an integral part of a relationship since no relationship exists except as two separate or differentiated individuals achieving social connection or separation (Baxter & Montgomery 1996: 9). The interplay of connection and separation is poised between 'unity or differentiation' (Baxter & Montgomery 1996: 79). In conceptualising face in terms of connectedness and separateness, FCT draws on a large body of research on relationships in interpersonal communication.

Although the theories of face have been discussed through the years, those which have been utilised in relation to Chinese face have neglected the interactional aspects of face. The following example is from Chen's (1990/91) study, which is one of the only studies which has indeed examined how face is interactionally achieved at the dinner table.

(5)

1   Host: Eat more? Come on; don't be 'keh chee' … Have more food, please have more …

2   Guest: No, thanks, I've eaten a lot already, really, thank you; I can't eat any more …

3   Host: Come on, more, just a bit more. You're the most important guest tonight … So 'keh chee' … How come eat so little? *(meanwhile rotating the Lazy Susan so that the new dish is in front of the guest)*

4   Guest: No, it's enough, really, really … I'm not being 'keh chee'; eat more yourself, *(rotating the Lazy Susan back so that the new dish is facing the host)*

5   Host: *(with enthusiasm)* Come on, don't be 'keh chee', you can afford to eat more … You ate too little. Just a bit more … *(rotating the Lazy Susan again)*

6   Guest: Alright, just a bit more … Thank you; too much food, so 'keh chee'.

The conversation was collected from a dinner table interaction between a guest and a host in Taiwan. The analysis starts with the explication of emic concepts involved in the Chinese table settings relating to *mianzi*, such as 'food', 'occasion' (*chang mian*), 'guest spirit' (*keqi*); it is later elucidated that there are social rules and duties involved in a general guest–host relationship in this setting. By faithfully orienting the prescribed social rules and duties derived from those emic concepts at Chinese tables, the host and the guest enact the ritual exchange of enthusiastic offering and restraint refusing in order to display their *sincerity* which is the core of the interactional ritual at the Chinese dinner table (Chen 1990: 134). The interactional performance of this ritual exchange at the Chinese dinner table thus is used to conjointly attend, maintain or even enhance each other's *mianzi* by following the culturally informed social etiquette. The sequentially enacted lines and actions of offer, refusal, challenge and acceptance between the host and the guest therefore play an essential role in attending to the social rules and duties arising from the host–guest relationship (Chen 1990: 136).

Chen employs a conversational analytic framework to describe how face is interactionally managed, enacted and negotiated in the flows of interactions at the dinner table, and thereby demonstrates the social practices inherent in Chinese 'face' (1990: 111). The analysis of the interaction indeed establishes a reliable and valid interpretation of Chinese 'face', which supports the notion that 'face' should be examined through interactions. On the other hand, this example from Chen's (1990) analysis has been used to highlight the relationship between the host and the guest, which has significant implications for studies theorising face. Face cannot thus be conceptualised as only 'identity-focused' as long theorised in the field of pragmatics, but the 'relationships' between the interactants should also be taken into account. Chen's study, therefore, has illuminated additional dimensions of interaction.

2.4.3 Face as emotively invested

According to Spencer-Oatey's (2000, 2007, 2008) rapport management, people develop preconceptions as to what frequently or typically happens in a given context and come to expect that behaviour. They may then develop a sense that others should or should not behave in that way, and prescriptive or proscriptive overtones become associated with that behaviour. As a result, people start perceiving rights and obligations in relation to them, with the result that if the expected behaviour is not forthcoming, those people may then feel annoyed (Spencer-Oatey 2008: 16). In other words, emotivity naturally arises when there is an expectation associated with social behaviour, and thus emotivity may also be involved in interactions where face becomes salient. Spencer-Oatey (2007: 644) points out that face can be associated with affective sensitivity, as 'our attention is captured because we are affectively sensitive to those evaluations'. If others' perceptions of one's behaviours are not in line with one's expectations, some emotional reactions which crucially impact on the perceived relationship are likely.

Ruhi's (2007, 2009b, 2009c) works also draw significant attention to the links between face, affect and the self-presentational choices that people make to effect outcomes in relational work that are in line with their goals both during and after an interaction. Those interlocutors sometimes display irritation and concern for the other through rising tones that clearly indicate the impact of affective responses to self/other-presentation. It also suggests that displays of feelings, that is, emotive discourse, can become an important dimension of face in social interaction, as showing feelings can be used strategically to achieve interactional goals (Chang & Haugh 2011b; Ruhi 2009c: 107). It is also argued that relational work will involve tensions between achieving one's interactional goals and attending to the feelings and expectations of interlocutors, with a strong tendency to appeal to people's inner, true selves with respect to both their emotions and their inner wishes and aspirations (Ruhi & Işık-Güler 2007: 706). In this regard, emotivity may crucially impact on face practices in the Chinese context, particularly in light of the importance placed on *ganqing, renqing* and other related emic concepts in the management of interpersonal relationships. There has been little research thus far, however, that has investigated emotivity in conceptualising face. The dimensions of emotivity and face are particularly important areas for investigation from an emic perspective explicating the interconnection between the two in relational work, and will arguably yield a more coherent theoretical framework of face in Chinese communication.

CHAPTER 3

An interactional pragmatics approach to investigating face practices

3.1 Data sets

A particular methodological approach is employed here, namely, Pan's (2011) *Grammar of Politeness*, which advocates the use of multiple analytical perspectives for investigating a particular pragmatic phenomenon. This framework involves four main methodologies, but this research mainly adopts the first three, which are (1) recordings of interactional data, (2) post-recording interviews and (3) ethnographic interviews, as discussed in the following sections. Three kinds of data were collected: (1) interactions among insurance agents, their marketing manager and their clients, (2) data from mediation sessions that involved various parties (insurance agents, mediation chair, in-conflict parties and advocates) and (3) post-recording interviews.

The first data set consists of audio(visual) recordings of naturally occurring interactions between insurance agents from an insurance company, their various clients and a marketing manager. This allows me to freeze time in order to focus on specific phenomena as well as avoiding the stereotypical findings of traditional pragmatics research, such as through the use of Discourse Completion Tests (DCTs). Forty-four audio(visual) recordings were collected, ranging in length from around 10 to 36 minutes. The amount of audio(visual) data recorded overall was approximately seven and a half hours. These recordings were gathered in the course of eight weeks of ethnographic observation (held over two separate periods in 2007 and 2010) of workplace interactions involving two different insurance agents and the marketing manager. The original aim was to record all interactional data audiovisually. However, some recordings were only audio recorded due to the issue of sensitivity. Particularly for the mediation interactions, the participants consented only to be audio recorded. I also recorded the ethnographic observations in note form. The main participant was approached through my relational connection, where agreement was sought before data collection began. As the data was based on a business context, an insurance company in Taiwan was chosen as the main environment for the data collection, since business agents in the Taiwanese insurance industry have plenty of opportunities to contact clients. Related clients who had their own business were also asked to have interactional recordings made in their workplaces. The insurance company provided indemnity for their clients if they had an accident, or there was damage to their clients' car or property.

As noted, two main types of interactional data were collected. One type of data was the dyadic business interactions between an insurance agent and his various clients. This type of interaction took place in the clients' homes or in their workplaces when the agents went to pass on the renewal forms for insurance, collect insurance fees or deal with insurance policies with their clients, or in the department store and in the workplaces of the sponsors of promotional events.

The other type of interactional data consisted of mediation sessions involving the insurance agent, at-fault party, injured party, chair of the mediations and other advocates recorded for investigation with regards to face issues, specifically for the mediation sessions in seeking a mutually agreeable indemnity for the car accidents. Compared with the dyadic business interactions, there were more roles in the multiparty mediation interactions, as the purpose of the mediation was to settle the amount of compensation for the injured party involved in a car accident. The roles and backgrounds of the participants involved in the mediation sessions are further explained in the analysis in Chapter 5. The recordings of the multiparty mediation took place mainly in the local government, which provides a committee to resolve a diverse range of disputes.[1] This type of interactional data broadened the interactions collected to include a larger range of different business contexts rather than focusing on the interaction of insurance-case negotiation only. Most of the interactions were conducted in the Taiwanese dialect, with some code-switching into Mandarin Chinese. Through repeated viewings of the recordings, in conjunction with the ethnographic and post-recording interviews, interactions in which face emerges as salient were selected for close interactional analysis. Seven key incidents were then transcribed according to standard conversation analytic transcription practices (Jefferson, 2004). The selected interactions were also translated into English for the convenience of English readers, but the Chinese/Taiwanese versions were used for analysis.

The second data set consists of 11 ethnographic interviews with native informants who had an association with a particular insurance company in Taiwan. I

---

1. The background of the mediation practices provided by the local government is further discussed in Chapter 5 in which the mediation sessions are analysed.

conducted my initial data collection of ethnographic interviews back in 2008, and those interviews were collected for my previous research project (Chang 2008). Some dyadic business interactions were also recorded, but they have not been thoroughly analysed. The informants in the interviews were approached through the social network of my personal contact in one insurance company. They were asked if they would be willing to be interviewed on the topic of human communication in business. The audio recordings of these 11 interviews ranged in length from 12 to 30 minutes. Five of the interviewees worked in that insurance company, while the remaining six interviewees were clients of that company. These clients all had their own businesses in Taiwan. All of the interviews were conducted either in the insurance company itself or in the workplaces of the clients. The data from these ethnographic interviews was first directly transcribed from the audio recordings, and then all transcriptions were translated from Taiwanese/Mandarin into English. The participants were interviewed in relation to their understanding of Chinese face (*mianzi*), in order to explore the concept of *mianzi* in business settings from the perspective of native speakers. The emic conceptualisations of *mianzi* were identified through these ethnographic interviews, although it is not limited in scope to just these folk understandings of face.

The third data set consists of a number of post-recording interviews, which were also conducted with the agents, the marketing manager and, where possible, with clients. This methodology originally attempted to elicit participants' perceptions and evaluations on the events where face-sensitivity is involved. This was intended to investigate the participants' uptake and interpreting of actions and meanings during the interactions and thus provide additional evidence for the analysis of emotive and relational aspects of the interaction. All of these interviews were conducted soon after the interactions finished. During the interviews, the participants were asked to make comments when I played back the videos for the purpose of refreshing the participants' memory of the interactions. They were free to ask for the video to be stopped whenever they felt like making any comments or felt uncomfortable (see also Spencer-Oatey 2009). However, it proved difficult in many cases to elicit their perspectives on these interactions, as such talk was found to be face-threatening in itself (see also Bargiela-Chiappini et al. 2007: 149; Pan 2008). Most of the participants were reluctant to make comments when I made an audio recording and played back the video clips, as they involved face-sensitive incidents. They appeared to be uncomfortable commenting on these moments where face-salient incidents were involved, displaying their discomfort through smiles or silence. The challenge of conducting post-recording interviews around highly sensitive issues thus arose at this point. The participants felt reluctant to proceed, and eventually their non-responses interrupted the flow of the interviews. For instance, in one interaction where the interviewee's behaviour had resulted in embarrassment for the co-participant, the interviewee was asked about his or her intentions or reasons for this conduct. The interviewee appeared embarrassed to respond to these questions. In the end, then, only nine post-recording interviews were collected, including seven that were audio-recorded and two that were made in note form. Being asked to comment on the (potentially) face-threatening incidents highlighted that the act of asking for such commentary is face-sensitive in itself. For those post-recording interviews which were successfully obtained, the interviewees mainly provided information about their relational history with the co-participants, the background information of the participants and the purpose of the interactions, and where there were no particular face-sensitive issues involved in previous interactions. Only in two cases did participants readily volunteer their views and feelings on the face-salient moments straight after the recording of interactions. It is also important to note here that not all the interactions allowed me to conduct the post-recording interviews with every participant involved due to some practical issues. Most of the participants, particularly from the mediation interactions, had no time to stay behind and showed no willingness to be interviewed at some other time after the interaction. All the post-event interviews of the interactions were conducted with the main business people/agents after they met with their clients. The post-recording interviews were attempts to elicit participants' comments on the interactions, more specifically, their perceptions and evaluations of the co-participant's meanings and actions in the interaction, so as to justify the interactional analysis.

Table 3. Summary of the total data set

Types of recordings		Number of recordings	Length of collection	Place of collection
Interactional data	1. Dyadic business interactions	41	Ranging from 20 s to 36 mins; approximately 7 hrs 30 mins in total	In the clients' workplaces or homes
	2. Multiparty mediation sessions	3	Ranging from 15 mins to 1 hr 15 mins; approximately 2 hrs 15 mins in tota	In the local government mediation department
Ethnographic interviews		11	Ranging from 12 to 30mins long; approximately 4 hrs 35 mins in total	In the insurance company or in the workplaces of the clients
The post-recording interviews		9, but 2 were in note form	Ranging from less than 1 to 8 mins; approximately 30 mins in total	In the car or in the place where the interaction occurred

Consent forms were provided to all the participants before the recording of the interactions, ethnographic interviews and also the post-recording interviews. The selected seven audio(visual) business interactions were transcribed according to standard CA practices. The audio recordings of ethnographic and post-recording interviews were transcribed with less detail, although recording and transcribing these interviews helped eliminate problems or shortcomings that many qualitative researchers may experience from the uncertain accuracy of notes, and thereby establish greater reliability for analysis in this study (Perakyla 2004: 285–286). Since the interactions and interviews were conducted in Mandarin or Taiwanese, a translation and morphological gloss of the conversations were also provided. Table 3 summarises the total data set collected in this project.

3.2 Theoretical framework

In order to explore how *mianzi* is interactionally achieved in Chinese social interactions, this research draws from recordings of authentic verbal interactions as they naturally occur in business interactions. In this research project, a theoretical and analytical framework that conceptualises face as a joint accomplishment of interlocutors emerging through the flow of conversation is employed. Consistent with Chen's (1990) earlier study of the accomplishment of *mianzi* in dinner-table interactions between native speakers of Chinese, this study focuses on the qualitative analysis of authentic interactional data. Taking an ethnographic approach not only enables me to understand the norms of face practices from an emic perspective, but also helps locate specific factors or problems which are relevant to participants that may deserve more analytic attention (Deppermann & Schütte 2008: 179–213). Therefore, this research aims to interpret Chinese face in terms of salient characteristics of human interpersonal relationships, through an analysis of how face is interactionally achieved in Taiwanese business contexts.

The research project makes a use of Arundale's (2006, 2009, 2010a) Face Constituting Theory (FCT) and Spencer-Oatey's (2005, 2007) theory of Rapport Management as the theoretical frameworks in which to ground the analysis of the interactional achievement of face in Chinese.

Arundale's (2006, 2010a) Face Constituting Theory (FCT) provides an integrated explanation of face and facework as both relational and interactional, explaining how participants interactionally achieve actions and relationships that coordinate with their producing and interpreting of the meaning(s) of sequences of utterances (Arundale 2010a). Face is conceptualised as a social phenomenon in which two or more persons conjointly co-constitute meanings and actions in talk-in-interaction (Arundale 2010a: 2091).

> [b]ecause individuals in interaction with one another constitute the social, just as social interaction is constitutive of individuals (Arundale 1999: 128; Stewart 1995: 27). Framing the individual and the social as dialectic provides an abstract framework for conceptualizing both the individual and the social phenomena involved as humans engage in relating to other humans. (Arundale 2010b: 139)

Thus, according to FCT, face and facework, which are dynamic in authentic communication, need to be treated as a conjoint product and so investigated through interactional data. Since Arundale (2010a) argues that relationality arises through the dialectical interplay of *connection* and *separateness*, through interaction the dialectic of connectedness and separateness play a central role within relationship as mentioned in Section 2.4.

FCT adopts an analytical approach of an interactional pragmatics informed by findings and methodology in conversation analysis (Arundale 2010a: 2094; see also Arundale 2005: 56–63; cf. Schegloff 2005: 474–475). Interactional pragmatics, similar to CA, has its focus on the analysis of participants' understanding and orientation to interactional practices, but it attempts to go beyond the scope of CA in providing more specific, theoretically motivated formulations of meanings, actions and evaluations (of persons and relationships). The formulations are second-order constructs, and they are informed by emic (first-order) understanding of meanings, actions and evaluations (of persons and relationships) (Haugh, Chang & Kádár 2015: 77). In other words, interactional pragmatics is to 'reach the theoretical second-order conclusions by means of analysis of data' (Kádár & Mills 2011: 8) which are not only consonant with participant understanding displayed in the course of particular interactions (Arundale 2010a: 2094–2096; 2010b: 155–159), but also consistent with the first-order understanding of the participants in the interaction being analysed (Haugh, Chang & Kádár 2015: 77). Since a key assumption is made that 'a basis for the demonstration [is] the evidence the participants themselves provide in the process of "displaying" for one another their interpreting of the other's talk' (Schegloff 1991: 50–53, cited in Arundale 2010a: 2095), the analyst should (1) provide evidence that the action or meaning is an influential component in talk-in-interaction, (2) demonstrate through specific and salient details of the interaction how participants are orienting to this phenomenon, and also (3) present details of interactions in terms of 'how the interaction proceeded in the way it did, how it came to have the trajectory, the direction, the shape that it ended up having (procedural consequentiality)' (Arundale 2010a: 2095). This analytic framework features not only the participants' displayed orientations in the interactions, but also the situational contexts invoked by the participants, the latter being able to validate the analysis of the interactional achievement of face interpreting in communication.

FCT provides a model for analysing face threat, face stasis (no change in face) and face support which are defined as *evaluations* that arise when participants interpret and project face. Evaluations of face as threatened, supported or in stasis are claimed to involve three types of face: (1) projected/interpreted face, namely, a participant's interpreting of the utterance or action currently in question 'with regard to the extent of both connectedness with and separateness from the other person', (2) evolving face, involving a participant's interpreting of 'the extent of both connectedness and separateness that characterise the relationship with this particular person, up to the current point in the interaction', and (3) contextual face, encompassing the participant's 'expectation for the interpreting of connectedness with and separateness from the other person that applies in the current context, as that context has been invoked or brought into play at the present moment by the participants in the conversation' (Arundale 2010a: 2092). In other words, evaluations of face interpretings as threatening arise when the proffered shift in face interpretings (viz., the perceived difference between the projected/interpreted face and evolving face) is not consistent with the situated shift in face interpretings (i.e., the perceived difference between evolving face and contextual face). Evaluations of face interpretings as supportive arise when the proffered and situated shifts in face interpretings are consistent, and evaluations of face interpreting as stasis arise when the situated and proffered shift has neither convergence nor divergence (Arundale 2010a: 2093). In this book, it is proposed that FCT is employed as the theoretical framework, combined with emic concepts which are drawn from emic notions in Chapter 2 to analyse face in interactions.

The use of ethnographic and post-recording interviews to supplement interactional analysis is consistent with Pan's (2011: 83) *Grammar of Politeness*, which involves four analytical perspectives: (1) member's generalisation, (2) individual case histories, (3) the objective or neutral view and (4) contrastive studies, aiming to illuminate data through the perspectives of the ethnography of communication, sociolinguistics and discourse analysis. The ethnographic interviews echo the first analytical perspective of the Grammar of Politeness, namely, eliciting member's generalisations 'regarding cultural beliefs'. It is worth examining how people 'often tell the others, especially researchers, what they believe they should say or what they think others want to hear' (Pan 2011: 17). While analysing the ethnographic and post-recording interview data, an interpretive approach was employed. By repeated listening to the audio recordings and examination of the transcripts, notes identifying key informant understandings of *mianzi* were made. In order to contextualise this interpretive process, these emergent themes were carefully analysed as jointly formed understandings, which reflect the participation footings of the interviewer and interviewee that were interactionally achieved at those points in the interviews (Potter & Hepburn 2005). As Pan

(2008) argues, interviews are interactional settings in and of themselves, where potential offence or face threats may arise, although, in the case of these ethnographic interviews, this problem was somewhat alleviated by the existence of a social network between the main contact and the interviewees. In this way, an emic conceptualisation of face from the native informants was drawn upon to support the analysis of interactional data in terms of participants' orientations to the interpretings of talk-in-interactions. Table 4 summarises the three methodologies employed in this research.

Table 4. The design of three methodologies employed in this research

Methodology	Collection approach	Participants	Aim
1. Interactional analysis	Naturally occurring interactions in office meetings, business negotiations, business visiting etc. Audiovisual recordings	Participants from the interactional recordings	To examine interactionally achieved meanings in terms of face in business communication
2. Ethnographic interviews	Open-ended questions with native informantsAudio recordings	Insurance agents, and related clients	To establish emic conceptualisations of face from the perspectives of native speakers to support the interactional analysis
3. Post-recording interviews	Straight after the interactional recordingsAsking the participants to comment on the event with regard to relational history, their feelings etc.Audio recordings/note-taking	Participants from the interactional recordings	To investigate participants' uptake and interpreting of actions during the interactions to provide evidence for emotive and relational claims made by analyst

3.3 Business context in Taiwan

As the data was based on a business context, an insurance company in Taiwan was chosen as the main environment for the data collection. The selected company is one of the most dominant companies in the insurance industry in Taiwan. Since insurance agents often visit their business contacts in the Taiwanese insurance industry, they have substantial opportunities to interact with their clients. Related clients who had their own business were also asked to have interactional recordings made in their workplaces, including a department store, retail shops, ironworks, repair workshops, factories and so on. The insurance company mainly provides indemnity in the event that their clients are the at-fault party in a car accident, or where there is any damage to their client's property due to theft or natural disasters in general. As explained in the section of data sets, numerous dyadic interactions between insurance agents and their various clients are recorded. It is a common practice that insurance agents visit their clients in person to hand over renewal forms, introduce/explain insurance packages or consult any issues regarding their insurance coverage, in order to establish interpersonal relationships rather than merely business relationships.

Mediation sessions are also a very common practice in Taiwanese society, particularly for people who often need a third party to be involved in negotiation sessions with regard to financial compensation. They are generally organised by local governments, which facilitate mediations as a civil practice over a diverse range of disputes, including family/marriage crisis, cases of traffic accidents and so forth. The establishment of a mediation committee functions as a conciliation organisation in order to resolve disputes and thus avoids people proceeding on to court cases resulting in a prosecution against the at-fault party. People involved in the dispute, no matter whether the at-fault party or the injured party, can always register for mediation service with the local government. Once the registration has been approved, the people involved will be notified of the time and location to attend the mediation session. The appointed mediator takes the lead in the mediation, endeavouring to find a mutually agreeable resolution, which is normally some kind of financial compensation, between the at-fault party and the injured party.

Insurance agents are frequently involved with such mediations, presenting on behalf of the at-fault party. One of the insurance agents, for instance, commented that attending one or two mediation sessions per day is a very common part of his job. The role of an insurance agent in such mediations is mainly to represent the at-fault party and to advise the injured party of the amount of indemnity they are able to claim according to the at-fault party's insurance coverage. However, in some cases where the at-fault party's insurance coverage is not sufficient to cover the entire medical or damage costs, seeking for a mutually agreeable extra amount from the at-fault party is also part of the insurance agent's task during the negotiations. People involved in a car accident often seek the services of a third party, namely, the committee members from local government, who assist in negotiations to find solutions to the dispute or agreement on financial indemnity. The system of the mediation committee is thus regulated by the Taiwanese government as an alternative solution for the at-fault party to compensate the injured party so as to avoid proceeding on to court or criminal prosecutions.

The chair of the mediation committee (the main mediator) is normally someone who has a large social network, a socially prestigious position or a high-ranking status, such as the head of a village, representative of a township, politician and member of local government and the like. Recognition of these broad social connections and entitlements that are associated with positions of high status can be considered as a means of gaining social face (*mianzi*), which can play a significant role in the mediation. Attaining or having social face (*mianzi*) can also be interpreted as attaining social achievement and success (Hu 1944; Hwang 2006). Through the acknowledgment of social face (*mianzi*), which is derived from social recognition of achievement or success, an individual can exploit this as a means to accomplish particular goals (Hwang 1987: 946) or to bring influence to bear on matters.

Although there is a fixed number of people on the committee panel who act as mediators, the chair of the committee takes the main role in managing the mediation process and is generally nominated by the local government, either at county-office or township-office level. Since the main mediator is normally someone with broader social connections such as a politician, there is a high likelihood that during the mediation process the main mediator will come across people whom he or she is familiar with. However, it is important to note that the committee serves as a civil organisation which aims to prevent people from bringing legal cases to court. This type of mediation is therefore quite different from the conduct of litigation. The mediation does not apply any legal procedures and provisions to the members involved, and thus familial connections are allowable in this setting. However, it is specifically stipulated that the insurance agents involved in the process are prohibited from taking any negotiation cases which involve any party related through family ties to the agent, since it might result in conflict of interest or impartial interference in mediation judgments on the part of the insurance company.

CHAPTER 4

Emic concepts of face

This chapter opens by first discussing the results of ethnographic interviews about emic face concepts in Taiwanese business interactions. It is suggested that eliciting folk understandings of emic notions of face can help ground the analysis of face practices in interaction, thereby further building on the distinction between emic concepts and practices proposed in Chapter 2. In the first part of this chapter, transcripts of ethnographic interviews with business people are carefully examined to investigate how native informants of Taiwanese Chinese conceptualise face when doing business, drawing from those informants' knowledge and experiences in relation to face. I first designed the questions for the ethnographic interviews, attempting to establish emic conceptualisations of face from the perspectives of native speakers to support the interactional analysis.

The informants were given notice of the interview time beforehand and were also advised about the purpose of this research as well as the procedure of conducting the interviews. Their agreement on participation was sought before they were asked to sign the consent form. They were recruited through the main contact in the target insurance company, either the insurance agent's colleagues or clients, who also worked as business people. All the ethnographic interviews were audio recorded for the purpose of transcription. The interviews are open-ended questions (see Chang 2008), and the interviewees were encouraged to explain and express themselves freely and were encouraged to provide any relevant personal experience. Therefore, a number of key folk notions were invoked during the interviews, and these findings are related to previous research on Chinese face, highlighting the significance of the ways in which *mianzi* is conceptualised, in particular in business settings. The folk notions mentioned by the native informants were compiled through the selection of relevant and salient findings from the ethnographic commentary in order to conceptualise face in Chinese. This analysis thus contributes to an understanding of what Taiwanese business people *say* about face, or what has been termed here emic face concepts.

It was previously argued in Chapter 2 that criticism can also sometimes be interpreted as 'having *mianzi*' in business settings. From the comments by native informants in ethnographic interviews, it appears that when a person is criticised, he or she does not necessarily interpret it as face-threatening conduct if the criticism has a positive or beneficial influence for him or her. In the course of that discussion some other underlying folk notions relating to face were highlighted, which are also involved in face practices in business settings, such as *guanxi* (social or relational network), *ganqing* and *renqing* (emotivity), *lizi* (profit) vis-à-vis *mianzi* (face). The following excerpts from the ethnographic interviews illustrate the complexity of emic face concepts in the Taiwanese business context.

Following on from the excerpt in Chapter 2 where a native informant claimed that criticism is not necessarily taken as a face-threatening act, other significant emic factors relating to this point also arose from the excerpts from the ethnographic interviews. Apart from *guanxi* (relationship), which is a significant element involved in the interactional achievement of *mianzi* in business settings, another important factor involving *guanxi* is *ganqing* (emotive quality), which encompasses both *renqing* (human emotion) and *jiaoqing* (friendly emotion). A number of scholars have proposed that the collective meanings of *mianzi*, *guanxi* and emotional components (*ganqing*, *renqing* and *jiaoqing*) in Chinese social relations need to be investigated in terms of their inter-relationships, as these components are inevitably intertwined with face in Chinese social relationships (Chang & Holt 1994; Gao, Ting-Toomey & Gudykunst 1996; Hwang 1987; Yang 1994), echoing Chang & Holt's (1994) argument that '*mianzi*, human emotion and interpersonal relations must be understood as a whole' (p. 103). *Renqing* is associated with the notion of *renqing zhai* (human emotion debt), meaning *renqing* is something that is expected to be contributed or returned through *guanxi*, whereas *jiaoqing* (friendly emotion) indicates the quality of the friendship, and is normally under consideration when employing *guanxi*. According to the informants, then, *guanxi* is closely related to issues of *mianzi*, in particular, when conducting business negotiations.

One of the informants, for instance, invokes a common Taiwanese saying and thus highlights the importance of *guanxi* in social contexts:

Extract 2: [EI-W1: 16: 40]

  8 I: *Na juede tan baoxian huo shi tan shengyi shangmian ni juede*
             women chang jiang guanxi huo shi kao guanxi hen zhongyiao ma?

             那覺得談保險或是談生意上面,你覺得我們常講關係,或是靠
             關係很重要嗎?

             [Do you think] the common saying about *guanxi*/relying on *guanxi* is very important during insurance business negotiations?

9   W: *Ou, hen zhongyao, erqie shi feichang feichang feichang de zhong-*
         yao, er, zhuanye lingyu ou, ta zhi shi ni gongzhuo biyao de dongxi
         eryi, zhuanye shi ni de biyao, yinwei na shi ni zhuanmen shengcai
         de qiju ma. Buguo zhe ge guanxi, zhe ge guanxi meiyou de hua,
         huo zhe ni lian guanxi dou kao bu liao de hua, ((Taiwanese)) Ná
         án-ne pháinn-sè lí nā-be tī siā-huē sing-tsûn, *keneng yao bi bieren duo*
         baifenzhi bashi de nuli. Na jintian ruguo you guanxi de hua, renjia
         shuo, ((Taiwanese)) 'nā tshuā tioh tsit-uī tshian-kim sió-tsiá, kiám hùn-
         tàu sann tsap nî. Kāng-khuán ì-sù a'.

         喔,很重要,而且是非常非常非常的重要,呃,專業領域喔,他只是
         你工作 必要的東西而已,專業是你的必要,因爲那是你專門生
         財的器具嘛,不過這個關係如果沒有的話,或者你連關係都靠
         不了的話,那不好意思,如果你要在社會上生存(台語),可能要比
         別人多百分之八十的努力,那今天如果有關係的話,人家說如
         果娶到一個千金小姐,少奮鬥三十年(台語),一樣意思啊。

         Oh, very important, and [it's] very very very important. Hmm, [in]
         professional area, it is just a necessity of your job. Your profession is the
         necessity because it is your tool of making money. However, if you do
         not have any *guanxi* or you do not know how to rely on *guanxi*, then
         I'm sorry. If you live in this society, you may have to put 80 percent more
         effort than others. If you have *guanxi*, [it's like] what people say, 'if you
         marry to a lady from a rich family, you can work 30 years less than oth-
         ers'. The meaning is the same.

In this excerpt the informant responds to a question about the importance of
guanxi from the interviewer (turn 8). He emphasises that *guanxi* is indeed very
important in business, implying that if one does not have *guanxi*, or does not
know how to employ it, then one is unlikely to be very successful (turn 9). He
goes on to emphasise the importance of *guanxi* by invoking a common Taiwanese
saying, which in this context means that the better *guanxi* one has, the more likely
one will be successful in business.

Another salient aspect raised by informants was the idea that *mianzi* is closely
linked in dynamic tension with issues of profit or gain (*lizi*), which arise as a matter of course in business negotiations. *Lizi* literally denotes 'inside', and so contrasts with the literal meaning of *mianzi*, which is 'surface'. The connotations of
lizi mentioned by the informants included that it involves substantive gains made
through business negotiations, such as purchasing the commodity at a lower
price, obtaining extra benefits or receiving additional services. Such gains can be
interpreted as *you lizi* (having *lizi*). While *mianzi* is characterised by informants
as involving an intangible attitude and positive feeling, *lizi* involves tangible profits. From the perspective of clients, then, if one gets a lower-priced service than

others, one would feel not only that one 'has *mianzi*', but also one 'has *lizi*', since a lower-priced service or product is what clients aim for. Thus, from the perspective of business people, it is extremely important to find a balance between *mianzi* and *lizi* during their negotiations.

One informant, for instance, talked about the need to strike a balance between maintaining the *mianzi* of the client as well as that of the company, and considerations of *lizi* in business negotiations.

Extract 3: [EI-H3: 19: 51]

10   I: *Ni juede baochi you mianzi hen zhongyao ma?*

你覺得保持有面子很重要嗎?

Do you think that is it very important to maintain 'having mianzi'?

11   H: *Dui women lai jiang, women tan liang ge bufen, yi ge mianzi, yi ge lizi, bici jiu shi yao zhuan dao qian ma, wo jiu shi guquan wo de mianzi bu zhuan dao qian meiguanxi. You shihou wo hui qu hengliang shuo, ruguo zhe ge dan* (amount of money) *hen da, na you shihou wo hui guquan lizi, bu yiding yao mianzi, zhiyao ta buyao tai guofen. Na tai guofen de shihuo, wo xiang renhe ren dou shoubuliao, na jiu hui shi buyao lizi yao mianzi.*

對我們來講,我們談兩個方面,一個面子,一個裡子,彼此就是要賺到錢嘛, 我就是顧全我的面子,不賺到你的錢沒關係。有時候我會去衡量說,如果這個單很大,那有時候我會顧全裡子,不一定要面子,只要他不要太過份。那太過份的時候,我想任何人都受不了,那就會是不要裡子要面子。

For us, there are two aspects [of business negotiations], *mianzi* and *lizi*. We want to make a profit from each other. Sometimes I only care about my own *mianzi* rather than making money. However, sometimes I might weigh up [the situation and] if there's a lot of money involved, sometimes I only care about *lizi* not *mianzi*, as long as he [the customer] doesn't go too far. If he goes too far, I don't think anyone can put up with it. Then [I'll] choose *mianzi* rather than *lizi*.

The informant responds here to the question of what 'having *mianzi*' means in the context of business by focusing on the balance she needs to find between maintaining *mianzi* and *lizi*. She points out that in business contexts making money (i.e., *lizi*) is clearly important, but this needs to be balanced with considerations of maintaining *mianzi*. In some cases she puts maintaining her *mianzi* first, over and above obtaining *lizi*, although if the *lizi* is potentially very large, then this may be favoured over maintaining her *mianzi*. However, she alludes to comments she made earlier in the interview claiming that she would favour maintaining her *mianzi* over even potentially large *lizi* in situations where she feels the client has 'gone too far', for example, by being overly demanding or not showing appropriate consideration. The dynamic tension arising in business negotiations from the need to find a balance between the two sides of a coin, namely *mianzi* and *lizi*, is thus a key consideration in decisions about whether or not to place emphasis on maintaining *mianzi* in business negotiations.

A related theme that also emerged through the ethnographic interviews was that maintaining *mianzi* during business interactions is crucial for obtaining business cases. Maintaining *mianzi* (*gu mianzi*) involves showing consideration for both one's own *mianzi* and the *mianzi* of others (Hinze 2002: 147). This means it is important to avoid *pohuai mianzi* (damage *mianzi*), particularly the *mianzi* of the clients, as claimed by one informant in the excerpt below.

Extract 4: [EI-Lan6: 4: 42]

6. I: *Ni renwei gen tongshi, kehu huo shangsi qiatan shengyi de shihou, gu mianzi shi hen zhongyao de ma?*

你認爲跟同事,客戶或上司洽談生意的時候,顧面子是很重要的嗎?

Is it important to maintain *mianzi* when dealing with business among your clients, colleagues or superiors?

7. Lan: *Na dangran. Ni buneng qu shanghai dao pohuai dao bieren de mianzi a, ni yao pohuai ta de mianzi, shengyi hui zuo bu cheng a!*

那當然。 你不能去傷害到,破壞到別人的面子啊,你要破壞他的面子, 生意會作不成啊!

Of course. You can't hurt or damage others' *mianzi*. If you damage his *mianzi*, you will even lose your business.

Here the informant responds to a question about the importance of maintaining *mianzi* in business negotiations by claiming that damaging the *mianzi* of others will result in losing business.

This theme of maintaining *mianzi* was expanded upon by another informant who outlined the importance of maintaining both the client's *mianzi* and that of the agent.

Extract 5: [EI-C9: 3: 40]

6. I: *Na nimen zai gen kehu jieshuo nimen de chanpin de shihou a, hui bu hui juede gu ziji de mianzi gen gu kehu de mianzi hen zhong-yao?*

那你們在跟客戶解說你們的產品的時候啊,會不會覺得顧自己
的面子跟顧客戶的面子很重要?

When you introduce your products to your clients, do you think that it is important to maintain your *mianzi* or maintain your client's *mianzi*?

7.   C: *Keneng zai yewu fangmian, chuli zhege hui bijiao yuanrong,* ((section omitted)) *jiu xiang women taiyu suo jiang de,* ((Taiwanese)) 'buah piah siang bīn kng', ((section omitted)) *xiang tong yisi.* ((section omitted)) *Gongsi de bufen shi yi ge mian, kehu de bufen yeshi yi ge mian, mianzi you de hua, lizi dajia dou you,* ((section omitted)) *na jintian ni chuqu shi daibiao gongsi, yao ba zhege chanpin xiaoshou chuqu, na ni yeyao qude kehu de rentong, yao rentong ni de gongsi ni de chanpin, ni cai you banfa ba chanpin xiaoshou chuqu, suoyi zhege fanmian liang bian dou yao gu.*

可能在業務方面,處理這個會比較圓融 ((部分省略)),就像我們
台語所講的, "抹壁雙面光" ((部分省略)),相同意思,((部分省
略)),公司的部分是一個面,客戶的部分也是一個面,面子有的
話,裡子大家有,((部分省略)),那今天你出去是代表公司,要把這
個產品銷售出去,那你也要取得客戶的認同,要認同你的公司
你的產品,你才有辦法把產品銷售出去,所以這個方面兩邊都
要顧。

Maybe in the aspect of marketing, while handling this, [we try to be] more flexible. ((section omitted)) It's similar to a Taiwanese saying, '*buah piah siang bīn kng*' (polishing the wall furbishes two sides). ((section omitted)) The meaning is the same. ((section omitted)) The company is one side [of *mian*], and the client is the other [side of *mian*]. If you have *mianzi*, everyone can have *lizi*. ((section omitted)) If you are [acting] on behalf of the company to sell this product today, you need to seek the client's recognition first. To enable you to sell this product, you need to have your clients recognise your company. Therefore, you need to maintain both sides [of *mianzi*].

This informant responds to the same question (extract (5) turn 7 above) by emphasising that in order to do business one needs to be 'recognised' by one's clients. This recognition is achieved through maintaining the *mianzi* of both sides in business negotiations. The Taiwanese expression mentioned by the informant, *buah piah siang bīn kng* ('polishing the wall furbishes two sides'), implies that it is vital to maintain your own *mianzi* as well as your client's *mianzi* and *lizi* at the same time. If a client does not obtain *lizi* (i.e., his expectations in regard to the business negotiations), he may feel his *mianzi* is being threatened or may even feel he is losing *mianzi*. Thus, even though obtaining *lizi* is of course a primary aim in business, the informants all emphasised the importance of building a good relationship by maintaining *mianzi* on both sides.

The emic concepts invoked by the native informants during the ethnographic interviews attempt to demonstrate and justify participant's orientation and procedural consequentiality in warranting their interpretations in the face-to-face interactions. The subsequent interactional analysis in this research, however, is *informed* but not *driven/constrained* by these folk notions, which are laid out as analytical tools to examine whether they are consonant with the underpinnings of participants's talk and conduct (Arundale 2010b). In the following analysis of interactional data, interestingly, there is an instance where both participants are not always oriented to maintaining each other's *mianzi*, and indeed at some points even threaten the other person's *mianzi*. Nevertheless, the agent ultimately gains the case (*lizi*) without damaging the long-term relationship between himself and the client. It is for this reason that a distinction needs to be made between emic concepts and emic practices, as we shall see.

CHAPTER 5

Emic practices of face: dyadic interactions vs multiparty interactions

This chapter includes incidents involving the interactional achievement of face in business contexts. The analysis of the interactional achievement of face in an extended audiovisual recording of authentic business negotiations provides insight into how face (i.e., *mianzi*) may be threatened in interaction, reflecting an example of what has been termed here emic face practices. The first half of this chapter starts with face and face practices in dyadic business interactions within the context of routine business interactions in which an incident involved strategic embarrassment of face threat projected by the insurance agent towards his client over a number of utterances in the sequence. This incident shows that the way in which business people talk about face (i.e., as a concept) is not necessarily consistent with their practices in actual interactions. It thus provides empirical evidence that grounds the theoretical distinction between emic concepts and emic practices in relation to face. The second half of this chapter involves two mediation interactions in which face and face practices emerged through negotiation of indemnity in multiparty mediation interactions. A number of face practices are identified in these two interactions and the analysis of how face is interactionally achieved is also demonstrated. The focus on the analysis of face practices, therefore, attempts to go beyond how face (i.e., *mianzi*) is conceptualised and thus provides an interactional view on emic practice, that is, how face and face practices actually emerge in business face-to-face interactions.

5.1 Face practices in dyadic business interactions

The analysis here focuses on how face and face practices emerge in dyadic business negotiations. These interactions were (audio) visually recorded when the insurance agents visited their clients (see Chapter 2). The interactions here are all one-to-one business interactions involving discussions regarding insurance policies and the organisation of marketing plans. While a number of face-related incidents arose in these interactions, a key face practice to emerge in the course of this analysis was that of occasioning strategic embarrassment through topicalising unmet expectations.

5.1.1 Strategic embarrassment of face threatening: topicalising unmet expectations

Strategic embarrassment involves the speaker occasioning embarrassment for the addressee by bringing up an instance where the speaker's expectations (usually arising from their previous interactions) have not been met by the addressee, something which the addressee is likely to want to be left unsaid. The speaker attempts to embarrass the addressee into doing what he or she wants by topicalising these unmet expectations, thereby implying a mild reproach or complaint (Drew & Holt 1988; Drew & Walker 2009; Schegloff 2005). Embarrassment is generally defined, following Goffman's (1956) seminal work, as a 'moment in face-to-face interactions where an individual becomes flustered, momentarily loses self-control, and is unable to comfortably participate in the systematically organised procedures that conversation requires' (Sandlund 2004: 162). Signs of embarrassment include blushing, blinking, hesitation, absent-mindedness, vocal pitch changes, stuttering speech (Goffman 1956: 265–266), as well as, fidgeting movements, shifting gaze, and ambivalent body postures (Heath 1988: 153; Lewis 1993; Sandlund 2004). According to Goffman (1956), embarrassment arises when 'the expressive facts at hand threaten or discredit the assumptions a participant finds he has projected about his identity' (Goffman 1956: 269), and crucially, that suffering embarrassment in social interaction displays the orientation of participants 'to shared norms of conduct' (Goffman 1956: 268; Sandlund 2004: 162). Embarrassment thus 'emerges in relation to a specific action produced by a co-participant' (Heath 1988: 154), either on the part of the speaker or addressee. One may embarrass oneself through one's own behaviour (e.g., loss of body control, social 'gaffes' and so on) (Goffman 1956: 268–269), or alternatively, one may trigger embarrassment in another co-interactant. The latter has been termed strategic embarrassment in cases where triggering embarrassment in others is built into turn design (Bradford & Petronio 1998; Gross & Stone 1964; Sharkey 1992, 1997): 'interactants sometimes use planned communication strategies for triggering embarrassment in a co-interactant … the instigation of embarrassment in others is designed to achieve certain interactional goals. Such goals may be designed to have both positive and negative outcomes, and are thus not always malicious acts to make others uncomfortable' (Sandlund 2004: 178–179).

A common focus of research in this area to date has been on teasing as a form of embarrassment elicitor (Sandlund 2004), and the ways in which it can be exploited to establish or maintain power, express sanctions of another person's behaviour, to discredit someone's presented identity, and to index solidarity (Bradford & Petronio, 1998; Gross & Stone 1964; Sharkey 1992, 1997; see also Haugh 2010a for an overview). In dyadic business interactions, however, topicalising unmet expectations was found to be a key way of occasioning embarrassment on the part of clients or agents and thereby giving rise to evaluations of threats to their face.

The interactional achievement of strategic embarrassment coordinates with constituting evaluations of face threat which can be observed, for instance, in the following incident which took place at the client's (Chen) business when an insurance agent (Lan) went to collect the annual insurance fee for Chen's property. Both participants spoke in Taiwanese for the entire conversation. The key incident involving strategic embarrassment occurs when Lan threatens their relationship as he attempts to persuade Chen to transfer the insurance for one of his cars back to Lan's company. Since Lan and Chen have known each other for more than 15 years, they have established a long-term relationship based on Chen buying insurance from Lan's company, although having such a long-term relationship does not necessarily imply closeness in the sense of intimacy here, but rather a sense of mutual obligation. Lan succeeds in persuading Chen to shift his car insurance business from another company to Lan's company through strategic embarrassment. As both Lan and Chen are demonstrably orienting to the threats to their relationship in this interaction, it is suggested that this strategic embarrassment is evaluated as face threatening. However, this face threat is allowable (i.e., treated as relationship-appropriate) because of the way in which Lan appeals to their *guanxi*.

Excerpt 2: IR-4 [1: 44]

```
1  L:    ah  lí  tsuèkīn  (.)  eh  lí  tann  tshia  sī  lóng  pan        dī
         PRT you  recently     PRT you  now   car    be  all   deal with  CP

         tó-uī  ah  khì°huh°<
         where  PRT CP  PRT

         'Ah where is your car [insurance] being dealt with recently?'

2  C:    tshia?  (0.2)°tshia ↓(0.1)  huètshia  °huè -( )
         guá  tse   to  >kiau-<
         car           car           van       van-    me  this  be  sedan

         kiau-tshia  ooh?=
         sedan        PRT

         'Car? car van van this is-, this is sed-you mean the sedan?'

3  L:    =tshia guá tann guá ah  bo  puànn tâi ah↑((swishing hand))>
         car    I   now  I   PRT N   half  C   PRT
```

```
lín   bú   a   tsit-leh kóng bé    ho   guá°bé   ho   guá°=
your  mum  PRT once      say  want give me  want give me
```

'Now I don't have any half of [your] car [insurance]. Your mother once
said she wants to give it [insurance business] to me'

((phone rings))

4   C:
```
=>ah tshia↑<((looking away))e::: guá  hit   tai huètshia(1.0)
  PRT car                    PRT  I    that C   van
ah↓guá hit  tai huètshia ho   guán giap-bu-a      pan
PRT I   that C   van          give our  business agent handle
lah(.)guán giap-bu-a        pan    lah
PRT   our  business agent   handle PRT
```

'How do I know. Er, that van. Ah, that is being dealt with by my business
agent, being dealt with by my business agent.'

5   L:
```
lín  giap-bu-a        kam   u-siánn-mih u  siánn-mih >hit-
lo--a?<
your business agent   could have what have what       that
```

'Your business agent, what what does [he] have?'

(2.0) ((chair squeaking)) ((looking into distance))

6   C:
```
ah: >tiu<   tiu:: ((patting envelope))=
PRT that's that's
```

'Ah, that's, that's…'

7   L:
```
                              =[lí] hit  tai tang-sî kàu-kî?
                              your  that C   when     due
```

'When is [the insurance of car] due'

8   C:
```
>guán hit  jà< tang-sî kàu-kî?
our   that C   when     due
```

'When is [the insurance of our car] due?'

((chair squeaking))

9   L:
```
kin-nî    tsuán toh tng  lâi°=
this year shift CP  back CP
```

'Shift back [the insurance] this year'

10   C:
```
                    = hó    lah   [hó    lah]
                    alright PRT   alright PRT
```

'Alright, alright.'

```
11  L:   ((walking away)) >[kaki ]<tsia-ê bô ma ka   sittsai::
                            ourself this   side N  also more down-to-earth
```
         'It's more reliable to deal with people on your side'

```
12  C:   hó      lah hó
         alright PRT alright
```
         'Alright, alright'

```
13  L:   heh    ah
         right PRT
```
         'Right'

```
14  C:   hó      [ah°]
         alright PRT
```
         'Okay'

```
15  L:   [hon hó]   hó     hó    án-ne                      guá lâi tsáu
         okay alright alright alright then ((walking away)) I  come CP
```
         'Okay? Okay okay, then I am going'

This excerpt begins when Lan brings up the topic of which company Chen insures his car with at present, which foreshadows the subsequent emergence of an implied complaint. In doing so, a sequence where Lan attempts to persuade Chen to shift his car insurance back to Lan's company is initiated (turns 1–15). The sequence begins with the pre-request 'Where is your car (insurance) being dealt with recently?', which establishes the grounds for making this request in turn 9 (Rue & Zhang 2008). Lan presupposes through his pre-request that Chen has given the insurance business to someone else instead of Lan, despite their long-term business relationship (*guanxi*). Chen responds in a hesitant and repetitive manner in turn 2 focusing ostensibly on fixing the reference for which vehicle they are talking about. Lan then goes on to say that he has not been given any car insurance business by Chen in turn 3, thereby implying a complaint that Chen did not keep his (previous) promise (to shift the insurance business to Lan) (Wu 2004). Chen indexes an embarrassed (*buhaoyisi*) stance in answering this question in turn 4 through his pausing and hesitation, and by averting his gaze away from Lan (Heath 1988: 145–146; Sandlund 2004: 163; Yang 2010: 195–198). Then Lan carries on to ask what Chen's business person has in turn 5 using the Taiwanese term *u siánn-mih*, which implies either that Chen's business person must have some kind of ability or, more likely, a special relationship (*guanxi*) with Chen. In doing so, Lan implies a second complaint as to why he has not been given the car insurance business by Chen, to which Chen expresses his reluctance to respond in turn 6, through averting his gaze away from Lan and his fidgety body language, thereby once again indexing embarrassment (Heath 1988: 145–146; Sandlund 2004: 163; Yang 2010: 195–198). In turn 7, Lan returns to the request sequence with another pre-request asking when the insurance is due, to which Chen responds by repeating the question, thereby showing hesitancy and nervousness. Strategic embarrassment is thus interactionally achieved through Lan topicalising his expectation that Chen will insure with Lan's company, and Chen's subsequent display of embarrassment. The fact that Chen does not answer Lan's question in turn 7 occasions Lan's pursuit of a response from Chen in turn 9 (cf. Pomerantz 1984) by directly asking Chen to shift the insurance back to him. Chen at this point responds with immediate agreement (turn 10). In immediately agreeing, Chen allows Lan to enact authority and power over him, thereby evoking their *guanxi* ('connection'). Lan subsequently employs the term *kaki* (Taiwanese) (cf. Mandarin: *zijiren*) or 'insider' in turn 11 to emphasise the importance of their in-group relationship through an appeal to their *guanxi* again. In turns 14 and 15, then, in response to Lan's imperative request, Lan and Chen reach an agreement that Chen will shift his car insurance back later in the year.

In the course of this sequence, Lan appears to accomplish a particular interactional goal (Spencer-Oatey 2005, 2009), namely, getting Chen to shift his car insurance back to Lan's company through invoking their long-term *guanxi*. The term 'interactional goal' in this data set is used broadly to refer to both transactional and relational functions, as these two are often interdependent given that the management of relational goals is required to achieve a transactional goal (cf. Spencer-Oatey 2005: 107). Given that this research aims to examine face practices in business contexts, the nature of business interactions thereby inevitably involves particular transaction-oriented tasks, such as obtaining insurance business, negotiation of the amount of compensation and so forth. However, alongside achieving such transactional goals, the management of relational goals might also need to be taken into account in business interactions, since the involved participants are relationally interconnected, either through business relationships, friendships or even both. The interactional goal here, therefore, is intertwined with both transactional and relational goals.

In this case, while Lan attempts to reach this interactional goal of requesting a shift of insurance business through their long-term *guanxi*, it involves moves that can be evaluated as face-threatening. Drawing from FCT, there are three face interpretings involved in the co-constitution of evaluations of face threat through the course of this sequence. In bringing up an instance where his expectations in regards to Chen buying car insurance from his company have not been met, and then going on to imply complaints about this (turns 3 and 5), Lan appears to project their relationship as having a lower degree of connectedness. Chen also appears to interpret these two complaints on Lan's part as implying that Lan is dissatisfied with this lower degree of connectedness (i.e., interpreted face), as he indexes an embarrassed stance through showing hesitation and reluctance to respond to Lan's line of questioning in turns 4 and 6. Up until this particular interaction, Lan and Chen have had a long-standing business relationship developed over the course of 17 years, which encompasses mutual obligations they are expected to meet (i.e., Chen has consistently obtained insurance from Lan's company, while Lan has maintained a personal interest in Chen's business). Their perceived degree of connectedness can thus be characterised as having been fairly high to date (i.e., their evolving face). In this particular interaction, both participants also understand that Lan's call is a business one, where naturally the aim is for them to make money in conducting their business, as well as to maintain good relations for future business dealings. There is nothing invoked in the current context, therefore, which suggests that their expectations in regards to their degree of connectedness are different from those they have previously had (i.e., contextual face). As Lan and Chen interactionally achieve strategic embarrassment, there is a proffered shift in face interpretings, that is, diverging interpretings between their projected/interpreted face and evolving face, as the former involves a lower degree of connection than the latter. On the other hand, there is no difference between their interpretings of their evolving face and contextual face, and thus there is no situated shift in face interpreting. As the proffered shift and situated shift in face interpretings are not consistent, Lan's projecting and Chen's interpreting of face are evaluated as threatening. In other words, as the two men interactionally achieve strategic embarrassment in the course of this sequence, both find their relationship or face to be threatened. However, while the interactional achievement of strategic embarrassment is arguably evaluated as face threatening, it does not negatively impact on their long-term relationship (i.e., evolving face). This is because Lan appeals to expectations about their relationship that he might reasonably have, namely, their *guanxi*, which thereby enables this face threat to be treated as allowable in that interaction. This analysis was further supported by Lan, who reported to me during the second round of data collection after two years that Chen's agreement to the shift the insurance business back to him was genuine and their long-term business relationship has continued since that interaction.

Notably, Lan's move to embarrass Chen about the car insurance through topicalising unmet expectations appears to be understood by the participants as occasioning an opportunity for Chen to fulfil these unmet expectations, thereby creating interactional space for Chen to repair this threat to their relationship, which Chen does indeed do through accepting Lan's request. In terms of FCT, the achieving of strategic embarrassment in effect changes Lan and Chen's evolving face in the direction of much reduced connectedness. However, both their contextual face that Chen will interpret the embarrassment as an opportunity to fulfil expectations involve relatively higher connectedness, resulting in a situated shift in face interpretings. Chen's subsequent acquiescence to Lan's request occasions an interpreting of greater connectedness, thereby leading to a proffered shift in face interpretings. As both the situated shift and the proffered shift involve convergence, their relationship or face is thus supported. In this way, while the strategic embarrassment initiated by Lan through topicalising unmet expectations is arguably evaluated as face-threatening, it subsequently occasions a response that is evaluated as face-supportive.

This incident thus involves the interactional achievement of strategic embarrassment through complaints implied by Lan in regard to unmet expectations. That this sequence involves the interactional achievement of evaluations of threats to their face is apparent from the way Chen becomes defensive and embarrassed by the line of questioning from Lan. Those threats to their face also involve Lan explicitly invoking the expectations that follow from the long-term relationship between himself and Chen which has been established over a number of years (i.e., their *guanxi*). In this way, the face threat is treated as relationship-appropriate and so allowable by Chen and Lan. This relationship is also the basis of evaluations of face support arising from Chen's subsequent agreement to shift the insurance business back to Lan's company. The incident therefore shows the importance of taking relationships into account when analysing face in interactions between Taiwanese, as it is through invoking relationship-bound expectations (*guanxi*) that Lan is able to enact power with regard to Chen and achieve his interactional goals.

The interactional achievement of strategic embarrassment can also be seen to emerge in another incident involving the same insurance agent going to another client's workplace. Here, the insurance agent, Lan, goes to Chu's factory to hand over a renewal form for annual property insurance. Both participants speak in a mixture of Taiwanese and Chinese Mandarin. Throughout the course of this excerpt Lan and Chu co-constitute evaluations of threats to their face. In the conversation preceding this excerpt, Lan has handed over the insurance renewal forms, to which Chu has responded by asking Lan why he did not give him the renewal forms before the expiry date. Lan then explains that the company car insurance will remain active as long as Lan has already renewed Chu's annual insurance. Following this explanation, Lan interrupts Chu and asks him about accident insurance for his employees in order to try to set up another insurance policy with Chu. In attempting to arrange another insurance policy, the interactional achievement of strategic embarrassment arises coordinate with co-constituting evaluations of face threats.

Excerpt 3: [IR-20: 1: 56]

```
26   L:    ((patting on C's shoulder, pointing outside))
           >°ah   koh   tsit-ê   hit-ê   siánn°<hit-ê::   %nimen yuengong
            PRT   more  one-C    that    what    that      your   employee
           shi bao    na    jia?% ((rubbing nose))
           be  insure which C
```

'There is one more thing. Which company do you insure your employees with?'

```
27   C:    %yuen::gong::?((putting his hand on his forehead and think-
           ing))
           Employee
           >Hongtu< (.)  >yiwai     wo<% lí   kóng [%yiwai    wo?%]
           (company name) accident Q    you say    accident Q
```

'Employee? Hongtu. You mean accident [insurance]? You mean accident [insurance]?'

```
28   L:    [°heh %yiwai%°]=((keeps rubbing nose))
            yes  accident
```

'Yes, accident [insurance cover]'

```
29   C:                    =gah   %Hongtu %      ê-khuán-=
                           seems (company name) seems
```

> 'It seems to be Hongtu [insurance company]'

```
30   L:                                        =tsit-má pí       guá
                                               now     compare  we
           tsia kuì      ah=
           here expensive PRT
```

'It's more expensive compared to ours now'

```
31   C:                                   =>ah guá m<wa m-tsai-iánn=
                                           PRT I   N I  N know
```

> 'I don't, I don't know'

```
32   L:                                        =?tsia siánn tshú-lí eh°
                                               This  who   handle  Q
```

> 'Who handles this?'

```
33   C:    tse: ing-kai ma  sī guá thài-thài tshú-lí eh=
           This should also be my  wife      handle  PRT
```

'This is supposed to be handled by my wife'

34 L: `````` =ah::°lí náe bô kiò
                          PRT you why N ask

guá lâi tshú-lí°=
me   come handle

'Ah, why didn't you ask me to take it?'

35 C: ```` =ah lí lí°> lí ài tsau i tsau i eh< guá si
                    PRT you you you need find 3sg find her PRT I be

m-tsai-iánn°
N know

'Ah, you need to ask her, I don't know [about it]'

36 L: hmm? guá u   kah pò-kè kuè leh ((looking into distance))
        Q   I   have give quote CP   PRT

'Mm? I have quoted the price [to her]'

37 C: (1.0)((nervous laughing))(h)m-tsai-iánn (.)heh ah (0.5)tan guá
                               N know   yes PRT   but ours
        he   si %shuyu e (.)you >you<liang zhong fanshi yi zhong
        that be belong PRT have have two   kind way   one kind
        shi (1.0) yi zhong shi% lán ê (.)tshiunn guá>tshiunn guá< e
        be   one kind be our ASSC like   we like   we will
        tiann tshut-tshai   ê   tsit khuán ê   tse mah(.)
        often on business trip ASSC this kind ASSC this PRT
        tse guá tsai-iánn si %Hongtu%(.)   >ah beh kóng< %quan
        this I   know   be (company name) PRT want talk   whole
        >quan ti<   yuengong% ê   tsit-kuah %baokua chang
        whole entire employee ASSC this kind include factory
        nei   de   zhe% guá to   m-tsai-iánn si m si %Hongtu%
        inside ASSC this I   then N know   be N be (company name)
        ah (.)ah si lín   ê   guá to   m-tsai-iánn
        PRT   or be your ASSC I   then N know

'I don't know, yes. But our one belongs to, we have two kinds of ways, one
is like that we have to go on business trips often. And I know this [kind
of insurance] belongs to Hongtu. If we talk about the insurance for all of
the employees and the insurance including the safety of the factory, then
I don't know whether it belongs to Hongtu or your company'

At the beginning of this excerpt, Lan interrupts Chu's ongoing speech in the
preceding turn and signals that he is going to change to a new topic by patting
on Chu's shoulder and pointing outside (turn 26). Lan then asks, 'There is one

more thing. Which company do you insure your employees with?', which topicalises a particular insurance policy, thereby initiating a request sequence where he attempts to persuade Chu to take accident insurance for his employees with Lan's company. Lan frames his pre-request, however, as tentative as he hedges the question with verbal tokens (*hit-ê*, 'that'), elongation, softening the speech, and rubbing his nose in a manner that displays hesitancy, and possible embarrassment (Goffman 1956: 264; Heath 1988: 153; Sandlund 2004: 163; Yang 2010: 206–211). Chu in turn responds to this pre-request by displaying discomfort and possible embarrassment through hesitation, elongation and repetition, as he ostensibly attempts to fix the reference for which type of insurance Lan is referring to (turn 27). Although Chu has already said the name of the other insurance company (Hongtu), he still seeks clarification about which kind of insurance Lan means, indicating that he may be reluctant to inform Lan which company he is insuring his employees with. This is evident from the fact that, in this context, the travel insurance for employees which is brought up by Chu is not particularly relevant, since taking out travel insurance for employees is only done when specific travel is imminent. Yet there is no specific indication in the context that Chen and Chu are referring to any employees who are going on a business trip. Thus, there are strong grounds to claim that Chu is displaying embarrassment rather than doing recalling or the like in this instance.

In his next turn, Lan continues to display nervousness through his continuous nose rubbing and weak tone of voice as he confirms that he means accident insurance for employees (turn 28). However, this utterance does not merely serve as a response to Chu's clarification, but also has an interrogative embedded within it, namely, inquiring which company Chu has insured his employees with. Chu's subsequent response in turn 29, where he confirms that it is Hongtu, is hedged with tokens (*gah...ê-khuán*, 'it seems like'), thereby positioning himself as uncertain about this. Nevertheless, Lan goes on in turn 30 to comment about the price of the other company, claiming that it is more expensive than his own, thereby implicitly criticising Chu for insuring with the other company. Chu's redundant verbal tokens are evidence of Chu's nervousness and embarrassment about Lan's claim and implied criticism (turn 31). Lan next asks 'Who handles this?', seeking to find out who is responsible for this matter in turn 32. Chu responds that his wife is the one who contacts the Hongtu company (turn 33). Lan then directly asks 'why didn't you ask me to take it?' in the following turn. In doing so, Lan presupposes that, since he has been managing the company car insurance for Chu's factory, he expects he should be the one to be relied on for other insurance business, thereby invoking their established business relationship. In his subsequent response (turn 35), Chu again denies direct knowledge of the case and shifts the focus to his wife by saying 'Ah, you need to ask her, I don't know [about it]'. Lan implies a complaint about this again in turn 36 in claiming that Chu's wife knows Lan's company offers cheaper accident insurance for employees. Chu then responds with considerable redundancy accompanied by concomitant nervous laughter (Glenn 2003) after a one second pause, in giving a long explanation to satisfy Lan's pursuit of a response (Pomerantz 1984). At this point, Lan abandons the request sequence since Chu's wife is not there at the factory, so nothing more can be said at that point.

In the course of this sequence, Lan attempts to accomplish a particular interactional goal, namely, getting Chu to shift his employee accident insurance back to Lan's company. However, this time he is not successful, at least not in the short term. Lan attempts to persuade Chu through topicalising unmet expectations, thereby interactionally achieving strategic embarrassment. These moves are also evaluated as face-threatening. In showing that he expects Chu to buy accident insurance from his company, and then going on to imply complaints about the fact that Chu has bought it from another company, Lan thereby projects a face threat to Chu as he designs the utterance. In contrast to the previous incident, however, Lan frames his pre-request (turn 26) and complaints (turns 30, 34 and 36) more tentatively by showing his hesitation or embarrassment to make them. Chen also appears to interpret these implied complaints as Lan expressing dissatisfaction with the lower degree of connectedness arising from these unmet expectations, as he shows hesitation and reluctance to respond to Lan's line of questioning, and indeed tries to shift the responsibility for that decision to his wife rather than himself (interpreted face). Similar to the previous interaction, Lan and Chu have developed a business relationship over the course of five years, during which Chu has obtained his insurance from Lan's company, while Lan has maintained a personal interest in Chu's business. Their degree of connectedness can be characterised as having been fairly high thus far (evolving face), although Lan's greater degree of tentativeness suggests that his relationship with Chu may not be as close as his relationship with Chen (which is a reflection of the length of time of their business dealings). There is also nothing invoked in the current context to suggest that their expectations in regard to their degree of connectedness are any different from those which they previously had (contextual face). It can be seen here, then, that the proffered shift in their face involves divergence between their interpreted face and evolving face due to Lan implying a complaint through topicalising unmet expectations, while the situated shift involves no divergence between their evolving face and contextual face. This difference gives rise to an evaluation of the current face interpreting as threatening to their relationship. However, once again, while this action is evaluated as face threatening, it does not negatively impact on their long-term relationship (evolving face). This is because Lan arguably appeals to expectations he might reasonably hold as a consequence of having had a long-standing business relationship through this move, with his appeal to *guanxi* also being alluded to in follow-up interviews with Lan. These implicit appeals to their *guanxi* thus enable this face threat to be received as allowable in that interaction.

In contrast to Excerpt (2), however, Lan is here unsuccessful, as Chu ultimately shifts the negotiations about this to his wife. Yet although Chu does not promise Lan that he will shift the insurance business to him at the end of the interaction, he states that he will find out more information about the insurance conditions from his wife later, and thereby demonstrates (at least on the surface) concern about Lan's questions. In this way, Chu's response, while not necessarily open to evaluation as face supportive, is at the very least not face threatening. Notably, Lan and Chu have also continued to have an ongoing business relationship since the recording was made.

This incident involves co-constituting threats to Lan and Chu's face. The threats arise from Lan's pursuit of a response through repeated questioning about employee accident insurance in Chu's factory, which appear to be an attempt to arrange further insurance for Lan's company. This line of questioning, through which he implies complaints, threatens their face in light of their long-term, established relationship with each other. However, it is apparent from Lan's nervous questioning and concomitant body language in the interaction that he is aware of the potential threats to their face. Yet he nevertheless persists in this line of persuasion, indicating that strategically embarrassing his client and thereby threatening their relationship and face constitutes a recognisable interactional practice in Taiwanese business contexts.

A similar practice was found in the multiparty mediation interactions (which are discussed in further detail in the following section). In the following excerpt from an interaction involving yet another insurance agent, who this time was the target of strategic embarrassment, for instance, strategic embarrassment also occasions evaluations of face threat. In this case, unmet expectations were topicalised by one of the representatives of two persons that were involved in a car accident where the insurance agent's clients were at fault. The interaction took place in a local government mediation department. In this mediation session, those present were the committee mediator (CM), the committee vice-chair (CVC) who is representing the people who were hurt in the car accident along with another representative, the insurance agent (Ying) and the clients of that agent who caused the accident. At this point in the meeting, the CVC is trying to get the insurance agent, Ying, to agree to increase the indemnity payment.

Excerpt 4: [100727001: 14: 51]

```
20   CVC:  ah  kah  tshú-lí-lí  eh  tse  lóng ma  ka-kīah
           PRT help deal with  PRT  this all  also self

           tàu-tīn  ê     lah  he   guán a-ku   lah
           together ASSC  PRT  that my   uncle  PRT
```

'Ah, help me deal with it. They are our people. That is my uncle'

```
21   Ying:  °tse° guá bô-huat-too lah  li  ài   khuànn ài
            this  I   N-solution  PRT  you need see    need

            khuànn ài   khuànn [i   ê-()]
            see    need see     he  ASSC
```

'I can't do anything. You have to see [the maxium] of (his   )'

```
22   CM:   [()>ÁN-NE<]  LI  BÔ-HUAT-TOO-  OOH=
               this     you N-solution    PRT
```

'You can't do anything [about it]?'

```
23   Ying:  =bô-huat-too=
             N-solution
```

'I have no solution'

```
24   CVC:  ah hiau-hīng ah  bô-huat-too beh-án-náh tshòng au-pái
           ah terrible  PRT n-solution  how        do    future

           pó     pat-king bô pó     Huaxing
           insure other C  N  insure (company name)
```

'It's terrible. What [can we] do if you can't do anything. [Let's] not insure
with Huaxing and insure with another [company] next time'

```
25         ((someone sniggering))
```

```
26   Ying:  hong-pian  tioh hó   lah hong-pian  khah hó    lah-
            convenient then good PRT convenient more good  PRT
```

'It's better to be more convenient'

The committee vice-chair explicitly invokes in turn 20 the familial relationship
he has with the injured parties of the car accident, namely, he is the nephew of
the injured parties. As he is also the committee mediator's son, he is also able
to implicitly appeal to the long-standing friendship between Ying and the committee mediator. In other words, he is able to ask for special favour due to the
presence of an intermediatory (i.e., his father) who mediates the *guanxi* ('connection') between himself and the insurance agent. Ying responds by claiming

that he is not able to offer a greater amount of compensation and starts to offer an account for this (turn 21). However, before he finishes this account the committee mediator interrupts in turn 22 with a reformulation of the committee vice-chair's previous explicit request as a question, which only implies a request for greater compensation. However, since this reformulated question has a negative polarity (i.e., 'can't do anything'), disconfirmation is the (structurally) preferred response (Heritage & Raymond 2012; Raymond 2003; Stivers and Enfield 2010), which Ying indeed provides in turn 23. In this way, it is confirmed that Ying's insurance company is not able to increase the amount of compensation. The committee vice-chair immediately responds in turn 24 with a strong negative assessment (*ah hiau-hīng*, 'it's terrible') in relation to his uncle having to pay the costs of medical treatment himself, and then implies that other insurance companies would offer better indemnity payments. In this way, he invokes an expectation that Ying should be able to offer a better indemnity payment. In topicalising this unmet expectation, then, the committee vice-chair is occasioning strategic embarrassment for Ying. The agent's subsequent response in turn 26 is disaligning, as it has no direct relevance to the committee vice-chair's previous turn, and thus arguably displays embarrassment on his part. The laughter of others (turn 25) also indicates that this topicalising of unmet expectations is indeed embarrassing for Ying.

This strategic embarrassment is interactionally achieved alongside the evaluations of a number of face threats in a similar manner to the examples previously discussed. The primary face threat arising in this part of the meeting, however, is the threat to Ying's relationship with his clients as a competent agent representing an insurance company that offers good services. In the course of the above sequence, the committee vice-chair attempts to negotiate a greater amount of compensation for the injured parties of the car accident he is representing through topicalising unmet expectations, namely, that they would expect that other insurance companies would provide a higher level of compensation. In interactionally achieving a negative assessment of Ying and his company in front of all those present at the mediation meeting, the committee vice-chair projects that Ying lacks the ability to offer good services as an insurance agent to others (and so impugns the reputation of his company more broadly). In this way, he projects a face threat to Ying's relationship with his actual clients as he designs the utterance. Ying has a long-standing relationship with his existing clients, and thus his degree of connectedness can be characterised as having been fairly high thus far (evolving face). There is also nothing invoked in the current context to suggest that their expectations in regard to their degree of connectedness have altered in any way. The proffered shift in face thus involves a divergence between the interpreted face and evolving face due to the committee vice-chair topicalising unmet expectations in regard to compensation, while there is no situated shift in face, since there is no divergence between their evolving face and contextual face. This difference between the proffered shift and situated shift gives rise to an evaluation of the current face interpreting as threatening to their relationship. Notably, Ying was not able to offer greater compensation during this meeting, and so in the end the case was passed on to another agent in his company.

In a follow-up interview with this insurance agent, Ying, he comments specifically on the actions of the committee vice-chair.

Extract 6: [EI-Y1: 1: 50]

1   Ying: *Na tongchang tamen de jiangfa le, jiu xianba baoxian gongsi daya, 'a baoxian gongsi henzao la', 'baoxian gongsi hen chajin la', 'hen ying la, peide buhao la', a buran jiushishuo, 'xiaci buyao bao tamen la'.*

那通常他們的講法咧,就先把保險公司打壓, '啊保險公司很糟啦', '保險公司很差勁啦', '很硬啦', '賠得不好啦',' 啊不然就是說, '下次不保他們啦。'

Then what they normally do, they will firstly suppress the insurance company on the basis of [his] position, saying 'the insurance is terrible', 'the insurance company is disappointing', 'very unyielding', 'bad indemnity'. Otherwise, they say, 'don't insure with them next time'.

2   I: *Suoyi zheshi hen tongchang de qingkuang lo?*

這是很通常的情況囉所以?

So this is a very common situation then?

3   Ying: *Zheshi hen tongchang de qingkuang, women shi tongchang buhui zuo suowei de bianbo. Yinwei jiang zhe dongxi shi meiyouyong de ma.*

這是很通常的情況,我們是通常不會做所謂的辯駁。因為講這東西是沒有　用的嘛。

This is a very common situation, and we don't normally do the so-called refutation because it's useless [to do so].

In turn 1, Ying generalises about the committee vice-chair's previous negative assessments and topicalising of unmet expectations, which has been characterised here as occasioning strategic embarrassment. He claims that this is something that people bringing indemnity cases against insurance agents 'normally' do. The interviewer then asks whether such a practice is common in turn 2, to which Ying responds in turn 3 that it is indeed common, and something which it is difficult for them to avoid. While follow-up interviews with participants were difficult to accomplish since questioning participants about face-sensitive incidents is face-threatening in itself, as previously noted in Chapter 3, these comments were volunteered by Ying in a discussion that followed the mediation meeting. They indicate his view that, while he does not necessarily like this practice of strategic embarrassment, it is something which is indeed commonly encountered in business interactions. Strategic embarrassment is thus evidently not only recognisable, but is also a recurrent face practice in business interactions.

The interactional practice that has been examined here, namely, strategic embarrassment and its relationship with face, is complex. It thus requires a relatively complex theory of face in which to frame an analysis of it. In particular, a theory of face which takes into account not only the interactional achievement of actions in a local context, but also the ongoing relationships of the participants, as well as particular aspects of the context that can be invoked by participants, is necessary in order to more fully explicate this interactional practice. It has also been argued that the threats examined here are directed at the relationships between the participants first and foremost, as they involve topicalising unmet expectations relative to their ongoing relationships. While implications for the interpretings of their persons are likely to have also arisen during the course of these interactions, these interpretings of their persons are only made relevant because of the ongoing interactional achievement of their relationships. Without relationships, whether they be close and intimate or only temporary, one's interpreted claims in relation to one's self-image are largely irrelevant. The analysis also illustrates that face threat and face support can co-occur in the same interaction since face is more about relationships rather than individual attributes. Although strategic embarrassment occasions on evaluations of threat to the participants' face, the opportunity is also given at the same time for the recipient to fulfil these unmet expectations and consequently to support their face. For this reason, the analysis here has focused primarily on the participants' interpretings of their relationships, here conceptualised as face, consistent with the re-conceptualisation of face as relational in Face Constituting Theory. This is not to say that an examination of participant interpretings of personal attributes is not important, but rather to suggest that the importance of face vis-à-vis relationships in interpersonal interactions has been relatively neglected in analyses of face threats thus far.

It is also important to note here that the analytical lens is broadened beyond how face (i.e., *mianzi*) is understood as an emic concept in Chinese. This is because, as seen in the case of strategic embarrassment of face-threatening, careful analysis of actual interaction indicates that interpretations and evaluations of face do not always emerge in ways that are consistent with folk claims about face (*mianzi*). Indeed, the term 'strategic embarrassment of face-threatening' is used here to describe an emic face practice because there is no readily available equivalent for the notion of face threat in emic discourses on face in Chinese, since to use the term *mianzi*-threat seems somewhat incoherent, for instance. Thus, in order to move into an analysis of emic face practice that is informed by emic concepts, but not constrained by them, the term 'face' and 'face practices' is used in a more technical, analytical sense, albeit one that builds on the understandings of the participants themselves.

5.2 Face practices in multiparty mediation interactions

5.2.1 Mediation about an injury caused by a car accident

This interaction from a mediation session took place at a regional government office in Yi-Lan City and involved eight participants negotiating over the case of a motorbike accident caused by Yang and Yu (the at-fault party) while they were reversing in a sedan around four months before the mediation meeting took place. The mediation session itself only lasted around 20 minutes, and the conversation is spoken entirely in Taiwanese.[1] The injured parties Fang and Fu, who sustained injuries including abrasions and broken teeth from the accident, are seeking compensation from the at-fault parties for the dental implants that were required as a result of the accident. Yang and Yu are the ones who called for this mediation session, hoping that the insurance company which they are insured with would be able to cover all the medical expenses for the injured parties so as to avoid paying extra compensation. Ying, the insurance agent from the Hua-Xin insurance company, represents Yang and Yu, the people at fault, to negotiate with the injured parties in order to reach a mutually agreeable settlement, which will be provided by the insurance company. The CM (committee mediator) Lin, who is the senior mediator allocated to this case, enlists the role of a third party to assist with this negotiation. However, the CM has both a legislative and a family relationship with the injured parties, namely, a legislative relationship as a mediator as well as a distant family relationship with the injured parties. Although there is no particular restriction preventing family members from being involved,[2] the CM nevertheless may be perceived as being biased towards the injured parties

---

1. As the majority of the business interactions and negotiations were spoken in Taiwanese, only the romanisation of the transcription is presented in the following excerpts in the analysis section. By using romanisation in transcriptions, I attempt to retain the original meaning of the Taiwanese data so as not to mislead by using Mandarin Chinese characters.

2. There is no specific regulation which stipulates that a family member shouldn't be involved, apart from the insurance agent being prohibited from taking any mediation where he or she has any relationship with the at-fault parties or the injured parties.

due to the existence of a (distant) family relationship, something which is explicitly commented on by Ying at the end of the interaction. Hsu (the committee vice-chair)[3] and Shih are asked by the injured parties to participate in the mediation as advocates because of their relational connections in order to assist with the negotiations. In terms of the family connections, Hsu is related both to the injured parties, who are Hsu's uncle and aunty (Fang and Fu), and also to the CM (Lin), who is Hsu's father; in other words, the CM is Fang and Fu's cousin-in-law.[4] As Hsu also serves as a public servant for the committee in the local government, his role in the mediation can be perceived as having social face (*mianzi*) that may enable them to accomplish their interactional goal through the recognition of his societal position (cf. Hwang 1987: 946), and it is that his social face (*mianzi*) carries weight in the mediation. Shih, a friend of the injured parties, is also present to assist with the mediation.

Ying has been asked to participate in this mediation by his colleague Wang, who is the main insurance agent Yang and Yu have been in contact with. As Wang has another meditation meeting to attend, Ying stands in for Wang to negotiate the amount of compensation on behalf of the insurance company. At this point, Ying has been notified that both Fang and Yu have received medical treatment and that Fang has had to have a dental implant due to broken teeth caused by the car accident. The injured parties were asked by Wang to bring their medical certificates and receipts to the mediation. The interactional goal of the injured parties in the mediation is thus to ask the at-fault party's insurance company to take responsibility for all the medical treatment, namely, to compensate all the medical costs incurred by the injured parties. However, the amount of compensation for dental implants is limited by the government, as the costs associated with dental implants can vary greatly, depending on the materials and techniques that are used. The compensation limits are specifically stipulated by the government so as to protect the insurance industry, preventing insured parties from over claiming the amount of compensation beyond the scope of their insurance cover. Thus, while Yang and Yu's interactional goal in this mediation is to ask the insurance company to reimburse all of the medical costs they have incurred and not to have to pay the excess beyond the limits of their insurance cover, this is not shared with Ying, who is acting as the at-fault party's insurance agent, since he was notified

3. Hsu works as a committee vice chair in the local government, and his job therefore deals with mediations to help people who have disputes as well. However, this case is allocated to the CM as the main mediator, so Hsu has no legislative authority to mediate, but is only taking an assistant role to help with the negotiations on behalf of the injured parties.
4. Although the familial relationship between the victim party (Fang and Fu) and the CM is quite a distant one, they are still considered fairly close in Chinese relationships. A more accurate translation from Chinese is actually that the CM is like the victim party's 'brother-in-law' (*biaojiefu*, cousinship).

by Wang (Yang and Yu's main contact) that the costs of the dental implants are beyond Yang and Yu's insurance cover. Thus, Ying's interactional goal here in this mediation is, first, to explain the regulations relating to compensation for dental implants and, second, to finalise the total amount of compensation the insurance company can provide.

The diagrams in Figures 5.1 and 5.2 show the relationships between the members involved in the meeting, identifying three types of relationships, namely, legislative, familial, and each member's position in the mediation. Members with legislative relationships take up the basic positions in the mediation process, namely the people at fault, the injured parties, the chair of the mediation and the insurance agent. The assigned insurance agent, Ying is there to negotiate the amount of indemnity which is to be provided by the at-fault parties' insurance company. The rest of the members involved act as representatives who have either friendship or family connections with the people in those basic legislative positions. It is also worth noting here the relationship between the CM and Ying. They have had a number of occasions where they have worked together on mediations in local government over the past few years, and have become well acquainted with each other through the years of collaboration in negotiating the compensation in such cases. The various positions and relationships of the people involved in this mediation are summarised below.

Summary of participants involved:
1. The parties at fault Yang and Yu (both late 50s, couple)
2. The injured parties, Fang and Fu (both late 60s, couple)
3. The insurance agent for the Hua-Xin insurance company, Ying (IA, male, 40s)
4. Lin, the committee mediator (CM, male, 70s) who has a familial relationship with Fang and Fu (Fang and Fu's brother-in-law)
5. Hsu, the committee vice chair (CVC), who is CM's son, and Fang and Fu's nephew (male, 40s)
6. Shih, Fang and Fu's friend (early 50s)

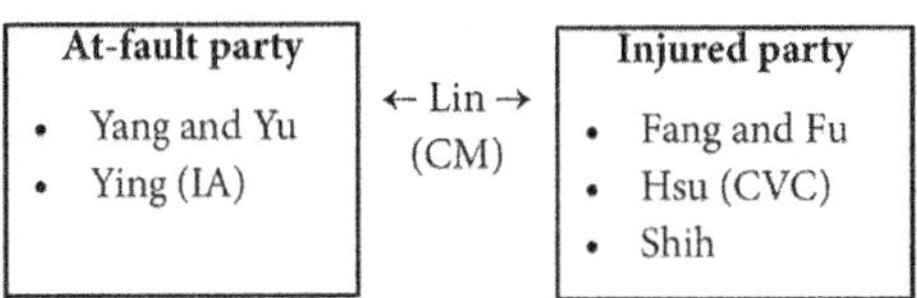

Figure 5.1: The structure of the mediation committee (1)

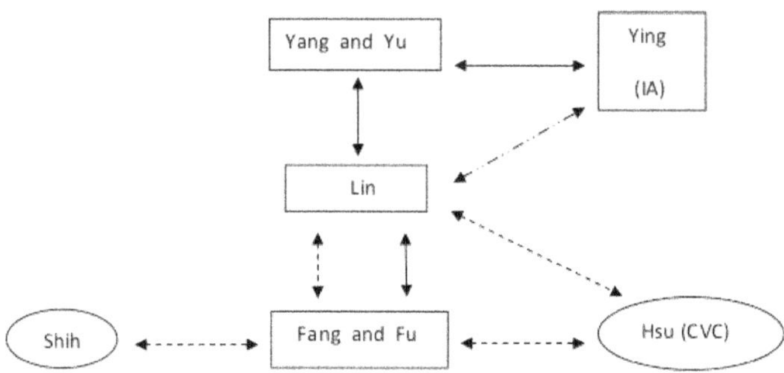

Figure 5.2: The relationships of the members involved (1)

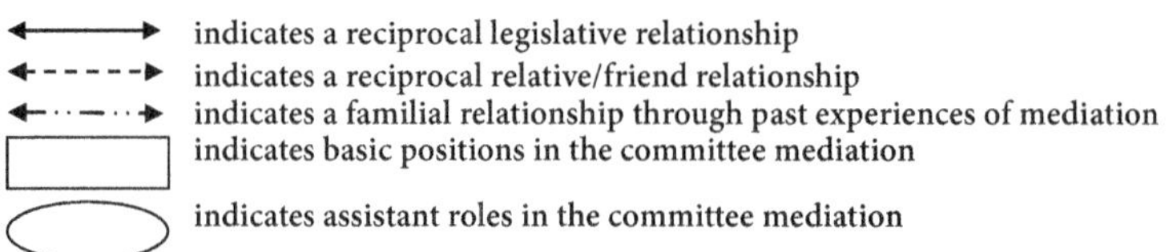

indicates a reciprocal legislative relationship
indicates a reciprocal relative/friend relationship
indicates a familial relationship through past experiences of mediation
indicates basic positions in the committee mediation

indicates assistant roles in the committee mediation

Prior to the start of the interaction, Fang and Fu have handed over to Ying their medical certificates and receipts for their medical treatment, including for dental implants and abrasions, in order to allow him to calculate the total medical costs. As mentioned earlier, Ying has already been notified that the injured party, Fang, has had the dental implant at this point. Ying has been asked to come and settle the negotiation relating to whether it is possible to reimburse all the costs of the dental implant by the at-fault party. The following excerpt begins immediately after Ying has worked out the total amount of Fang and Fu's medical expenses. The CM initiates the following sequence by asking Ying whether the indemnity from the insurance company could cover all the costs of dental implant.

[100727-001: 11: 40]

```
1   CM:    heh  lah   guá  sī  kóng  >tsham<  tsham
           yes  PRT   I    am  say   add-up   add-up

           i   >tse<  tse  tuānn  kî-kan  ê      sún-sit    li
           3sg  this   this  C     period  ASSC   loss       you

           kā  (.)   ha'h  ha'h  ua       kāh        >kāh<
           give-him  add   add   together  help-him   help-him

           kóo       khuànn   [ê     kau    bô]
           estimate  see  if       can  reach  N
```

> Yes, I am saying [that can you] add up his loss during this period, add up
> [all the medical costs] together, and see if [they] can reach [the amount
> of indemnity]

As a mediator, the CM first initiates a request in turn 1, asking Ying to estimate
Fang and Fu's total medical treatment fees, while Ying just finishes going over
the receipts and calculation. [*k*]*āh kóo khuànn ê kau bô* ('help him estimate see
if [the medical costs] can reach [the amount of indemnity]') is thus framed as an
implied directive, by means of the intonation and imperative manner, through
which the CM makes known his entitlements. He has three types of interpretable
entitlement arising from the relationships involved in this mediation: as the chair
of the mediation, through having a familial relationship with Ying, and as being
distantly related to the injured party. Thus, through the formulation of a directive
for compensation action, rather than by means of a tentative request, the CM
appears to display a strong entitlement to suggest that Ying reimburse the full
amount of the indemnity. The display of this high degree of entitlement, moreover, reveals the perceived asymmetric relationships involved. First, Ying has a
familial relationship with the CM, who is much more senior in the mediation
context. In the context of this familial relationship, Ying, as a junior member and
an insurance agent, has a certain degree of obligation to comply with the directives of his senior and the chair of the mediation. Ying, at this point, is thus treated
as the one who will be held accountable, namely, he is responsible for reaching an
agreement about the compensation on behalf of the insurance company. Second,
while the injured parties (Fang and Fu) can be regarded as side participants here,
they actually occupy the principal footing for this directive, since this directive is
made for their benefit. As there is a relative connection between the CM and the
injured party, the CM has the entitlement in their relative relationship to make
a directive and advocate on behalf of them for their benefit. Third, by making a
directive (rather than a request), it also reflects the CM's entitlement as the chair
of the mediation session, demonstrating that he holds a legitimate position to
make such a directive.

Thus, we can see how, in a multiparty mediation, multiple layers of speaker
meaning can arise. In other words, additional implicatures arise in this turn
through the CM invoking his entitlements, drawing on the different relationships
involved. On the one hand, the addressee of this turn, Ying, who is the target
for this directive, is implicitly directed to meet the injured party's interactional
goal, that is, to agree to cover all the costs of Fang and Yu's medical treatment
on behalf of the insurance company. On the other hand, drawing on the footing
of the injured parties as side participants, the CM relationally implies that he is
attempting to fulfil his obligations arising from their relative connection. However, before the CM completes his turn, Ying contests the implied directive by

arguing that the disparity between the feasible indemnity and the actual medical costs is too large, with an overlapping utterance in turn 2.

2   IA: [AH::: TSHA] SIUNN TSĒ LAH ah-oo   huat-=

            PRT   differ too   much PRT PRT-have solution

The difference is too big. [How can I] have solutions?

This indicates that the actual costs of the medical treatment are in excess of the compensation which could be provided by the insurance cover. Ying, at this point, thus holds the CM interactionally accountable for the directive, when he explicitly orients to the implicature in saying '[How can I] have solutions?' (*ah-oo huat*). This rhetorical question generates a reverse epistemic gradient where Ying implicitly asserts he has greater epistemic rights with respect to the knowledge domain of compensation while asserting that the CM has less (Heritage & Raymond 2012). Ying's epistemic rights to make this assertion are linked to the legitimacy of his entitlement to make such assertion in his professional capacity (Heritage 2002). It is also evident through the prosodic cues with which Ying displays his frustration: rejecting the CM's implicature, the elongation, the increased volume, and the emphatic tokens in this overlapping turn signify that to compensate the full amount of the medical costs is beyond Ying's ability (Selting 1994).

In the next turn, the display of the CM's strong emotive stance can be observed through the formulation of another rhetorical question in response to Ying's prior turn, as well as through the latching of the rhetorical question concomitant with the prosodic features of loudness and stress in this sequence.

3   CM: =LONG-TSÒNG KAH GUĀ-TSĒ (.) TSÁP BĀN

          total   CP how much   ten   ten-thousands

          TO   BÔ TĪNN LEH >GUĀ-TSĒ<=

          even N full PRT how much

       How much [of the difference] in total? [It's] even less than one hundred thousand, how big [the difference is]?

The rhetorical question occasioned by the previous one through which Ying asserts his epistemic entitlement, once again, generates a reverse epistemic gradient where the CM implicitly asserts he has greater epistemic rights with respect to the knowledge domain of compensation, while simultaneously asserting that Ying has less (Heritage & Raymond 2012), and an assertive challenge is thus invoked through the formulation of this negative interrogative form (Heritage 2002). It mirrors the assertive challenge of the CM's epistemic rights in the implicit directive in turn 1, and so defends the legitimacy of his entitlement to make such directives within the context of their relationship (Heritage 2002). However, the formulation of the rhetorical question occasioned by Ying's declination in the previous sequence is here employed as a pre-negotiation strategy, through which he asserts a condemnation of the prior turn. This condemnation appears to be related to the rejection of the CM's epistemic entitlement by Ying in the previous turn, and in this way he attempts to reclaim his epistemic rights here. In other words, the relational separation projected by Ying is interactionally perceived by the CM at this point. That is, by rejecting the CM's implicit directive, Ying simultaneously asserts his epistemic entitlement, through the formulation of an assertion, that he is not able to fully compensate all the costs. Relational separation thus arises from the assertion of his epistemic entitlement, as through it Ying displays a stance of disaffiliation towards the CM. Critically, challenging these asymmetric entitlements in the context of their relationship can be perceived as a potential threat to the CM's separation face. In other words, the CM's entitlements to direct the negotiations are being challenged by Ying at this point.

Thus, through the latching of this rhetorical question, along with the prosodic features of loudness and stress in this sequence by the CM, it appears that the CM displays a strong emotional stance (Chafe 2002; Goodwin & Goodwin 2000; Selting 1996) in responding to Ying's rejection of the CM's implicit directive that Ying covers the disparity, that is, compensate the full amount of medical costs. The epistemic rights displayed in this rhetorical question, along with the concomitant strong emotive stance, therefore blocks the possibility of Ying straightforwardly rejecting this claim. The CM thus simultaneously attempts to challenge Ying, as well as reclaim his entitlement to issue directives in the context of their relationship (*guanxi*). On the other hand, the CM implies once again a demand that Ying agree to fully compensate the total amount of the injured party's medical costs thereby reasserting his entitlements. On the other hand, the condemnation formulated through the rhetorical question is simultaneously potentially face-threatening to Ying, in two different ways: first, a threat to Ying's connection face with the CM arises, as the CM implies that Ying's refusal to fulfil the obligations of their relational connection is offensive; second, a threat to Ying's separation face as a competent insurance agent who is entitled to negotiate on behalf of his company also potentially arises.

An orientation to the potential threat to both their connection face and separation face arising in this turn can be seen in the subsequent uptake by Ying in turn 4.

```
4  Ying:   =hmm-eh tch (0.5) sian  mā    bô-huat-tōo lí  kin-á-ji't
            hum-eh INT        deity also N-solution  you today

            nā kóng i  ê (3.0) i  ê     %shangshi% hooh
            if talk his ASSC    his ASSC injury    PRT

            %chule      yachi zhiwai% hooh %a   nage  qitai
            except for  teeth besides Q    PRT  that  other
```

```
de    bufen% kóng ya   gou-ū      hit-lou (.) hooh
ASSC part   talk also also-have that        PRT
%mei you  a%  i  ê    %shangshi% (1.5) khah
N    have PRT he ASSC injury            more
pháinn-sè   lah hooh% shou shi jiu >jiu  jiu<°
embarrassed PRT PRT   say  be   just just just
shi cashang  la  ah  li  cashang% beh  khì
be  abrasion PRT PRT you abrasion want go
tshíng hia - ê qita %de   feiyong oh% tioˈh-bô
apply  those other  ASSC fee      PRT right Q
kāng-khuán ah >li   tann<tsit-má >li   tsit-hia<
the same    PRT you now    now       you now
li  ka-kī khan tioˈh bô
you self  see   right Q
```

Yeh tch (an exasperated 'oh'), even deity has no solutions, either. If you talk about his injuries today, except for [his] teeth, [he] doesn't have other injuries. His injuries, [I feel] embarrassed [to say], [the injury] are just abrasions. Then how [is he going] to apply for other indemnity, right? Same thing. Now, [the medical certificates] are here and you can have a look at them

The formulation of the rhetorical question by the CM about the discrepancy in turn 3 is perceived as a condemnation or an accusation by Ying, as evident in the subsequent dispreferred response in turn 4. Here Ying explicitly makes a pronounced outbreath, with an irritated sigh, and also visibly cuts off his eye contact with the CM, thereby displaying a strong emotional stance which indicates that the condemnation is judged as unacceptable by Ying. More specifically, Ying appears to evaluate the previous rhetorical questions by the CM as threatening to Ying's face, both his separation face as a competent insurance agent and his connection face with the CM (i.e., the implication is that he has failed to fulfil the obligations in their familial connection). The display of irritation occasioned by this face threat is followed by subsequent justification or self-defence by Ying (Couper-Kuhlen 2012: 461), and thereby implies that the previous implied directive by the CM is inapposite (Drew, Walker and Local 2011). The invoking of a metaphor after his display of exasperation, *sian mā bô-huat-tōo* ('deity even has no solutions'), is used to justify the stance that the CM's directive is impossible to achieve, namely, to cover the entire costs of the injured party's medical treatment. Since a deity in Taiwanese folk belief has the power to fulfil people's wishes beyond a human being's capabilities, Ying therefore implicitly rejects the possibility of providing the full compensation to cover the costs of Fang's dental implant. The defence arising from the previous implicature comes later, when Ying further explains that Fang and Fu's injuries are only abrasions, apart from the dental implant. Ying also displays reluctance and discomfort through the significant long pauses, repetitions, compressed tokens, as well as the token of *pháinn-sè* (lit., 'embarrassed'), which frames his assertion as a dispreferred first, thereby indicating that the following statement could be a potential threat to the face of the injured parties, namely, a threat to their separation face. That is to say, he indicates his awareness that he is threatening Fang and Fu's entitlement as the injured parties to seek full financial compensation for their medical treatment through this dispreferred first formulation. On the other hand, this token can also simultaneously project a potential threat to the connection face between the CM and Ying, as it can be perceived as threatening to the relationship that Ying and the CM have built up over the years they have been working together in negotiation sessions. The subsequent justification by Ying can be interpreted as disaffiliative with the CM's prior turn, where he attempts to get the injured parties' medical costs fully covered. By justifying his display of exasperation in suggesting that the injured parties' injuries are just abrasions, Ying's acknowledgment of their minor injury also simultaneously signals another declination, thereby occasioning a possible threat to the separation face of the injured parties, since the acknowledgment appears to be downgrading the severity of the accident and thus challenges their entitlement to claim full compensation. Ying then subsequently issues an imperative request, asking that the CM examine the medical certificates that record Fang and Fu's injuries as being only abrasions. Through this imperative request, Ying thus implies that asking his company to cover all the compensation is beyond his ability, and therefore Fang and Fu can hardly justify claiming full reimbursement of their medical costs.

The CM subsequently attempts to direct Ying to have a look at other medical costs in turn 5. However, Ying interrupts the CM in turn 6 and initiates another rhetorical question *tioh-bô* ('right'?), and the concomitant '[it's] the same', which refers to the other receipts the CM attempts to ask Ying about. In this way, Ying implies they are the same as the other medical costs, which are mainly from the injuries sustained through abrasions.

```
5   CM:    hmm (.) Ah i  ê     leh i [ê?]

           hmm     PRT he ASSC Q   he ASSC
```

　　　((*pointing to another medical certificate*))

　　Hmm. What about his–

```
6   Ying:                        [oh]tio'h-bô kăng-khuán

                                 oh right Q  the same
```

```
            ah (.) >li   tann< tsit-má >li    tsit-hia< li   ka-kī
            PRT      you now   now       you  here     you self
            khan (.) tioˈh-bô
            see      right Q
```

Right? [It's] the same. [The medical certificate] are here, and you can
have a look at them now. Right?

Through the formulation of this rhetorical question, Ying thereby asserts his
epistemic rights in this matter, as well as pursuing the CM's agreement with his
implied stance, namely, that the injured party should not be over compensated
for simple abrasions. He then re-emphasises his epistemic rights and projects the
implicature once more through the formulation of another rhetorical question at
the end of turn 6.

At this point, Hsu steps into the conversation through formulating an interrogative question, *li tak tsít king* ('which [company] are you [from]'?), in turn 7.
This occasions a brief side sequence that ostensibly interrupts the progressivity of
this negotiation. It also occasions an interactionally marked response from Ying.

```
7   Hsu:    >li< li  tak   tsit king=
            you you which one  C
```

Which [company] are you [from]?

```
8   Ying:                      =>guá %Hua-xin        baoxian%<
                               I     (company name) Insurance
```

I [am from] Huaxin Insurance.

```
9   Hsu:    Huaxin          oh=
            (company name) PRT
```

Huaxin

```
10  Ying:                      =>heh sī<
                               heh yes
```

Yes

Ying responds to the question from Hsu immediately in turn 8, but in doing so
he code-switches from Taiwanese to Mandarin to give his company name. This
code-switching, as Su (2009) argues, has particular relational import, through
which he asserts the social distance between himself and Hsu. Code-switching can
be employed to negotiate interpersonal relationships in (potentially) face-threatening situations (Su 2009: 18–19). Here, Ying is switching from the Taiwanese
dialect to Mandarin Chinese, which is considered to be an official language used
more frequently in more formal settings. In other words, Ying's uptake in turn 8
of Hsu's previous interrogative about his company name is treated as sequentially

incoherent, that is, interrupting the progress of the negotiation. It also appears to be interpreted as a potential threat to Ying's separation face, since Hsu's attempts to get involved in the negotiation implies a challenge, whereby Ying's entitlement to assert full compensation for the injured party is deemed impossible (i.e., Ying's following implicature in turns 4 and 6). Ying thus switches from the dominant language of Taiwanese to Mandarin Chinese in this interaction to evoke a more formal social relationship with Hsu, thereby managing the face-threatening situation by creating greater relational distance (cf. Su 2009: 19).

Hsu then starts referring to similar experiences he has had in turns 11–19 that follow.

```
11   Hsu:   eh guá tíng-pái   long tsit-ē    mā    sī án-ne=
            eh I    last time hit   one time also be this
```

     I had the same [situation] last time

```
12   Ying:                                           =heh
                                                      Heh
```

     Yah

```
13   Hsu:   °(khiâ ootobai)° >khì-honnh   tsit-ê< kâu-gín-á
               ride motorbike  be-passive one   C  monkey-kid
            gah        guá long=
            be-passive I   hit
```

     [Someone] rode a motorbike. [I] was hit by a damn kid

```
14   Ying:                       =heh
                                  Heh
```

     Yeh

```
15   ((someone laughed))
```

```
16   Hsu:   tnˉg  nnˉg khí:: =
            break two  teeth
```

     [I] broke two teeth

```
17   Ying:                 =↓mm mm?
                            mm mm
```

     mm mm

```
18   Hsu:   pó-hiám    kong-si  mā   sī tsóng tshú-lí.(.) dongtai
            insurance company  also be all   deal with   (company name)
            ē=
            ASSC
```

     The insurance also dealt with all of it. Dong-tai [Insurance company]

```
19  Ying:  =mm↓(0.5) >tse   si bô liáu-kái   lah tse- guá si
            mm                this be N  understand PRT this I   be

       bô liáu-kái   lah li  guá m tsai-iánn li   kóng

       N  understand PRT you I   N know      you talk

       ē    hit-leh >siánn< li  kóng  ē   %zhuangkuang

       ASSC that     what  you talk  ASSC situation

       tāi-khài% si án-náh<=

       generally be what
```

[I] don't know, [I] don't know, [I] don't know what the situation was like

After the exchanges between Ying and Hsu confirming Ying's company name in turns 9 and 10, Hsu launches a story-telling sequence in turns 11, 13 and 16, narrating how he encountered a similar situation when he was injured in a motorbike accident by a young man who caused him to break two teeth. Ying responds with minimal acknowledgment tokens (e.g., *heh* and *mm*). The account concludes with an implied contrast with Ying's company and thus a complaint directed towards Ying's prior assertion that they cannot completely cover the full costs of dental implants arises in turn 18. Hsu frames these implications by stating that another insurance company was able to cover all the dental costs and thereby projects an implicature of irresponsibility on the part of Ying's company. In implying that Ying's company cannot offer the same compensation as another company, Hsu thereby projects a threat to Ying's separation face as a competent insurance agent vis-à-vis the rest of the participants, as well as to the group face which involves Ying's relationship with his company as a joint unit (Spencer-Oatey 2007: 641), for being unable to claim the entire medical costs for the injured parties.

This threat simultaneously challenges Ying's entitlement to refuse, that is, to claim that the entire medical costs cannot be covered. Concurrently, the story-telling sequence is used as a deferral strategy, postponing production of an occasioned or sequentially implicated bargaining sequence (Maynard 2010: 139), soon after Ying declines the CM's request, foreshadowing the implicative request that emerges in this sequence. The evoking of similar personal experience is thus used to insert a seemingly relevant account so as to position Ying's previous refusal as unreasonable. In other words, an indirect request is simultaneously formed through the story-telling sequence by Hsu, who implicitly requests that Ying offer a similar resolution in what is asserted to be a similar situation.

Ying responds to Hsu with the acknowledgment tokens *yeh* and *mm* as weak agreement markers in the course of Hsu's story-telling sequences in turns 14 and 17 (Gardner 1997). However, by turn 19 it becomes clear that, while these acknowledgment tokens are aligning (i.e., they contribute to the progress of the account), they are not ultimately affiliative (i.e., expressing agreement with Hsu's stance). In turn 19, Ying rejects the potential complaint as well as the implicative request with the repetition of epistemic markers disclaiming knowledge of such events, *bo liáu kái* and *m tsai-iánn* ('don't understand' and 'don't know'), which functions as a deter move that sidelines the relevance of Hsu's telling for this negotiation. By suggesting uncertainty in regard to the relevance of Hsu's personal experience via this epistemic stance, this deter move appears to be used to manage Hsu's expectation through the formulation of this dispreferred response, and thereby implies that he cannot agree to the implied request in this particular case (Maynard 2010: 137). On the other hand, the epistemic markers of uncertainty also imply that Hsu's prior turn is irrelevant, illegitimate or inapposite, and thereby declines to take responsibility for responding to the implied complaint or indirect request (Keevallik 2010). Therefore, this indirectly reflects that the prior turns by Hsu constitute an implied complaint as well as a complainable sequence. This disaligning response therefore indexes a disaffiliative stance with regard to Hsu's previous account, and thereby potentially projects a threat to Hsu's separation face, which is his entitlement in this context to take the role of speaking on behalf of the injured parties. This face threat becomes more apparent in Hsu's subsequent response in the following excerpt.

```
20   Hsu:  =ah: kah  tshú-lí-lí eh  tse  lóng mā   ka-kī
            ah  help deal with  PRT this all   also self

            tàu-tīn °ē°  (.)  he   guán a-kū  lah:=
            together ASSC     that my    uncle PRT
```

Ah, help me deal with it. These are our people. That is my uncle

```
21   Ying:                                =°heh° guá bô-huat-tōo
                                           that I   N-solution

            lah li  ài   khuànn ài   khuànn ài   khuànn
            PRT you need see    need see    need see

            [i   ê    (   ) ]-
            3sg  ASSC
```

I can't do anything. You have to see [the maximum] of his xxx (subdued speech). I can't do anything

```
22   CM:    [()>ÁN-NE<]  LI  BÔ-HUAT-TOŌ OOH=
             this    you N-solution  PRT
```

You can't do anything [about it]?

```
23   Ying:                              =bô-huat-tōo=
                                         N-solution
```

I have no solution

With the prosodic cues of the latched and elongated token of *ah*, Hsu displays his frustration through the directive of *kah tshú-lí-lí* ('help [him] deal with [it]') in turn 20, attempting to re-negotiate Ying's degree of entitlement to issue a refusal. The repetition of the last syllable *-lí* also indexes Hsu's emphasis on appealing for action to be taken to deal with the matter; in other words, to strengthen the directive force to appeal for Ying's help to cover the entire amount of compensation. Subsequently, Hsu appeals to the insider relationship with the injured parties, Fang and Fu, by stating that they are *ka-kī tàu-tīn ē* ('our people [who are] together'), and he explicitly invokes the familial relationship he has with Fang, namely, he is the nephew of the injured parties. By acknowledging the insider relationship with the injured parties, Hsu claims a mutual bond between them, and thereby shows emotional support towards Fang and Fu, as the relationship of insiders is generally understood as more affection- and obligation-oriented (Hsiang 1974: 57; Chang & Holt 1994: 109). Meanwhile, through the acknowledgment of their relationship, Hsu attempts to evoke emotional support from Ying as an emotive strategy, that is, to take their connectedness into account, and thus support the connection face between Hsu and the injured party at this point. Ying subsequently responds by claiming he is not able to offer a greater amount of compensation and starts offering an account for this in turn 21. However, before he finishes this account, the CM interrupts in turn 22 with a reformulation of Hsu's previous explicit appealing request as a question, through which he only implies a request for greater compensation. Nevertheless, since this reformulated question has a negative polarity (i.e., 'can't do anything'), disconfirmation is the (structurally) preferred response (Heritage & Raymond 2012; Raymond 2003; Stivers & Enfield 2010), which Ying indeed provides in the latched turn 23. In this way it is confirmed that Ying's insurance company is not able to increase the amount of compensation.

Hsu immediately responds in the latched turn 24 with a strong negative assessment (*ah hiau-hīng*, 'it's terrible') concomitant with an emphatic style in relation to his uncle having to pay the costs of medical treatment himself.

```
24 Hsu:   =ah hiau-hīng ah  bô-huat-tōo °beh-án-náh tshòng°

           ah terrible  PRT n-solution   what to    do

           āu-pái pó     pa't-king bô pó     Hua[xin]

           future insure other C  N  insure (company name)
```

It's terrible. What [can we] do if you can't do anything. [Let's] don't insure with Hua-xin and insure with other [companies] next time

```
25  Shih:                                   [hehehe]hehehe
```

He then implies that other insurance companies would offer better indemnity payments, and also indirectly projects a complaint about Ying's insurance company, that is, treating the refusal by Ying as a complainable matter (Drew 1998; Schegloff 2005). The implicature and the indirect complaint by Hsu is made in front of all the participants, and thus the rest of the interactants are treated as side participants, although Ying is the direct addressee. In this way, he invokes an expectation (and perhaps also from the side participants, particularly Fang and Fu as the at-fault parties) that Ying should be able to offer a better indemnity payment. Hsu thus projects the act of topicalising this unmet expectation which invokes the obligations that accompany ongoing relationships (*guanxi*). Hsu is occasioning a face threat of strategic embarrassment for Ying by topicalising the unmet expectations originating from the relationship (*guanxi*) involved in this mediation (Chang & Haugh 2011b: 2959). Hsu thereby projects a threat to Ying's separation face, as well as connection face with the CM and his clients (Fang and Fu). In this case, Ying's separation face is his image relative to his clients, even to the rest of the participants, as a competent insurance agent who represents his insurance company to provide a satisfactory indemnity in the mediation, while his connection face refers to his relationships with the CM with whom Ying has a long-term relationship, as well as with the at-fault parties who are actually long-term clients with Ying's company. In other words, Ying's relational entitlement with the injured parties for making a judgment about the indemnity as well as Ying's *guanxi* vis-à-vis his clients as a reliable insurance agent were both challenged at the same time. As previously noted, long-term relationships are understood to involve a certain degree of obligation and display of affection, and therefore Ying's face is threatened, since he is evaluated as failing to fulfil his obligations to these long-term relationships through the complaint as well as failing to show his emotional support.

The agent's subsequent delayed response in turn 27 is thus disaligning, as it has no direct relevance to Hsu's previous turn with a significant silence in between, and thus arguably displays embarrassment on his part.

26   (2.5)

27 IA: hong-piān tioh hó   lah hong-piān khah↑ hó   lah=
          convenient then good PRT convenient more good PRT

          It's better to be more convenient

Specifically, Ying's face is threatened at this point, namely, his separation face with his clients, that is, his image as a competent insurance agent representing his insurance company is jeopardised. His connection face is also threatened as he is treated as failing to fulfil his obligation within both his relationships with the CM as well as with the at-fault parties. He responds to the strategic embarrassment indirectly so as to avoid reiterating the refusal thereby expressing his reluctance to further threaten their face. In other words, he attempts to avoid reiterating the undesired outcome on the side of the injured parties, namely, being unable to reimburse the entire amount for the medical costs of the injured parties. A threat to his connection face with his client arising from his failure to fulfil the expected obligations is thus avoided by responding indirectly. Since this embarrassment is occasioned in the presence of all the participants, there are other possible threats to Ying's face, including evaluations of threats to Ying's long-standing friendship with the CM, as well as his potential relationship with possible future clients present at the meeting. The laughter by Shih in turn 25 at this point is also arguably occasioned by the act of embarrassing Ying and thus is framed sarcastically. It therefore indicates that the act of topicalising of unmet expectations is indeed a threatening to Ying's separation face, something which is also evidently shown in turn 27, where there is an apparently irrelevant response to Hsu's previous turn.

However, even though Ying has displayed embarrassment on his part, Hsu responds with a strong negator, concomitant with an emphatic elongation in turn 28, deflecting the disaligning stance of Ying.

```
28   Hsu:   =bô lah::  tsīn-liōng          ē-sái tshú-lí    >tioh

            N   PRT    as far as possible  can   deal with  then

            kā<        tshú-lí   ah:  tann m̄ sī tsha

            help him deal with PRT  now  N  be difference

            tsin- guā-tsē ah

            very  much    PRT
```

No, [if you can] do your best to deal with it for him, the difference [between the loss and the indemnity] is not so much

He then continues with another directive request that Ying increase the indemnity payment, along with an assertion that the disparity between the actual medical costs and the amount the insurance is supposed to cover is not that much. The directive Hsu initiates here displays his entitlement from his status as a representative of the injured parties, which once again mirrors the asymmetrical relationships involved between the at-fault parties and the injured parties in the mediation. In other words, by projecting his entitlement on behalf of the injured parties, Hsu attempts to challenge Ying's entitlement to make a refusal in the previous disaligning turn.

When Ying subsequently checks the disparity between the indemnity offered by the insurance company and the actual medical costs in turn 29, the CM attempts to intervene in the negotiation between Ying and Hsu.

```
29   Ying:   [TSHA:: ]  ((Ying looks at the receipts))

             difference
```

The difference [is about]

30   CM: [I TSE-]
              3sg this

              His this

31   (1.0)

32   Ying: tsha   >put-lí< tsē bān
                      difference quite   much ten thousands

              The difference is more than ten thousand

However, Ying quickly glances through the receipts again and then responds that
the difference is more than ten thousand dollars in turn 32. Ying suggests that
the disparity is quite significant through the tokens *put-lí tsē* ('quite a lot'), and
thereby implicitly argues that the disparity is too much to be covered by his insurance company. In this way, Ying disaffiliates with Hsu's prior turn.

Thereafter follows a short discussion of their personal experience and common understanding of the prices of dental implants amongst the CM, Hsu and
Ying (data not shown). At the end of the omitted section, those three speakers
reach a consensus that prices of dental implants can vary. When Hsu mentions
there are even more expensive dental implants than the one Fang has, Ying then
initiates the following sequence.

(13: 18)

41   Ying: =heh:: lah:: >tse lo   mi-<   sóo-í kóng
            right PRT   this kind thing- so   say

            sóo-í kóng >li kóng< li zhiya   ooh ni
            so   say   you say   you dental implant PRT you

            %zhiya   zai (1.5) baoxian   zhege
            dental implant in   insurance this

            zai zhege qukuai°youmeiyou°(.) ta banlai
            at   this area   yes-or-N   he originally

            jiushi meiyou zai zuo suowei   de   zhege(.)ta
            that is N   have at do so-called ASSC this   he

            dongzuo >weishengme< tebei   yachi you zhe
            action why   especially teeth have this

            yige zhege tebei   de yige guifan% (.)ah
            one-C this-C especially ASSC one-C regulation PRT

            tse sī tsìng-hú honnh lâng ê   %guifan% (.)
            this be government PRT   people ASSC regulation

            tō sī kā li kui-tīng kui-tīng án-ne
            then is give you regulation regulation this

```
SIŌNG-KUÂN   tō    sī  hia-ê  ah(1.0)ah  tio'h
the highest   then  be  those  PRT     PRT  right
bô  (3.5)  >TSIK-Á<  LÂI
Q          uncle    come
```

 So [when] you say dental implant, the [indemnity of] insurance about dental implant is not covered. Why there is a special regulation for dental [implant]? This regulation is from the government to regulate the maximum [of the indemnity], right? Uncle, come [here]

In this turn, Ying displays a strong affiliative stance with the consensus that the costs of dental implants can vary, marked through the prosodic features of an emphatic intonational style and elongation in turn 41, by further offering an account as to why the government regulates the policy in terms of the costs for dental implants. He asserts that since the costs of dental implants are quite diverse due to the variety of different materials used in the treatments, the government has introduced regulations for insurance companies relating to indemnity payments, specifically regulating the maximum cover for dental implants. That is, the total costs are not able to be covered by Ying's insurance company according to government regulations. Ying once again displays his strong stance through the emphatic token *siōng-kuân* ('the highest [cover]'). This implies that Ying's insurance company can only cover the amount which is stipulated according to the regulations, and thus he cannot help any further. Through the rhetorical question that follows, Ying thus projects his epistemic rights in making the claim that the regulations are made by the government, thereby asserting his professional insurance agent's knowledge through the design of the tag question ('right'). On the other hand, Ying simultaneously distances himself from the principal role of taking responsibility for the level of compensation by invoking the institutional authority of a third party (i.e., the government). This functions as a deter move in negotiation to avoid the injured parties from trying to further initiate a counter proposal (cf. Maynard 2010).

After offering an account as to why they are unable to cover the entire medical expenses, Ying asks the CM to step outside and have a backroom negotiation through an imperative formulation. This is a common practice in mediations, that is, where the mediators (and/or sometimes their clients or their representatives) will have backroom negotiations to seek a possible acceptable amount of compensation, rather than negotiating over the indemnity in everyone's presence, which could be considered highly sensitive and thereby project potential face-threats towards everyone involved. However, instead of calling the CM's name or position, Ying addresses the CM as *tsik-á* ('uncle'), although they are not actually kin. By addressing the CM using kin terms in a non-kin relationship, Ying attempts to invoke a relational connection within their long-term relationship

(*guanxi*), and thereby turns the outside relationship into an inside one (Pan &
Kádár 2010: 82). In this way, the insider-relationship invoked here appears to
be foregrounded, and thereby the involved obligation, favours and authority are
implied to be relevant for the subsequent backroom negotiation.

However, as Ying and the CM are about to leave the mediation room, Hsu
appeals to the familial relationship (*guanxi*) he has with the CM in turn 43,
namely, he is the son of the CM.

```
42            ((IA waving to the CM and walking out to the door))

43   Hsu:   he    guán A-PAH  LAH::  tshiau    tsi't-ē tshiau

            that  my   father PRT   deal with a bit   deal with

            tsi't-ē=

            a bit

            That is my father, [help] deal with it, [help] deal with it

44          (([°hhehh]hehh°))

45   Ying:       =[GUÁ] TSAI LAH  guá [tong-liân  mā   tsai-iánn lín

                  I     know PRT  I    of course  also know      your

            a-pah  koh m̄ tsai  guá tio'h hāi – khì] ah

            father if  N  know I   then  screwed    PRT

            I know [that]. Of course I know that's your father. I am screwed if I don't
            know [about it]

46          ((°hhhhhhhehh°))

47   Shih: [I KOH(h) M TSAI LÍN  A-PAH  YA   HÂI(H)  AH]

            he if     N know your father then screwed PRT

            He is screwed if he doesn't even know he is your father

48   Fang: [i koh m̄ tsai lín  a-pah  tio'h hāi      ah]

            he if  N  know your father then  screwed PRT

            [He is] screwed if he doesn't even know he is your father

49   Hsu:  kang-tîng     hiám        tsuân pó    lín

            construction insurance all   insure your

            Hua-xin         ê

            (Company name) NOM

            [We] insured all of our constructions with you Hua-xin
```

As Hsu is the CM's son, he is able to seek special favours due to the presence of the
mediator (i.e., his father) who mediates the connection (*guanxi*) between himself
and Ying through the long-standing relationship (*guanxi*) between the insurance
agent and his father. This act of appealing to *guanxi* is therefore consonant with

the following directive request, imperatively asking them to deal with or resolve the issue, namely, to increase the indemnity payment as they wish. This implies that Hsu's understanding of the *guanxi* involved in this mediation has granted him the entitlement to direct Ying's actions (Craven & Potter 2010: 437), as evidently seen in the emphatic use of an term of address with increased volume and elongation. The latching and increased volume of Ying's response in turn 43 allows him to acknowledge the act of appealing to the *guanxi* involved by Hsu through the emphatic epistemic token of *guá tsai lah* and *tong-liân* ('I know' and 'of course'). More specifically, Ying displays a strong epistemic stance towards the action of appealing to the relational connection through those emphatic tokens, thereby invoking the presupposition of askability (Stivers 2011). In other words, through the sarcastic mocking of himself and these epistemic markers, Ying treats this relationship and attendant obligations as apparently already salient, and thus Hsu's appeal is redundant. Interestingly, at this point, Shih and Fang, who are side participants in this sequence, take the floor through overlapping utterances that reformulate the 'obviousness' of the appeal to their *guanxi*. In other words, Shih and Fang also acknowledge the act of Hsu's appealing to *guanxi* (i.e., the *guanxi* between Hsu and the CM), thereby implicitly suggesting the significance of taking their *guanxi* into account.

Hsu subsequently appeals to the family connection with Ying again, with an account of his business relationship with Ying's company, which he claims has been given all the construction insurance business by Hsu, or someone who is related to Hsu. Although the subject was omitted in the original text, Hsu apparently invokes *guanxi* through the business relational connection with Ying's company, which was given favours for having their business, thereby implying that Ying has a certain degree of obligation as a consequence of these relational connections. Therefore, Hsu's last statement indirectly requests that Ying fulfil these obligations, that is, to fully cover the medical costs for the injured parties.

The outcome of the backroom negotiations between the CM and Ying, however, was that Ying decided to conclude this mediation session at this point, since they could not reach an agreement on the amount of compensation. He declared that it was first necessary to report to his company before he could proceed to make any further decisions. Therefore, at the end of this mediation session, the CM agreed with Ying's proposal that another mediation session would be needed once the at-fault parties were informed by the insurance company.

The interactional practices that have been examined here include strategic embarrassment, responding indirectly, and 'invoking formality' through code-switching. The face practices identified here, therefore, have highlighted that the ultimate goal the involved participants attempt to achieve is an interactional goal, namely, to reach a mutually agreeable amount of indemnity for the injured parties. By employing these practices, the participants attempt to attend to their connection face and separation face, which are their interconnected *guanxi* and relational entitlements respectively in the negotiation setting. *Guanxi* is in particular frequently appealed to in the course of this mediation interaction. Address terms are used numerous times to suggest the interconnected relational connections between the participants, thereby invoking a sense of mutual obligation between the participants. On the other hand, the participants' relational entitlement also becomes salient in this interaction, particularly when the face practices of responding indirectly and 'invoking formality' through code-switching arise. These two face practices are employed to claim and challenge Ying's relational entitlement vis-à-vis the other participants, namely, as a competent insurance agent in the eyes of the other participants in this particular context. This analysis further indicates the importance of *guanxi* and relational entitlement as cultural construals of connectedness and separateness in Chinese.

5.2.2 Mediation about a death caused by a car accident

This mediation took place at a regional government in Yi-Lan County, and involved a committee of 13 people to negotiate financial compensation for the death of the injured party's son in a car accident. In cases of manslaughter caused by car accidents in Taiwan, the prosecution of the at-fault party is always launched by the court within three months after the accident. The purpose of holding mediations is therefore to seek a mutually agreeable financial compensation between the injured party and the at-fault party before prosecution is launched by the court and thus avoids prosecution of the at-fault party in a civil suit concurrent with criminal proceedings for the manslaughter charges arising from the fatal car accident. In such cases, the party at fault is always the one who applies for a mediation session so as to provide a satisfactory financial compensation for the injured party within the official three-month time frame thereby avoiding a civil lawsuit. If the injured party agrees to accept the negotiated financial settlement, the civil suit part of the criminal proceedings can be waived by the injured party at their discretion prior to the at-fault party being charged in the criminal lawsuit.

There are three types of relationships between the members involved in this kind of mediation meeting, namely, legislative, relative or friend and electoral relationships,[5] based on which member takes up a position in the mediation. People who are members of a legislative council were explicitly invited to act as representatives in this mediation because they are the electoral representative of one

---

5. Electoral relationships (*xuǎnmíng guānxì*) refer to the relationships between local politicians and local residents. As the politicians are elected by their local residents, they have a certain degree of societal expectation and obligation to help out with local matters or speak up for their local constituents.

of the parties involved in the mediation process. The people at fault, the injured party/ies, the chair of the mediation and the insurance agent are the basic members in the mediation. The assigned insurance agent is always the one representing his/her client who is the at-fault party. The at-fault party negotiates the amount of indemnity which will be provided by the insurance company, the amount of which will depend on the extent of the insurance cover. The remaining members involved act as representatives who have either friendly/familial connections or even electoral relationships with the at-fault party or the injured party.

It is also necessary to briefly note the process of forming a mediation session here. First of all this type of mediation session is always called by the at-fault party, who needs to seek an alternative solution to a civil lawsuit within three months of a fatal car accident, such as an offer of financial compensation for the injured party. The financial compensation for cases of death caused in a car accident involves mainly three types of compensation: compulsory insurance, third-party insurance and the excess. In accordance with Taiwanese law, every car owner should purchase compulsory insurance in order to compensate the injured party if there is a death caused in the car accident. The regulated amount of compensation for death caused by a car accident from compulsory insurance is 1,600,000 Taiwanese dollars (around US$55,000). Second, there is third-party insurance, which is optional cover, and the amount of indemnity is determined by the insurer according to how much cover the insured takes out with the insurance company. Lastly is the excess, which is often provided in the case of death in a car accident, especially when the cover from third-party insurance is insufficient to compensate the injured party. When the injured party is notified by the mediation committee through the local government, the injured party first pre-determines a desired approximate amount of financial compensation prior to the mediation session. The role of the representatives on the side of the injured party is to advocate for the injured party and thus negotiate with the at-fault party on behalf of them, attempting to get them to agree to compensate the full amount proposed by the injured party. In terms of the overall purpose of the process, the injured party and their representatives expect the outcome to be that the at-fault party will agree to the amount of financial compensation proposed by the injured party. In this particular case, that is to say, the injured party expects the at-fault party to pay an excess on top of the insurance indemnity. On the other hand, the representatives on the side of the at-fault party play a role advocating for them, acting to assist them to accept or decline the injured party's proposal. The chair of mediation (CM) is thus acting in a role of mediating between the two parties in order to settle on a mutually agreeable amount of financial compensation so as to avoid the at-fault party being prosecuted in a civil suit alongside the criminal proceedings by the court, and to help the injured party to obtain a satisfactory amount of compensation without bringing the case to court. The insurance agent

(IA) is required to participate in the mediation on behalf of his/her client when the at-fault party is the one who is responsible for providing the financial compensation. The IA's role is to provide the maximum amount of indemnity, according to his/her client's insurance cover, and then help the at-fault party to come to an agreed amount of excess on top of the financial compensation provided by the insurance company. In other words, the IA thus plays a role, on the one hand, to represent his/her company to offer a regulated indemnity, but on the other hand, to help the at-fault party come up with the excess, in the situation where the indemnity from the at-fault party's insurance cover is inadequate.

Investigation of this particular interaction that occurred as part of the mediation process in terms of face-related issues requires a brief summary of the background to the fatal accidental that is the subject of the mediation. The car accident occurred approximately two weeks before the mediation. Liu, the deceased victim, was riding her motorbike on the way home around 6 pm when Kuo crashed into her. It was confirmed by police that Kuo was responsible for the accident and that he was drunk while driving his pickup truck. Liu was taken to hospital immediately after the accident but passed away two days later. In accordance with Taiwan's criminal law, Kuo was charged with being drunk while driving and causing a fatal accident (i.e., manslaughter). This case was also the subject of a civil lawsuit initiated by the victim's family to determine financial compensation for her death. In order to avoid bringing this civil case to court and therefore having to pay an even greater amount of compensation and legal costs, Kuo and his wife, Kong, called for a dispute conciliation at the regional government, asking that a committee be formed to mediate a financial resolution through a more peaceful interaction that would allow room for negotiations by both parties to reach a mutually agreeable amount of compensation for Liu's family members (Lu and Chiu).

Throughout the entire mediation process, the at-fault party (Kuo and his wife Kong) and representatives of the victim had minimal interaction. It was mainly the representatives who spoke on behalf of both parties involved in the accident, acting in facilitating and supportive roles. This is because it is common that people involved in a mediation process involving accidents usually have little experience in negotiating proposals, requests or refusals. Moreover, they also tend to avoid overt discussion or conflicts, as the meditation could be highly emotionally sensitive. Those who are regarded as representatives of one of the parties involved in the mediation are therefore requested by the people involved in the accident to assist with negotiations, helping with offers of compensation, proposals for resolution, making requests, or explaining their perspectives on the incident. These representatives are sometimes people who have extensive social connections, prestigious positions or even merely have family relationships with the people involved in the accident. It should be noted that there are no specific regulations or restrictions on the numbers of representatives that each party can request to participate in the mediation.

Kuo invited two people to help represent him in the negotiation process: Luo, a relative, and Lin, a friend. Tsai, who is a councillor in the legislative council of Yi-Lan County, was another individual invited by Kuo to join the negotiation. He is distantly related to and also has an electoral relationship with Kuo and Kong. Although Tsai showed up and briefly greeted everyone before the negotiations started, he left the room to attend to personal work and thus did not stay for the entire meeting. However, with his title as a councillor in the legislative council of Yi-Lan County, it is assumed that with the social face gained through Tsai's well-recognised position, Tsai's name would have also carried weight when the other representatives advocated for the at-fault party during the mediation, despite his absence during the mediation process.

There were also a number of representatives on the victim's side involved in the mediation process. Aside from the deceased victim's son (Chiu) and older brother (Lu), there were three other representatives assisting in the negotiations, namely, Chen, Peng and Hu. Chen, who is also a councillor in the legislative council of Yi-Lan County, is a distant relative of the victim and is also the elected member of Chiu and Lu's district in the legislative council. Chiu and Lu also asked Peng, the head of Yu-Tian village, to be involved in the mediation process. The involvement of politicians is considered an effective mechanism in facilitating the mediation process as well as having a potentially positive impact on the party in the negotiations. Hu, a good friend of the deceased was also asked by Chiu and Lu to participate in the mediation.

The persons involved in this mediation and the relationships between them are summarised below.

Summary of participants involved:
1. The person at fault, Kuo (husband, 30s) and Kong (Kuo's wife, 30s)
2. Insurance agent (IA hereafter, male, 40s)
3. Luo (male, Kuo's relative, 55)
4. Lin (Kuo's friend, late 50s)
5. Tsai (the member of legislative body of Yi-lan County; has distant relative as well as electorate relationship with Kuo and Kong; had left before the mediation started)
6. Liu's (the deceased) brother, Lu (late 50s) and Liu's son, Chiu (early 20s)
7. Chen, the member of legislative council of Yi-Lan County (Liu, Lu and Chiu's representative; is a distant relative as well as having an electoral relationship)
8. Peng, the head of Yu-Tian village (male, 60s; Liu, Lu and Chiu's representative)

9. Hu, Liu, Lu and Chiu's friend (female, 50s)
10. Wu, a former member of the legislative council[6] of Yi-Lan County (the committee mediator of this negotiation, hereinafter Wu; male, 70s, has a family relationship with Kuo, Kong and Chen)

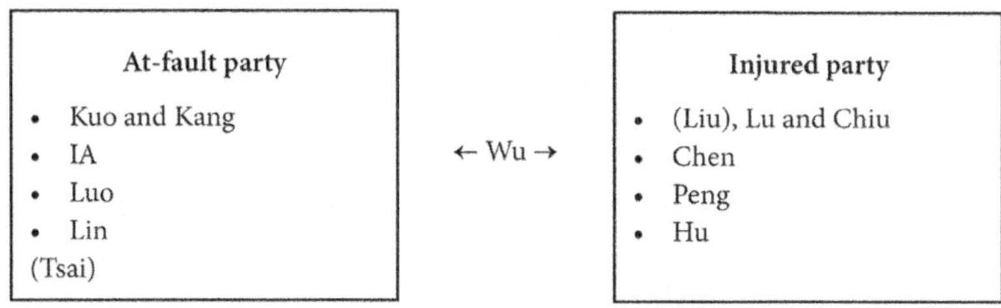

Figure 5.3: The structure of the mediation committee (2)

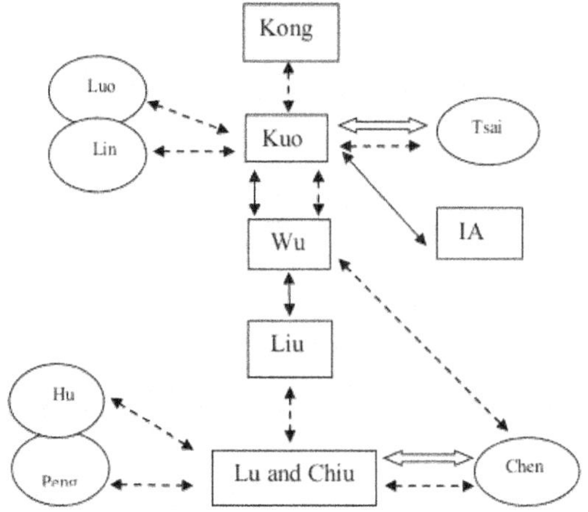

Figure 5.4: The relationship between the members involved in the mediation

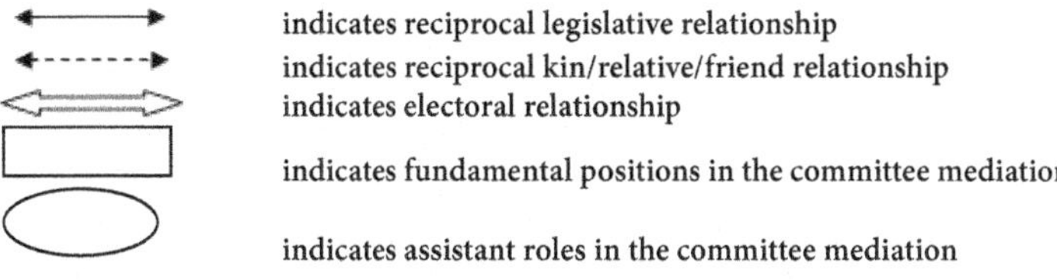

indicates reciprocal legislative relationship
indicates reciprocal kin/relative/friend relationship
indicates electoral relationship

indicates fundamental positions in the committee mediation

indicates assistant roles in the committee mediation

6. The legislative Council of county exercises autonomy as part of local government, reflects the opinions of the public, and provides resolutions on local affairs. The councillors of legislative council are elected by the residents of that county.

Prior to the main process of mediation, the participants enter the mediation room, one after another, and briefly greet each other. People who know each other engage in some small talk before the actual mediation starts. As a general rule, mediation meetings can take place across more than one session, depending on whether or not both parties are able to reach a consensus or resolution and are satisfied with the settlement of the dispute. In this particular case of a mediation held at the regional government, however, the participants only met on the one occasion, as they reached a mutually agreeable amount of indemnity at the end of the mediation interaction. All the participants sat down and some began having casual conversations; Chen, a member of the legislative council of Yi-Lan County and also Kuo's distant relative, interrupted the conversation between Wu and Peng and also asked that the group commence the mediation session. The following turn was thus initiated when Wu started giving his opening remarks and introduced the participants involved in the interaction.

[100727_12: 3: 08]

```
1  Wu:   %Ci  ci%  to  woo  kuí    jîn    tāi-piáu  ah  guá (.)  i   sī
          this time then have several people represent PRT I         3sg be

          kiò guá kū-kong    ah  lí  tse  tsik-kong līng-guā  mài tsham
          call me granduncle PRT you this granduncle in addition N   mix

          tī  tsia luī hònn (.)  ah  to   guá í  kuân-puè lâi  >kā<
          ASP here CP  PRT        PRT just I  as senior   come ASP

          tàu-kuan-sim tsit-tsām tāi-tsì hònn(.)ah  to  guan tāi-piáu lâi
          help concern this C   matter  PRT     PRT then we  represent come

          kā  lín lâi- gī-uân tann ū    tāi-tsì sin    tsáu ah (.)  hònn
          ASP you come MLC    now  have matter  first  leave PRT      PRT

          sóo-í guá tī siūnn- kóng kin-á-jit >khuànn ē-tàng tú-hó< khuànn
          so    I  ASP think  CP   today      see if   can   just   see if

          ē-tàng tú-hó tak-ke- >tak-ke-< ū    tsit ê (.)%Chiu xiensheng%
          can     just everyone everyone have one  ASSC (surname) Mr

          mai- %women do  buyao keqi   hònn jiran fasheng do  yijing
          N    we    ASP N     modest PRT  since occur   ASP already

          shiqing
          matter

          fasheng dajia    jiu(.)yao(.)lai zenmeyang lai  jiejue% hònn(.)
          occur   everyone then  need come how        come resolve PRT

          ah  guá siong-sìn lí  a-kū tī tē-hng siōng kā  lán tsiah
          PRT I   believe    your uncle ASP local ASP   with we  these
```

```
tak-ke    long tsin kuan-sim tē-hng ah  guá khuànn (.)hoo  lín
everyone all  very care      local PRT I   see          give your
a-kū  lái  lái  kóng tse  uē    ah  guan  lín
uncle come come say  some words PRT our  (surname)
tāi-piáu         hònn >lai<(.)lai  siang  hong-bīn lái
representative PRT    come   come mutual sides      come
%go-tong%  tsit-ē        >ah lán< ū    būn-tê    bô-kín tak-ke
communicate a little bit PRT we   have questions okay everyone
thê-tshut-lâi thó-lūn ah  guá tse  tsok su-gî  sing gah  lín
raise CP      discuss PRT I   this as   emcee first help you
khui-tiûnn hònn ah  lín tsài tshiánn lín- °(    )°
open       PRT  PRT you then please  you-
```

This time we have a few representatives. Me, he called me granduncle (maternal) ((pointing to the Kuo and Kong)) and you [call me] granduncle (paternal) ((pointing to Chen)). But [we] don't mix [the relationship between Chen and me] here. I, as a senior, come to help care about this matter. We represent [on behalf of the victims and the people at fault] to come to … the MLC[7] (Tsai) has something on so he has already left. I am thinking that if today everyone is able to have a … Mr Chiu, don't be *keqi* (modest/to hold back), since this matter has occurred, [let's see] how to resolve [this issue]. I believe that your uncle (D) and we all care about the local (matters). I think, let your uncle speak [first] and let Representative Lin host the mutual negotiation with everyone. It's okay if you have any questions. Everyone can bring up [your questions] for discussion. I, as the emcee, take the opening [speech], and all of you please –

The excerpt begins when the chair of the committee, Wu, takes the hosting role and gives an official opening speech, along with a brief introduction of himself and the participants. By doing so, Wu starts by acknowledging the footings of the involved participants in the interaction. Particularly in the case of multi-party interaction, when there are numerous participant footings, multiple meanings and evaluations can arise (Haugh 2013; cf. Goffman 1981). Therefore, in this introductory turn, Wu sets up the participation framework through three main actions.

First, he establishes the way he should be addressed by the co-participants. Wu explicitly states his relationship to Kuo and Kong (in the at-fault party team) and then Chen (in the injured party team) in this negotiation before the mediation formally begins. The context and the social distance thus become salient through use of the address terms employed in the introduction (Su 2009: 329). In this case,

7. MLC, Member of Legislative Council

it highlights his insider relationship with the participants (Pan & Kádár 2011), as well as decreasing the social distance between himself and the named participants at the same time, since terms of address are drawn on to establish associations or connections between the participants in the mediation. In other words, the use of addressing terms mirrors the psychological connections, and thereby implicitly suggests interconnectivity amongst the participants, as well as minimising the relational distance in order to engage the participants in the mediation (Yang 2007; Ye 2004). On the other hand, Wu also specifies himself as an 'elder member' within both their family and legislative relationships, and thereby casts himself as having a superior role in this context. According to Chinese traditional beliefs, a person with a superior or an elder role should be highly respected (Sung 2001; Sung & Kim 2009). When introducing the representatives involved in the mediation, Wu also particularly names Tsai, who is also an MLC, who came to the mediation area but left earlier to attend to personal matters. The act of addressing an absent MLC of the local government also invokes the electoral relationship between the at-fault party and Tsai, who is asked to be a representative by Kuo and Kong, and therefore has the face (*mianzi*) that can potentially bring about a positive impact, even though he is absent from direct involvement in the negotiations.

Second, Wu, code-switches to Mandarin Chinese to address the son of the victim, Chiu, who is in his early-twenties, presupposing that Mandarin Chinese is Chiu's dominant language (Su 2009: 320), as it is the most common dialect among younger people in Taiwanese society nowadays. Wu asks Chiu not to be *keqi* during the mediation, which refers to not showing any 'restraint in expressing one's wants or acknowledging one's own abilities' (Haugh 2006: 20; cf. Chang & Haugh 2011b). This imperative directive involves asking Chiu to not restrain himself from expressing his opinions or the desired amount of compensation, and thus leaves open negotiation space for Lu and Chiu. This directive thus serves as a politeness strategy and an implicit acknowledgment of Chiu as the beneficiary of the compensation, showing concern for Chiu's speaking rights in the mediation.

Third, Wu subsequently code-switches back to Taiwanese dialect in the talk that follows and, in doing so, acknowledges Lu's participation in the mediation, and Lu's concern and care about this matter. At this point, it appears Wu is treating Chiu as the direct recipient of the comment and yet, simultaneously, Lu is evidently treated as the indirect addressee through the code-switching back to Taiwanese,[8] thereby implicitly assuming Lu will speak up for Chiu as he is his senior (i.e., being Chiu's uncle). Instead of being invited to speak, Chiu is welcome to ask or raise any concerns in the discussion following between Lu, the IA (the

---

8. Taiwanese is the dominant language amongst the older generations in Taiwan.

insurance agent) and Lin (Kuo and Kong's representative). In other words, Wu creates a particular participation footing for Lu, as occupying the primary negotiation role in this interaction on the side of the victim. The comments indirectly addressed to Lu thus implicitly serve as a compliment and give face (*mianzi*) through elevating Lu's personal character by alluding to his voluntary participation in the mediation. On the other hand, by means of the compliment of giving the next speaking turn to Lu, Wu at the same time attributes institutional authority to himself by asserting the right to select the next speaker. In other words, simultaneously Wu displays his entitlement to take the leading position in this meditation context, as well as highlighting Lu's and Chiu's entitlements that arise from having family connections to Liu, and being the beneficiary respectively. Wu thus endorses interactionally what might have been previously assumed by the participants in relation to their participation footings. However, Wu goes further in complimenting a side participant, namely, Lu, which evidently serves as a politeness strategy in order to achieve particular situational goals in the mediation.

The setting up of a participation framework by Wu's three key actions in his opening turn acknowledges the roles and the attendant responsibilities of the participants, but also acknowledges their entitlements as well as the speaking rights of the involved participants. Managing the participation footings and rights in institutional contexts is expected in Chinese settings (Gu 2011), and so failing to define the situational goal might be considered as a failing on the part of the institutional mediation system. In other words, it is critical to recognise the interrelated connections, entitlements and speaking rights of the participants involved so that they are able to act accordingly without violating their perceived institutional entitlements and obligations and thus achieve the interactional goal in a more harmonious manner (Spencer Oatey 2005; 2009). The setting up of the participation framework is arguably interpretable as orienting to face and so constitutes a face practice in the negotiation context, since invoking the participants' footings appropriately is critical for acknowledging their entitlements, that is, to properly enact their rights or obligations while negotiating their expectations without unduly breaching the interactional relationship.

After Wu's opening speech, Lu then takes the floor to start the negotiations from the victim's side.

```
2          (2.0)

3  Lu:    lán tú-tsiah    hònn >lán<lán kóng sit-tsāi sī tsit-tiûnn
          We  just before PRT   we  we  say  honestly be one  C

          tshia-hō   huat-sing ooh(.)ē-tàng kóng hoo pó-hiám kong-si kah
          car accident occur PRT able   say  let insurance company help
```

```
lán tàu  tann     tsit-sut-á tse  tsînn (.) kim-tsînn hong-bīn
we  help  shoulder a little   this money    money    part
(.)bô    tann(.)sí ah  kiò bē tńg-lâi(.)ah: (.)tú-tsiah: (.)lín
otherwise now die PRT call N back       PRT   just before    Lin
tāi-piáu     ū    kóng kuè(.)kóng tse-leh pó-hiám kong-si ê
representative have say  CP   say  this    insurance company ASSC
pōo-hūn (.)%qiang-zhi-xian%      tō   hit-loh it-tīng    ū
part       compulsory insurance then that    certainly have
ê    mah hònn (.) pah-   lak=
ASSC PRT PRT      hundred six
```

Honestly, we just talked about the occurrence of a car accident, [we hope] the insurance company is able to compensate us, in terms of money. Now, the deceased [one] cannot be called to come back. Just before the Representative Lin has said [we will] certainly have the compulsory insurance [compensation], one million six-hundred thousand dollars

4   Lin:

```
                                        =Pah-lak
                                        hundred six
```

one million six-hundred thousand dollars

5   Lu:

```
iáu-ū tse-lê: (.)%di-san-ze-ren-xian%  i  ū   tsit-pah (.) guá
also  this        third-party insurance it has one hundred  I
tsit-má tō  sī kā  guan- tō sī kóng(.)koh  hōo  sū-tsú (.)
now     then be CP  my   then be say   also make peo-
ple at fault
tsò  nng-pah
make two hundred
```

It also has [the compensation of] one million. Now I [talk] to my– to make the person at fault [pay] two million more

When Lu is given the speaking turn after a two-second pause, he first starts with a statement about their expectations, that is, his hope that the insurance company will be able to compensate them for the victim's death. Through the token word 'honestly' at the beginning of this announcement, he is claiming that the statement that follows is said with honesty or sincerity. What is implied by this is that they will not need to be compensated by Kuo, the person at fault, if the insurance company is able to compensate them. As we are aware, the mediation is held for the purpose of seeking a mutually agreeable civil compensation between the parties representing the victim and the person at fault, thereby avoiding bringing this case to the civil court. However, Lu's opening statement conflicts with the function of this meditation meeting. It is thus arguable that this opening statement can be evaluated as a politeness strategy, eschewing a bold demand about the amount of compensation at the very beginning. In other words, it is interpretable as polite because Lu avoids first directly bringing up specific amounts and also allows the at-fault party more room to avoid additional responsibility and providing extra compensation by first suggesting that the insurance company has to take responsibility. The following expression about the deceased made by Lu, that one 'cannot be called to come back', is idiomatic, meaning that the deceased has passed away and thus no amount of money could possibly compensate adequately for her life. He subsequently uses reported speech, displaying his understanding of the amount of compensation, which is the indemnity from both the compulsory and third-party insurance, based on a short conversation he had with Lin prior to the mediation. This reported speech is thus employed, on the one hand, to confirm that his understanding of the amount of compensation is correct, and on the other hand, to project a possible dispreferred response, such as a counter offer or a rejection of that amount of indemnity (Maynard 2010: 140). Therefore, the direct addressee of this turn is Lin, who has explicitly offered this amount of indemnity. The indirect addressee of this turn is the IA (insurance agent), who has the authority to agree to the indemnity amount on behalf of his company. In other words, while Lu is seeking confirmation from Lin, he is also using the reported speech by Lin to avoid possible rejection or counter offers by the IA, as the amount of indemnity can in fact be increased depending on different situations.

While Lu is confirming the amount of indemnity from the insurance company in turns 3 and 5, he also acknowledges that they will receive compensation from Kuo's compulsory and third-party insurance, which amount to one million six-hundred thousand dollars and one million dollars, respectively. At the end of turn 5, Lu then makes a direct request in an embedded form, asking for compensation through an imperative formulation from Kuo, who caused the car accident, *koh hōo sū-tsú tsò nng-pah* ('to make the person at fault [to pay] two million'). The formulation of this as a directive for compensatory action rather than making a request constitutes a display of Lu's entitlement to direct the addressee for indemnity, thereby restraining the recipient's choices of acceptance or refusal (Curl & Drew 2008; Craven & Potter 2010: 426, 437). The display of this high degree of entitlement reveals the asymmetric relationship in this mediation, where the people siding with the victim's party appear to demonstrate that they are more entitled to assert their dominant position in the negotiation. Thus, the restraint of choices of acceptance or refusal affords a low degree of contingency for Lin/Kuo, which might be interpreted as a possible threat to Lin/Kuo's separation face, who are afforded low entitlement and contingency in making their choices freely (Arundale 2006: 204).

The interpretation of this directive as potentially face-threatening can be substantiated through analysis of Lin's uptake of this utterance in turn 7. The following sequence is continued by Lin, who first starts by confirming the proposed amount of compensation mentioned by Lu after a long pause.

6   (3.5)

7 Lin:

```
Ná-m-tō hām      pó-hiám   án-ne ooh(.)sì-ah-lak(3.0)siú-sian-
Then    including insurance this Q   forty-six       first of all

hònn (.) lán tuì bong-tsiá-ooh tì    tsit-ê >hit ê< khiàm-ì lah
PRT     we to deceased one   offer one C that  apology PRT

(.)hònn in-uī sènn-miā sī(.)bû kè-ê lah: ah  lán kóng-uē (.)ah
   PRT because life    be priceless PRT PRT we speak      PRT

tann (.)tāi-tsì tō       huat-sing ah >ì-guā     huat-sing ah<
now    but     already occur    PRT accident occur       PRT

tsóng-sī ài  tsē loh lâi kóng mah (.)sènn-miā iōng kè  lâi kah
always   need sit down CP talk PRT    life     use price CP CP

kóng án-ne hònn (.) ah lán °mā sī ài ka tsun-tiōng tsit-ê° ah
talk this PRT       PRT we also be need ASP respect a little PRT

(.)kî-sit (.)lán tī  kóng lah hònn kim-tsînn ē-tàng kái-kuat ē
actually    we ASP  talk PRT PRT  money     able resolve ASSC

hònn án-ne sī siōng hó lah (.) ah sū-tsú      tsit-pîng hònn
PRT  this  be most good PRT    PRT people at fault this side PRT

(.)guá tī siūnn lah i  ka-kī mā   ū  hit-ê  sîng-ì   lah hònn
   I ASP think PRT 3sg self also have that C sincerity PRT PRT

ah: (.)tān-sī lán mā  khó-lū tsit-ê kóng >ah< i-ê ling-lik  ē
PRT    but    we also consider a little say PRT his ability ASSC

hit-lō-ah hònn sī-m-sī lán (.) hit-leh (.) lái thé-liōng tsit-ê
that      PRT  be N be we    that        CP consider a little

án-ne(.) lán lái tsò tsit-ê hiap-siong tsit-ê
this     we  CP  make one C negotiation a little
```

Then the insurance [indemnity] is included? Four million six-hundred thousand dollars. First of all, we pay [our] apology to the deceased one because life is priceless. We discuss … as the accident has occurred, we need to sit down and discuss [about it]. We are using money to negotiate over a life, so we need to pay respect [toward the deceased one and whose family]. In fact, it's the best if we can resolve [this matter] through indemnity. On the side of the people at fault, I think, he also has sincerity. But we might need to consider one issue, which is his [financial] capac-

> ity. Can [we/you] show a little consideration? Then we can make a little
> negotiation

In this subsequent turn, Lin does not respond to Lu's directive through either immediate acceptance or refusal. Instead, he first starts with a confirmation of the amount in a delayed manner. This deviates from the preferred response projected in the prior turn and so constructs in this turn a disaligning response (Wu 2004). The long pause could be considered interactionally significant and thus displays possible tension (Tannen 1984: 2973), which potentially arises here from the previous request. The delay and overtones of disalignment in Lin's turn marks it as a dispreferred response, thereby indexing Lin's treatment of the request as a face-threatening request. More specifically, a threat to their separation face is constituted through his refusal to orient to Lu's proposal, which, on the one hand, serves to resist the low contingency attributed to the at-fault side through Lu's formulation of the directive, and on the other hand, challenges Lu's display of high entitlement. It is also evident that this directive has created an interactional dilemma for Lin, who represents Kuo (and Kong) in reaching the interactional goals which are, on the one hand, to avoid bringing this case to the court and, on the other hand, to avoid paying extra indemnity over and above their financial capacity. Simultaneously, Lin also needs to please or satisfy Lu and Chiu with regard to the amount of compensation offered, so as to fulfil the obligation residing in this asymmetric relationship, which underpins Lu's (and perhaps also Chiu's) display of entitlement evident in the formulation of the directive.

Instead of accepting or refusing the request, then, Lin initiates an apology towards the representatives of the victim, addressing the cause of the accident. Through the apology and addressing the cause of the accident, as well as through showing respect and empathy by saying *sènn-miā sī* (.) *bû kè-ê lah* ('life is priceless'), Lin is affiliating with the victim's stance. On the other hand, Lin starts defending Kuo, who he asserts has *sincerity* to compensate Chiu through prosodic stress of this word. This prosodically marked emphatic style also displays Lin's emotive involvement and stance, thereby contextualising a sequentially implicative request (Selting 1994: 380), namely, asking the co-participant to sympathetically take Kuo's sincerity into account during this negotiation scenario. In terms of *sincerity* (*sîng-i*), it is often argued that it can be expressed through offers of gifts, apologies or expressions of gratitude to display the initiator's genuine intention (Hua, Wei & Yuan 2000: 99). In other words, Kuo is claimed by Lin to have a genuine intention to pay the proposed indemnity. Thus, the expression *quá tī siūn* ('I think'), spoken on behalf of Kuo, is used as a device to boost the emphasis on the speaker's belief, that is, Kuo is believed to have *sincerity* to resolve this issue, which in turn strengthens the force of this request for sympathy. However, this expression simultaneously indicates that the following opinions might be actually or potentially projecting a threat to or conflict with the recipient's opinions or stance (Endo 2013). This is because emphasising Kuo's *sincerity* could also be a perceived as a strategy to bargain for a decrease in the amount of indemnity through evoking the co-participants' sympathy.

This becomes evident in the next utterance, where Lin makes a request to *thé-liōng* (*ti-liang* in Mandarin, 'to show consideration'). The token *thé-liōng* is actually a marked expression in which a particular cultural concept is embedded. According to the definition in the Chinese dictionary by Gang and Hua (1965), *thé-liōng* means 'to be able to examine and understand other's real situation or difficulties and thus *forgive* the other' (1965: 1928, emphasis added). Lin thus explicitly starts evoking the co-participants' emotive stance by formulating an imperative request for them to *thé-liōng* ('show consideration') towards Kuo in terms of his financial capacity, which is also evident from his prosodic emphasis on the token of Kuo's financial capacity (*ling-liik*). This emphatic style, once again, displays an emotive involvement, triggering a further sequentially implicative request. More specifically, by invoking the co-participants' emotive stance, namely, sympathy for Kuo's limited financial capacity and forgiveness for his wrongdoing, a request to decrease the amount of indemnity is implicitly conveyed.

This action of responding indirectly by Lin in turn 7 is occasioned by Lu's display of high entitlement and low contingency through the formulation of the preceding request in turn 5 and so treat it as inapposite in the same way (Craven & Potter 2010; Walker, Drew & Local 2011). Lin thereby postpones the production of an occasioned or sequential action, namely, an agreement to the request (Maynard 2010: 139). This is because Lin faces a dilemma between assisting Kuo (and Kong) to accomplish their interactional goal, that is, avoiding civil charges as well as bargaining for a decrease in the amount of the compensation, and yet at the same time satisfying Chiu and Lu's expectations for compensation. Therefore, he attempts to solicit emotivity from Chiu (as well as from the people representing the victim's party), seeking a sympathetic or empathetic stance towards Kuo's financial capacity. This action of soliciting emotivity is arguably a relational practice whereby Lin indirectly refuses the request, as a defer-type move in order to avoid impeding Lu's (and Chiu) entitlement within this asymmetric relationship (Maynard 2010: 130).

After Lin's indirect refusal prompted by the indirect request, Lu continues the subsequent turn with a story-telling sequence.

```
8  Lu:    guan sió-muē-ah    tsiah gōo-sip-sann huè    (.)>oh tsit-kuí
        I   little sister  only  fifty-three   years old   PRT these

        kang heh-< i  huat-sing í-tsîng tiānn long   kóng >kóng kóng<
        day  PRT  3sg occur   before  often always say    say  say
```

```
kóng hit-ló uē  >tō  bô kóng< tîng-tánn ē   ah (.)tio huân-ló
say  that words then N  say    normal ASSC PRT    always worry
guan tuā-tsí ( )  tsiànn bô kè-tat oh siàu-liân >tsò kah< sun
my   elder sister very  N worthy PRT young     work until grandkid
nng ē long tuā-hàn ah kiánn long long ē    thàn-tsînn ah i
two C both grown-up PRT son  all  all  able make money PRT 3sg
tsiah ē    an    lah >TIU-TIU<  ÁN-NE LIĀM(.)°hònn°(.)ah tō
then  able settled PRT just just this  talk   PRT     PRT then
kóng guan tuā-tsí (.) eh::: (0.1) kah hia-ê kiánn kau-tài kóng
say  elder sister      PRT        CP  those son   remind  say
tuā-tshù bé   hoo suí-suí i   tsit-sì-lâng tō   tik-tioh hit-ê
grave    want ASP pretty 3sg one life time just get CP    that
(.)guan nā   án-ne-KAH GUAN KÓNG (.) a-hiann lí  nā kah
   I    then this CP   I    say     brother you if be-Passive
guan pān-ê-tioh hònn guan sī bé  lâi sang-óng-hng ( ) oh: (0.1)
I    deal ASP   PRT  I    die want come (cemetery name) PRT
inn jī-só       mā  kah mē  sam-pat leh (.)kóng jī-só       ah
her sis-in-law also CP scold nonsense PRT  say  sis-in-law PRT
(.)lí  ná-ê sam-pat   kóng hit-ló uē    siánn-mih (.) heh: -
   you why nonsense say  that    words what            PRT
>kánn-ná< %ming-ming-zhi zhong% ū tsit-ê tī  tshui: kāng-khuán
  seems    imperceptibly         have one C ASP urge    seem
(.)tann gōo- sip-sann huè      (.) lán    kóng (.) m-tat:  sī
   now  fifty-three  years old     people say      N worthy be
sènn-miā bô-khì tsiânn m-tat (.) ah: (.) tse-ê iah   tsiah
life     gone   very   N worthy PRT      this  still very
siàu-liân (.) sí-ê    lâng  í-king (.) siánn-mih long bô ah
young         deceased person already     what     all N PRT
(0.1) he   sī tsit-ê mí-póo=
      that be one  C compensation
```

My younger sister was only 53 years old. Oh, these days, before the accident, she'd been talking something abnormal. She'd been worried about my elder sister. It's such a waste [i.e. her death]. She'd been working since she was young – [now] two [of her] grandchildren have grown up, [and her] sons are now able to make money, and now this accident occurred. She'd been talking … and asked my elder sister to tell her children to buy her a nice grave. This is what she wanted for this life. [She] told me so, 'brother, if you can fulfil my wish, I would like to be buried in the *sang-*

> *óng-hng* (name of the graveyard).' Her sister-in-law [who heard this] also scolded her saying, 'sister-in-law, nonsense!' It seems to me [the accident] was destined to happen. She was [only] 53 years old. [Her] death such a waste. This one is still so young ((pointing to E)). The deceased one has nothing left. That [indemnity] is only for compensation

Interestingly, the subsequent turn 8 by Lu also constitutes a disaligning response to Lin's request. In other words, Lu responds indirectly (turn 8) to Lin's prior move of responding indirectly (in turn 7) to Lu's initial request (in turn 5). This is evident that the subsequent disaligning narrative (turn 8) about the deceased victim does not directly respond to Lin's previous implied request. It indicates that an evaluation by Lu of Lin's appeal for sympathy or empathy could be under consideration. Lu begins with a narrative regarding his sister before the accident occurred and expresses the idea that the car accident seems to be a predestined incident. He then stresses prosodically that her death was *tsiànn bô kè-tat oh* ('such a waste') in that she passed away at such a relatively young age. Continuing on at the end of this utterance, he reiterates her age, saying 'only fifty years old', which had already been mentioned. This is accompanied by the comment that '(her) death is such a waste'. An embodied reference is made by pointing to Chiu while asserting that Chiu is still young and then lamenting the 'deceased has nothing left'. Lu thus attempts to provide more explicit accounts to justify a greater amount of compensation. He does so by claiming the injured party's entitlement to this, as well as attempting to elicit a sympathetic and empathetic stance from the at-fault party. In other words, by evoking an emotive stance of showing sympathy or empathy towards Chiu through the narrative story-telling and the accounts, Lu is also projecting an indirect refusal of Lin's previous request as a defer-type move, and concurrently making an implicit request for them to agree to the proposed indemnity (Maynard 2010: 130). Meanwhile, Lu also displays his (and Chiu's) entitlement within the relationship to implicitly request through stating '(the deceased) has nothing left' (*siánn-mih long bô ah*) at the end of this turn, presupposing that the request from Lin is inapposite (Walker, Drew & Local 2011), and therefore paying the expected amount is the only way to compensate them for their loss. It is thus evident that evoking co-participants' emotional stance in the situation is exploited as a negotiation strategy to bolster the request for the desired amount of compensation, as his response echoes his previous request. It is also evident in Lu's subsequent claim, *he sī tsit-ê mí-póo* ('this is only for compensation'). In other words, soliciting of emotivity on the part of Lin could be interpreted as inapposite by Lu, as Kuo's financial capacity might be outweighed by Lu's (or even Chiu's) concerns (Walker, Drew & Local 2011), since in the asymmetrical relationship here, the injured party has a greater entitlement.

The interpretation of Lu 'responding indirectly' to Lin's request, thereby treating it as inapposite, draws not only from the long pause, but also from his own subsequent appeal for sympathy for his sister.

The indirect refusal in turn 8 is occasioned by the indirect request from Lin in turn 7. By responding indirectly to an indirect request, Lu diverts attention from the at-fault party to the injured party. It is thus suggested that this reflexive indirectness is constructed through the formulation of the indirect request leading to the indirect refusal that shifts the figure or the target of the aforementioned action, and thereby occasions transformative answers (Stivers & Hayashi 2010). That is, an implied request, initiated by Lu asking the at-fault party to show an empathetic or sympathetic stance, is embedded in this narrative story-telling sequence. Lu thereby very indirectly accomplishes a refusal of the prior request, or perhaps it would be more accurate to say, transforms an anticipated indirect refusal into an indirect request.

Lin then projects an affiliative stance in the following turn through expressing agreement at the conclusion of Lu's story-telling sequence, and subsequently initiates another action of soliciting emotivity from Lu.

```
9   Lin:   =tioh lah tse  sī %wang-yang-bu-lao%          hit-lō ah (3.0)
           right PRT this be  taking precaution after loss that    PRT

           ah: (.) tioh lah lán mā sī: (.) siūnn kóng sènn-miā tō  sī (.)
           PRT     right PRT we  also be    think CP   life    just be

           tsún kóng eh >tng< TNG:    TSE-LEH sî-tsūn tng tsing-hua niâ=
           like CP   PRT exactly exactly this time   exactly essence PRT
```
Right, this is just taking some precautions after the loss. We also think [her] life only just [reached to] the peak

```
10  Lu:    =tioh ah
           Right PRT
```
Right

```
11  Lin:   ah tān-sī huat-sing tsit-tsióng ì-guā    tak-ke    mā   long
           PRT but     occur     this kind   accident everyone also all

           bô-guān-ì lah (.) %shei yuan-yi kan dao zhi yangzi% (.)hònn ( )
           N  willing PRT     who  willing see  CP  this kind        PRT

           tsóng-sī heh-leh: (.) bô uân-siān lah ah  mā-sī ai  lâi (.)tsò
           invariably that      N  perfect  PRT PRT still need CP    make

           tsit ê mí-póo      ah hònn tak-ke  tuì tse-ê mí-póo   heh-leh
           one  C compensation PRT PRT everyone ASP this compensation that

           °hong-bīn sī m  sī lán tshiánn:: heh-leh: lán (.) siū-hāi-tsiá
           Aspect be N  be we ask that        our         victim     this
```

```
tsit-pîng hònn (.)lái thé-liōng tsit-ê   khuànn ē-thang°

this side PRT    CP  consider  a little see      able
```

But no-one wanted to see this accident [happen]. Who would have wanted to see it happen? [The compensation] is not ideal, [yet we] still need to redeem [the loss]. Can we ask– the side of the victim to show more consideration [towards the people at fault]?

The latching of turn 9 by Lin displays strong agreement through the token of 'right' (*tioh lah*) as well as the Chinese idiom *wangyang bulao* ('taking some precautions after the loss'), which displays his understanding of Lu's implied request, which was accomplished through an indirect refusal, that meeting their expectations about the amount is the only way to achieve satisfactory compensation. The Chinese idiom implies that financial recompense is the only way to compensate for their loss, and by reiterating it here, it confirms Lu's previous implied request in turn 6. Lin's stance on the victim's death is shown in another emphatic manner, through the prosodically marked tokens of *tng tse-leh sî-tsūn* ('exactly [at] this time') in turn 9, which indexes an affiliative reaction implicative of shared feeling (Selting 1994: 392). However, Lin subsequently signals potential contrast with what Lu has previously implied through the token 'but' at the beginning of turn 11, indicating that the following statement could differ from what is presupposed by Lu's implied request. Lin proposes a generalised assumption that no-one actually wanted the accident to happen, implying that no-one is excluded from feeling that way, thereby implying that they all share the same feelings as Lu and Chiu. Through acknowledging their mutual feelings and sorrow for the accident (and again in turn 11), Lin projects an emotive involvement, or takes an emotive stance towards the co-participants through this generalised assumption. In other words, Lin displays his empathy towards Lu's previous claim about his sister's death.

The display of an emotive stance can also be observed through the formulation of the rhetorical question that follows. Such questions generate a reverse epistemic gradient where the questioner has more epistemic rights with respect to the knowledge domain, while the respondent has less (Heritage & Raymond 2012). The rhetorical question thus presupposes that the generalised claim is an opinion which everyone shares, rather than being a personal assertion only. It thereby blocks the possibility of rejection of this generalised claim with greater force, as well as making this claim less disputable. In other words, the at-fault party's mutual feeling of sadness and sorrow is claimed to be not open to question. This rhetorical question is arguably employed as a pre-negotiation strategy, foreshadowing the subsequent counter proposal, namely, asking for them to show consideration towards Kuo's financial capacity in return. Moreover, the generalised claim not only aligns with the displayed entitlement of Lu (and Chiu) (i.e., showing sympathy for their loss through orienting Lin's feelings towards the victim of the accident) (Du Bois & Kärkkäinen 2012: 440), but also sets up the expectation of a reciprocal display of empathy. In other words, Lin appears to be eliciting emotivity through showing his aligning stance towards Lu (and Chiu), but for a different purpose from Lu, namely, in order to reduce the amount of the excess. However, it is apparent that Lin is aware that this request for Lu (and Chiu) to attend to the reciprocal entitlement for empathy might possibly conflict with the injured parties' claims about the desired amount of the indemnity, as is evident from the hedges, elongation and softened speech through which Lin displays possible discomfort. These prosodic cues thus display Lin's emotive stances and involvement in his expectations about this series of requests, which might trigger the co-participants' sequential evaluation or assessment (Selting 1994: 391; cf. Retzinger 1991), namely a potentially threatening act to the separation face of the people on the side of the injured parties in terms of impeding their claim for their expected amount of compensation.

At this point, Chen intercedes in the negotiation, as seen in turn 12 below.

```
12   Chen:   bô lah (.) tsit-má mā-sī kāng-khuán lah lí it-tit kóng: (1.0)
             N  PRT      now        also the same    PRT you keep  say

        lâng    í-king    bô-tī    ah (.) tsit-má  m-sī kóng iōng kè-tsînn

        person  already   deceased PRT      now    N be say  use  price

        lái >kóng an-na< tsuè-khí-má lí    mā   ài   piáu-sī tsit-ê   kóng

        CP   say  this   at least    you also need show    a little say

        lí    ū  siánn-mah (.) mí-póo     ê    hong-sik (.) kóng lái tsò

        you have what         compensation ASSC way          say  CP  as

        tsham-khó khuànn (.) °hònn°

        reference CP          PRT
```

No. Now [the situation] is the same. You keep saying that 'the victim has passed away, [and] now [we are] not negotiating [over a life] with a price'. But you also, at least, need to indicate what ways of compensation [you can provide] for our reference.

That Lin's request in turn 11 above is interpreted as a face-threatening act can be inferred from the subsequent response in turn 12, when Chen, the representative of Chiu and Lu, self-selects as the next speaker to join in the conversation and immediately disagrees with Lin's previous implied request through the token of *bô lah* ('No'). This token is used to reject the unsaid or implied meaning arising from the previous turn, meaning something like, 'No, it's not the case' or 'No, it's not like that'. The utterance of 'Now it's the same' (*tsit-má mā-sī kāng-khuán lah*) is in response to Lin's implicature that they reduce the amount of compensation. The 'sameness' here refers to the request to show consideration, implying that they are also asking for the same consideration, i.e., a request to show consideration from the party at fault to the victim's side who suffered the loss. This corresponds with the subsequent argument against Lin's earlier claim about not negotiating over the price of a life, but asking for a reduction in the amount of compensation, and thereby implicitly criticises Lin for being contradictory in his own argument. Through echoing Lin's earlier claim in turn 6, Chen thus draws attention to the contradiction between what has been said and what is implicitly requested by Lin. With a critical and questioning attitude, Chen thereby frames this utterance by Lin as ironic, which is generally argued to project a mismatch between what is expected and what is actually said or done (Clift 1999: 536). Irony is used here to evaluate what has been said negatively, and is thereby used to subvert the prior turn (Clift 1999: 540). In other words, the irony occasioned here indexes Chen's disaffiliative stance towards Lin's previous request. Therefore, Chen's explicit rejection of the implied request, the irony, as well as the subsequent direct interrogative request that Lin proposes an amount of compensation that meets the expectation of the victim's party can be interpreted as projecting another threat to the separation face of Lin, who represents the at-fault party. In this sequence, Chen thus displays his high entitlement in this asymmetric relationship through his strategic use of footing. He casts himself as the animator of this utterance, and yet Chiu and Lu are the principals of this sequence, and therefore he attempts to highlight the asymmetric relationship between the party at fault and the injured party. The sequence of face-threatening utterances therefore projects the low entitlement, the low contingency and restriction on the options for Lin (inclusive of the at-fault party) and therefore constitutes a disaligning response to the implied requests of the at-fault party (Walker, Drew & Local 2011) as well as projecting a disaffiliative stance towards Lin.

That this constitutes a negative evaluation is evident in Lin's subsequent turn 13 where there are repetitive hedges (e.g., *heh-leh, hònn*) in his response through which he displays his discomfort in responding to Chen's prior turn.

```
13  Lin:  =in-uī guan í-uī    sī siūnn kóng ah  heh-leh pó-hiám >hònn< ē
          because we thought be think CP   PRT that   insurance PRT  can

          khah kuân (.) tsīn-liōng        pó-hiám  khuànn pó-hiám   i
          more higher as much as possible insurance see   insurance 3sg

          °ē  pōo-hūn hònn ē-thang khah kuân tsit-ê  bô° (.) ah  tāi-tsì
          can part   PRT able  more higher a little Q      PRT but

          lán liáu-kái  pó-hiám  kong-si tī  tsia hònn i   mā   phài lâng
          we understand insurance company ASP here PRT 3sg also send person

          lái  in-uī   lán %ji-xien% tō   sī (.) kah: heh-leh: (.) tsit-ê
          come because we   limit    then be     up   to that      one  C
```

```
tsit- pah    tsit-ê  pah-lak    tse (.)  i    heh  tō   sī
one million one C  hundred-six  this    3sg   that then  be

%qiang-zhi xien%    heh-leh pōo-hūn heh-leh sī pah-    lak hònn (.)
compulsory insurance that   part    that   be  million-six PRT

ah heh-leh: %ze-ren xien%          heh-leh tsit- pah    hònn (.)
PRT that       third-party insurance that    one hundred PRT

a-nah (2.0) i an-ne ê: hit-loh-ah hònn sit-tsāi sī (0.5) sui-liân
if       as this ASSC  that       PRT   really  be          although

sī heh-leh: (.) TSO-SîNG ì-GUĀ    hònn sī (1.0) lán tī  kóng khah
be that         cause   accident  PRT  be        we ASP say  more

kuè-sit khah hit-loh-ah (.)°>ah<°(.) hū-tam mā  sī °>khah< >khah<
sorry   more that           PRT      burden also be     more  more

khah tāng tsit-sut-á° (2.0) lín  ê   kám-kak an-ne- (.) ah  bô
more heavy a little         your ASSC feeling how        PRT N

lán tshiánn pó-hiám   ko(hh)ng-si khuànn-(.)lí pó-hiám   kong-si
we  ask     insurance company     see       you insurance company

kah hit-loh-ah >>bô lí  tsha-<< lí  kah lí   kong-si hit-loh-ah-
CP  that        N you then      you CP  your company  that
```

Because I thought that the [indemnity] from the insurance [company] could be higher. [I hope the insurance company] can [offer] as much as [they can]. [I hope] the part of his [indemnity] can be a bit higher. However, we understand that the insurance company is here. It has sent [their] agent here. Because there is a limit [of the indemnity], [the total indemnity from the insurance company is] up to only one million [dollars] and one-million and six-hundred thousand dollars. That is compulsory insurance. This part is one million and six hundred thousand dollars and then [the indemnity from] that third-party insurance is one million dollars. It's really ... although [the people at fault] caused the accident and we are sorry for it, his burden is a little bit heavy. What do you think? We can ask the [agent of] the insurance compa-ny-((turning to the insurance agent)) your insurance company-

Lin subsequently explains that he expects the insurance company to offer more compensation so that Kuo will not need to pay the rest, beyond his financial capacity. By doing so, Lin thus shifts the footing as the target of Chen's previous claim to the insurance company, implying that the insurance company will be the one determining the amount of compensation. In this way, Lin shifts the attention to the insurance agent, who is argued to be principally responsible for the compensation, and thereby simultaneously treats the insurance agent as the indirect addressee who is thus indirectly requested to provide better compensation as Lin alludes to their expectations about a bit higher indemnity being possible (*tsīn-liōng pó-hiám khuànn pó-hiám i°ē pōo-hūn hònn ē-thang khah kuân tsit-êbô,* ('[I hope] the part of his [indemnity] can be a bit higher'). On the other hand, from the pauses, elongations, cut-offs in talks and a number of hedges in this turn, i.e., *heh-leh, hit-loh-ah, an-ne* and *heh* ('that', 'this'), it is evident that Lin displays discomfort about providing a response to Chen's previous turn, and also responds indirectly to Chen's request that they first propose the amount. In other words, this indirect response is occasioned by the combination of Chen's irony and the direct request for them to make a proposal about compensation, which engenders a footing shift that occasions yet another implicit request, this time directed at the insurance agent. While Lin repeats the amount of indemnity that the insurance company is offering, there are actually two actions Lin attempts to accomplish here: one is to confirm the specific amounts of compensation that the injured party will receive from the insurance company, and the other is to indirectly shift the speaking turn to the insurance agent (IA) since the sequential evidence foreshadows Lin's nomination of the IA to speak and further explain the amount of compensation through his implicit request.

On the other hand, Lin acknowledges the fault on behalf of Kuo again, and at the same time implicitly asks Chen (including the injured party) for consideration with regard to Kuo's limited financial capacity, by stating Kuo's financial burden, which is 'a little bit heavy' since Kuo still needs to pay the extra indemnity in order to avoid bringing this case to civil court. By asking for consideration for Kuo's limited financial capacity to pay the extra indemnity, Lin is once again soliciting emotivity from the injured party, a practice which is arguably occasioned by Chen's negative evaluation in turn 12. This soliciting of emotivity is also evident through the emotive stance displayed in an overly soft volume and using understaters. The lexical modification of the understater (*tsit-sut-á*, 'a little') is used to modify the illocutionary force in order to minimise the force of the request (Rue & Zhang 2008: 42). This can be evaluated as decreasing the possibility of projecting a threat to the victim party's separation face, namely, their perceived entitlement. Lin's uptake of Chen's face-threatening interrogative can also be observed in this uncompleted turn and his selection of the IA to be the next speaker concomitant with the use of hedges.

While the IA is given the speaking turn by Lin, he begins turn 15 with an apology.

```
14              ((coughing in the background))

15   IA:    pháinn-sè lah   hònn e:   >gī-uân< kok-uī tāi-piáu tshuan-tiúnn
            sorry     PRT   PRT PRT   MLC      every  representative HV

            >>lah hònn<< (.) in: uī: (1.0) pó-hiám    giah-tōo sī lâng-kheh
            PRT PRT          because        insurance amount   be customer

            kuat-tīng ê     lah m-sī(.)pó-hiám   kong-si kuat-tīng ê     lah
            regulate  ASSC PRT  N  be  insurance company regulate ASSC PRT
```

(.)ah tong-liân i   ê   pó-hiám   giah-tōo (.)bô kàu hia-ê (.)
     PRT certainly 3sg ASSC insurance amount   N reach there

tse: (.)guan tsit-pîng (.)lí kóng %xiang-yiao bang-mang ye
this   we   this side   you say want   help   also

li-you-wei-dai   la% hònn (.)ah %zhi shi shuo(.)e::: (.)tao
strength N enough PRT PRT   PRT this be say   PRT   quote

yi ju gang-cai   dai-biao   suo jiang de   hua   la (.)
one C just before representative ADV say   ASSC words PRT

fa-sheng shi-qing dai-jia bu yuan-yi la (.)oo na   dang-ran
occur   matter   everyone N willing PRT   PRT then certainly

shi e:: >liang zhao yao<LIANG ZHAO hònn liang zhao duo yao (.)
be PRT two   side need two   side PRT two   side both need

huxiang   ti-liang   yi-xia hònn(.)danxia de xinqing(.)danxia
each other considerate CP   PRT   moment ASSC feeling   moment

de xinqing la (.)oo wo juede zheyanzi shi(.)bijiao(.)%ok%
ASSC feeling PRT   PRT I think this   be   more   okay

yidian la (.) ˚hònn˚ a na jiran jintian nage: (.) (())e::: (.)
a little PRT   PRT   PRT PRT then since today that   PRT

shuohaizhe zhibian   ye   tichu   suowei   de (.) chule
victim   this side also propose so-called ASSC   except

baoxian   busuan   de   hua dagai   shi suowei   de (.)
insurance N-counted ASSC if approximately be so-called ASSC

((cough))liangbaiwuan de   peichang (.)na women jiandan jiang
         two million ASSC indemnity   then we   simply say

hònn (.) %total% jine jiu shi sibai   liushi wuan (.)
PRT   total   price thus be four million six-hundred thousand

na   sibai   liushi wuan   de hua lei(.)hònn a:
then four million six-hundred thousand ASSC if PRT   PRT PRT

zai zhe yi ge jine de   kaoliang   shangmian ne: (.) nage (.)
ASP this one C price ASSC consideration upon   PRT   that

Kuo   xiensheng zhebian   hònn (.) yinwei qishi   women
(surname) Mr   this side PRT   because actually we

jintian zai zenme tan hònn (.) dao   shihou (.)nage yali
today   ASP how   talk PRT   until then   that pressure

yiding   hui dao ni zhe bian lai% (.) hònn %bijin   women
certainly will come you this side CP   PRT After all we

shi dangshiren% (.) hònn(.)%zhege ye   pau   bu diao
be person involved PRT   this also escape N CP

```
de% (.)hònn %ni  ziji dagai   xin    li      yao  you  ge di
ASSC  PRT   you self roughly heart  inside  need have C  bottom
(.)yao xiang yixia shuo women dagai you   duoshao  de    nengli%
   need think CP   say   we    roughly have how much ASSC ability
(.)>hònn<  %neng lai chuli zhe  ge shiqing (.)jiang nanting
      PRT     able ASP deal  this C  matter      say  unpleasant
yidian    la%(.)hònn (.)>>nā bé   tshú-lí bē   tshân    bē
a little  PRT   PRT        if want deal    sell farmland sell
hng       mā   ài   tshú-lí lah ah  nā bài tshú-lí tsit- sen
property also need deal     PRT PRT if N  deal    one   cent
gōo  gín    lóng bián puê<<
five dollar all  N    compensate
```

Sorry, MLC, every representative and Head of the village, because the amount of insurance [indemnity] is decided by the customer, not by the insurance company, of course, I cannot help much if the insurance [cover] is not enough even I wanted to. [I'd like to] quote what the representative just said, that no-one wanted this [accident] to happen. Of course, those on both sides need to show consideration for each other's feeling at this moment. I think this is better. Since the people on the victim's side have proposed a two-million indemnity in addition to the insurance indemnity,[9] the total indemnity will be four million and six hundred thousand dollars. In terms of the amount of the indemnity, Mr Kuo ((turning to Kuo)), no matter how we discuss the matter today, you [are the one] bearing the pressure. As you are the person involved, you cannot escape from this. You will need to be prepared and think about how much capacity you have to deal with this matter. To put it unpleasantly, if [you] want to deal with this matter, you will [even] sell your farmland or property. But if you don't want to deal with it, [the people on the side of the victim] will not even get a penny.

In turn 15, the IA starts with an apology Illocutionary Force Indicating Device (IFID) (*pháinn-sè*, lit. 'embarrassed'), foreshadowing that the forthcoming statement could be perceived as impolite or offensive. However, although this apology IFID is made in front of everyone, it can be interpreted differently depending on the footings of the recipients, and thus appears to project multiple layers of meaning in this multi-party meeting. First, the IA apologises to the at-fault party. By responding to Lin's prior turn, he implicitly rejects Lin's shifting the footing of principal to the IA, and in this sense *pháinn-sè* ('embarrassed') is employed as

9. The insurance indemnity involves two separate amounts of insurance cover: the compulsory insurance (the amount of compensation is $NT1,600,000) and the third-party insurance (the amount of compensation is $NT1,000,000).

an indicative token to imply that the subsequent claim will deviate from the preferred response. This corresponds to the IA's following statement:

> *in uī pó-hiám giah-tōo sī lâng-kheh kuat-tīng ê lah m-sī pó-hiám kong-si kuat-tīng ê ah tong-liân i ê pó-hiám giah-tōo bô kàu hia-ê tse guan tsit-pîng lí kóng xiang-yiao bang-mang ye li-you-wei-dai la hònn* ('because the amount of insurance [indemnity] is decided by the client, not by the insurance company, of course I cannot help much if the insurance [coverage] is not enough even I want to').

This is used to explicitly distance the insurance company from the party who decides the amount of indemnity and thereby shifts the footing of principal back to Kuo, who is the insurer in this case. While the IA declines the displayed entitlement projected by Lin, namely, the indirect request to increase the compensation on behalf of the insurer (Kuo), he also projects separation from the at-fault party, who he implicitly claims should hold the principal footing in this case. Second, the IA also apologises to the injured party, as he shows regret at not being able to meet their expectations through his rejection of taking the principal footing here, and thus claimed inability to take responsibility for offering a higher amount of compensation. By stating *xiang ya bang mang ye li you wei dai la* ('I can't help much even I wanted to'), the IA furthermore implies he is in a powerless position and thereby shifts the footing of principal back to the at-fault party. This corresponds with the following account, where he claims that the amount of compensation is determined by the condition of insurance cover, thereby also implying that the amount of compensation lies in the insurer's hands (Kuo). Through this multi-layered apology, then, the IA thus displays a disaligning stance towards both parties. However, while shifting the footing of principal back to Kuo, the IA attempts to mediate the tension arising from the negotiation between the party at fault and the injured party at this point. The IA then proposes that it would be a better idea for both parties to show consideration, alluding to turns 12 and 13, where both parties are seeking for consideration towards each other's feelings, namely, to come to a compromise regarding their expectations about the amount of the compensation. Through intonational emphasis and repetition of the words *liang zhao* ('both parties'), the IA explicitly shifts the focus onto both parties to get them to reach an agreement as to whether they decrease or increase the amount of indemnity, and thereby distances himself from making the decision. Both lexical and prosodic cues are apparent in this utterance, thereby indexing an emphatic style in this activity (Selting 1994: 380), namely, the suggestion that both parties show consideration. In other words, the amount of compensation can only be finalised by both parties, rather than himself as an insurance agent. While the IA offers this advice, this turn is qualified by the hedge *wo juede* ('I think') in the middle of this utterance. In this way, the IA distances himself from the claim by 'mark[ing] a lower degree of speaker commitment to claim' (Endo 2013: 9), through the token of *wo juede*.

Prior to this mediation meeting, the injured party had proposed an extra excess of two million Taiwanese dollars, in addition to the indemnity (i.e., in addition to the compulsory and third-party insurance provided by the insurance company). At this point, the IA reiterates the figures in order to confirm both parties' understanding of the amount of the total compensation. The IA then turns to Kuo, proposing that Kuo is the one who will need to decide whether to accept the injured party's proposal, no matter how this negotiation ends, as he is the one who caused this accident. By physically orienting to Kuo, the IA treats him as the direct addressee in this turn, while the rest of the participants are treated as indirect ones. The IA therefore displays his strong entitlement by means of his body movement, shifting the present attention to Kuo, who is subsequently positioned in the footing of principal. By displaying his strong entitlement to epistemic territory through the formulation of a direct statement which emphasises his epistemic status regarding the insurance cover condition (Asmuß & Oshima 2012: 83), the IA thereby projects separation from the at-fault party by arguing that his footing is not the same as Kuo's in terms of deciding on the extra compensation proposed by the injured party. When the IA points out that it is Kuo who needs to consider how much indemnity he needs to pay to compensate the victim, he makes reference to a Taiwanese idiom *nā bé tshú-lí bē tshân bē hng mā ài tshú-lí lah ah nā bài tshú-lí tsit-sen gōo gín lóng bián puê* ('if [you] want to deal with this matter, you will [even need to] sell your farmland or property. But if you don't want to deal with it, [the victim's party] will not even get a penny'). Prior to this utterance, the IA explicitly framed it as *jiang nanting yidian* (lit.: 'not pleasant to hear; to be offensive'), a formula which is used to acknowledge that the forthcoming suggestions can be potentially evaluated as offensive or even face-threatening to the recipient, namely, the subsequent implicature embedded in the Taiwanese idiom, which alludes to the possibility that Kuo will be not able to pay the indemnity if he is lacking in sincerity, and consequently will not be able to meet the injured party's expectations. This alliterative Taiwanese idiom implies more specifically that, if the at-fault party has *sincerity* to resolve this dispute, he will even sell his farmland or property. However, if the at-fault party has no *sincerity* to resolve the dispute, he will not even pay a small amount of compensation. In other words, the later interpretation is that the injured party might end up obtaining the indemnity from the insurance cover only, but no extra amount of compensation from the at-fault party. This idiomatic implicature thereby attempts to elicit the at-fault party's sincerity and thus accept the injured party's proposal, namely, to agree to the amount of extra indemnity of two million

Taiwanese dollars, or at least to provide an agreeable amount of compensation, in order to settle this dispute and avoid the victim party bringing this case to court. The insurance agent's evoking of sincerity is arguably a relational practice, which is occasioned by the assumption that Lin's shifting of principal footing to him in the prior turn implies a possible lack of sincerity on the IA's part. The sincerity referred to here is thus a euphemism for money, namely, the amount of compensation or a concrete figure for indemnity.

In the course of this sequence, the insurance agent appears to accomplish a particular goal through three steps of interlocking interactional and relational practices, i.e., evoking a sympathetic stance from people on both sides, evoking sincerity from the at-fault party, as well as distancing himself as a representative of the insurance company from the potential pressure to provide extra indemnity by shifting the responsibility for this back to the at-fault party. In order to reach this interactional goal, the IA's interactional and relational practices involve relational separation work, that is, marking his entitlement to display separation in this relational context and thereby projecting a potential threat to his connection face with the at-fault party, where the role the IA plays is as a representative of the at-fault party with whom he has an ongoing business relationship.

There is robust evidence that a face threat indeed was interactionally achieved from the pause and Lin's subsequent response in turn 17, where Lin's denial is accompanied by an increase in volume, which signals emphasis, indexing Lin's evaluation of a contradiction between his expectation and the reality represented in the IA's prior turn (Selting 1994: 384). In other words, through his uptake in response to the IA's statement, Lin displays a negative evaluation of the IA's prior proposal and thus an evaluation of it as face-threatening.

```
16          (1.0)

17   Lin:   heh[ HEH  SĪ bô khó-lîng lah (        )]
            that that be N  possible PRT
            That, that is impossible
```

After a one second pause, Lin responds in an emphatic manner in turn 17, suggesting that the scenario alluded to through the idiom will not happen. With prosodically marked talk, Lin explicitly rejects the implicature that Kuo might not have enough sincerity to pay the extra expected compensation and thereby claims that having no sincerity to resolve this issue is unthinkable.

After Lin rejects the implicature, the IA continues on with an account of his previous claim in an overlapping turn.

```
18   IA:    [hònn tse  sī sū-sit oh (.) TIÓH  BÔ] (.) M SĪ (.)NĀ-BÉ
            PRT   this be fact   PRT   right PRT   N be    if want
```

```
TSHÚ-LÍ LÁN KÓNG TSÌNG-KING LÍ  TŌ- >GUÁ Ê    Ì-SÙ
deal    we  say  seriously  you  then  I  ASSC meaning
SĪ KÓNG(.)LÍ TŌ BĒ  TSHÂN  BĒ  HŇG     MĀ ÀI
be say    you need sell farmland sell property also  need
TSHÚ-LÍ LAH <HÒNN: (.) %a  yao you  nage xin  la (.)yao you
deal    PRT PRT        PRT need have that heart PRT  need have
nage xin   A: jiang nanting  yidian  zhende mei you  qien jiao
that heart PRT say unpleasant a little really N have money ask
ni  qu sha ren    fanghuo        zhege ye   bu
you go kill people set places on fire this  also N
keneng%(.)hònn: (.)
 possible PRT
ni  ziji kaoliang yixia (.)wo benshen you  duoshao
you self consider a little I  self    have how much
%nengli   shibushi% (.) hònn (.) ē-sái tam      tsit-ē    bô
capability be-N-be        PRT      able  shoulder a little Q
(.) >ah tsīn-liōng    tam      tsit-ē<(.)lí(.)siūnn khuànn
PRT as far as possible shoulder a little  you  think CP
māi ah  tsit-ē(.)hònn ah: lán nng ê tshut-lâi guā-kháu
CP  PRT a little PRT  PRT  we  two C come  CP   outside
gián-kiù tsit-ē   ā-sī >kah  lán tāi-piáu       gián-kiù
discuss  a little or    with our representative discuss
khuànn māi tsit-ē<=
see    CP  a little
```

 This is fact. Right? No. If [you] want to deal with [it], to be serious,
you then, I mean [that you] need to deal with [it even you need to] sell
farmland or land. [You] need to have the heart. [You] need to have the
heart. [It's] unpleasant to say [that] asking you to kill people or set places
on fire is also impossible if you don't have money. Is that right? You need
to consider a bit. 'How much capability do I have?', 'Am I able to shoulder (the extra indemnity) a bit?' Try your best to shoulder some (extra
indemnity). Think about it. We two come outside to discuss or discuss
with our representative

Through an overlapping utterance of *tse sī sū-sit oh* ('this is a fact') concomitant with prosodic emphasis of the rhetorical question *tióh bô* ('right'), the IA
once again stresses that the situation alluded to through the idiom does in fact
happen in reality according to the IA's previous mediation experiences. However,
the implicature arising from the idiom can also be interpreted along the lines

that the injured party might not receive adequate compensation, or the at-fault party might need to try very hard to compensate the injured party. Through a rhetorical question formulation, the IA asserts this as a generic claim, and thus a belief which everyone could share and evaluate, rather than being a personal assertion only. The subsequent token of *m sī* ('No') with an increased volume and prosodic emphasis is arguably an emotional cue of frustration (Selting 1994), which responds to Lin's prior interpreting of the idiom. It is in this sense used to mitigate somewhat the potential face threat arising from the idiom, suggesting it might be possible that the at-fault party could be seen as being not sincere enough. However, the IA then repeats the idiom again, but only the first half of it. The reiteration of only the first part of the idiom thus also mitigates the possible negative interpretation of the insurance agent's talk as implicitly accusing Kuo of having no sincerity. By saying that *lí tō bē tshân bē hŋ mā ài tshú-lí lah* ('you [need to] deal with [it even you need] to sell farmland or land'), the IA implies that Kuo might indeed have sincerity to provide compensation with his utmost efforts, thereby mitigating the previous potential face threat, as well as affiliating with Lin's stance, i.e., to negotiate along his presently realised stance and Lin's prior stance through showing his affective orientation derived from the emphatic tokens (Du Bois & Kärkkäinen 2012: 440). He subsequently attempts to elicit Kuo's sincerity again, by arguing that *yao you nage xin* ('[Kuo] needs [to] have that heart') with stress and repetition, implicitly asking Kuo to show his sincerity in terms of the amount of excess. In the course of eliciting *sincerity* and *heart*, it is arguable that *sincerity* stands metaphorically for money and therefore *heart*, *sincerity* and money exist in a metonymic relationship here. Kuo is thus implicitly requested by the IA to accept the two-million-dollar proposal or to provide an alternative amount for compensation. Interestingly, the IA once again displays an aligning stance towards the at-fault party by making reference to an analogy, suggesting that 'asking you to kill people or set places on fire is also impossible if you don't have money'. Through this analogy, he is suggesting that 'we are not asking you to do bad things in order to get money to compensate the injured party'. At this point, the IA explains what he meant by the idiom in the prior turn in order to clarify his meaning. Further evidence of his affiliation with the at-fault party's stance lies in the token at the beginning of this analogy, when the IA claims the analogy is *jiang nanting yidian* ('unpleasant to say'). This token indicates that the forthcoming statement could be offensive or potentially face-threatening, as the IA displays an affiliative stance towards the at-fault party through the analogy that it should not be possible to request Kuo to compensate beyond his financial capacity and force him to do bad things in order to get the money. He thus explicitly acknowledges that the analogy may be offensive to the injured party by establishing grounds for Kuo's account for not being able to afford the injured party's proposed amount of compensation. In other words, by affiliating with Kuo's presumed stance, he justifies the possible negative assessment arising from his previous use of the idiom, and thereby mitigates the face threat arising from the idiom. On the other hand, through increasing the volume and emphasis of the tokens, in making a denial and claim (*nā-bétshú-lí lán kóng tsìng-king*, 'if [you] want to deal with [the situation], let's be more serious/honest') at the beginning of this sequence, the IA thus positions himself as an experienced advisor who is entitled to make a series of suggestions as well as inviting Kuo, Lin and Wu to have a private discussion outside the mediation room. He thereby indexes his relational separation from the rest of the participation and constructs his own expert identity within the participation framework underlying this mediation.

In the following excerpt, the IA then suggests that the at-fault party step outside and have a private discussion about the amount of compensation in order to provide a counter proposal for the injured party.

19   Lin: =bô [lah]

       N   PRT

       No

20   IA: %[bijing]   lai   zhebian haishi yao   tan   yixia la%

             After all come here   still   need talk CP   PRT

       After all [we] come here for negotiation

21   Lin: guā kah sûn-mn-g [tsiít-ē]

       I   CP ask   CP

       I ask [him first]

22   IA: [án-ne] hó   bô hònn

       this   good N Q

       Is this okay?

23   Chen: lín sing   tâm   khuànn lah::

       you first talk CP   PRT

       You [guys]talk first

24   Peng: kóng tsit-ē kah   tsìng-king

       Talk CP   more serious

       Be more serious

25   Wu: lán   guá sī tsin tsìng-king

       person I   be very serious

       I am very serious

26   Peng: ((hhhehhheh))

> *(Kuo, Kong, Lin, IA and Wu stepped outside to discuss the amount of*
> *indemnity)*

While the IA invites Kuo, Lin and Wu to step outside in order to have a private conversation among themselves at the end of turn 18, Lin at first rejects the IA's invitation (turn 19). Nevertheless, the IA keeps talking to Kuo (turn 20), paralleling the account of his invitation with Lin's alternative proposal, that is, suggesting that they settle the amount of compensation privately. Chen subsequently agrees in turn 23 that the party at fault should first have a discussion about whether Kuo can afford to offer the proposed amount.

Although Lin at first refuses to have a private conversation in the IA's presence, he eventually relents when Chen agrees that they should go along with the proposal to have a private conversation amongst the people at fault. As Kuo, Kong, the IA, Lin and Wu are about to step outside the room, Peng self-selects at turn 24, asking them to be more serious about the discussion. Peng's talk actually orients the IA's previous claim, implying that what the IA suggested or claimed with the idiom or analogy is not serious or even offensive by making a non-serious complaint. The implicature is embedded in an imperative within a mocking frame, which is constructed and interactionally achieved through their laughter in turn 26. In addition, while it is constructed within a humorous or teasing frame, Peng also indirectly requests that they have a serious discussion about offering a decent level of indemnity for the injured party. Through this indirect request, he is simultaneously implying that what has been negotiated does not constitute satisfactory progress on the side of the at-fault party, which can be evaluated as a solidarity face-threatening act (cf. Chang & Haugh 2011b), as it eases the tension through a non-serious accusation. Interestingly, the footing of the subsequent turn has then shifted from the IA as the principal recipient to Wu, as it is Wu who responds, ostensibly in a serious way, to this turn on behalf of the IA in order to attend to this mock seriousness on the part of Peng.

The following excerpt occurs when the at-fault party steps outside in order to have backroom negotiations. This discussion is between Chen and Luo, who are saying that people at fault in general should ensure they have a greater level of insurance cover in order to avoid a situation where a person at fault is not able to afford the required degree of compensation, so that the insurance company can fully cover the compensation for the injured party. Here, in turn 27, Chen is complaining about people (who he has helped with similar experiences) who only insure for a very minimal level of cover and so are unable to fully compensate the injured party.

```
27  Chen: TSIN-TSĒ LÂNG  HÒNN TSHIA-HŌ   TÀK-PÁI   GUÁ KÓNG LÍ  ING-KAI
           many    people PRT car accident every time I   say  you deserve
```

```
LAH LÍ KA-KĪ BĒ   TSHUT TSÎN HÒNN (.) LÍ  TŌ  PÓ-HIÁM  KE
PRT you self want pay    money PRT     you then insurance CP
PÓ     >TSÌT-SUT-Á< NNG TSHING  KŌH:: KĀ  LÍ PÓ     TSÌT-
insure a little   two thousand dollars with you insure one
TSHING  KŌH   TŌ  TSHA  TSIN-TSĒ [AH]
thousand dollars then differ very much PRT
```

I told many people [who had car accident] every time, saying 'you deserve it, you want to pay [extra] money yourself'. You just need to insure your car with better coverage. Two-thousand dollars [of the annual fee] can make a big difference [in the indemnity], compared with one-thousand dollars [of the annual fee]

While Chen complains about people who do not take out sufficient cover, he stresses that just a further one thousand Taiwanese dollars in the annual insurance premium could make a huge difference to the amount of indemnity payable by the insurance company. With the stress and increased volume in this utterance, it is evident that he is confident in making this claim. In this way, he constructs a positive image of himself as an advisor with experience in dealing with disputes over car accidents, thereby displaying an entitlement to make such a claim. This is particularly evident when he condemns people by saying *lí ing-kai* ('You deserve it', i.e., deserve to pay extra compensation in the situation where people have minimal insurance cover) with an emphatic style as well as through the subsequent generalised imperative. Chen thus apparently casts himself in the principal role, displaying his high entitlement through this condemnation (Asmuß & Oshima 2012: 82). On the other hand, through a generic complaint about his past experience, Chen simultaneously projects an indirect criticism about Kuo who now encounters a similar situation. The generic complaint about others thus at the same time implies that, if Kuo had paid a higher premium for his insurance cover, he would not have had this trouble in negotiating the extra compensation, as the indemnity from the insurance company would have been sufficient for the compensation. By displaying entitlement through the generalised complaint as well as the implicature, Chen thereby attempts to highlight Kuo's role as the one needing to take responsibility for the extra compensation, and thus positions Kuo as having a low degree of contingency to reject the proposed amount of compensation at this point.

In the following turn, Luo displays an affiliative stance towards Chen's claim through an overlapping utterance.

```
28  Luo:  [PING]-SIÔNG KIÁM KHAI
          Everyday     less spend
```

```
TŌ   Ū   AH  LAH  (.)  TIÒH  BÔ AH  LI  AH  KÓNG KIÒ  AH-  (.)
then have PRT PRT      right N  PRT you PRT say  call PRT
TĀI-TSÌ HUAT-SING TSHIŪNN LÍN LÂI ÁN-NE TSHÚ-LÍ TŌ   KHAH KÌN
matter  occur    like    you come this deal    then more quick
KÁI-KUAT
resolved
```

[If you] have spent less [money] everyday, [you'd have] had [enough
money to pay for better insurance cover]. Right? [If something] happened like this and then you were asked to come [to help], it can be
resolved quickly

Luo endorses Chen's complaint in turn 28 by commenting that if people spend
less on other everyday things, they would be able to afford better insurance cover,
and so avoid situations where they need to pay extra indemnity. By displaying
emphatic agreement through overlapping and increased volume, Luo displays an
affiliative stance with Chen's experience and feelings towards similar negotiation
cases (Selting 1994; Stivers, Mondada & Steensig 2011). By subsequently complimenting Chen by saying, *tāi-tsì huat-sing tshiūnn lín lâi án-ne tshú-lí tō khah kìn
kái-kuat* ('[if something] happened like this and then you were asked to come
[to help], it can be resolved quickly'), Luo is echoing Chen's claimed high entitlement (*mianzi*) through ratifying Chen's experience so as to seek for a possible
mutually agreeable amount of compensation. In other words, Luo attempts to
attribute Chen's separation face (here glossed as *mianzi*) in this relational context,
and so this complimenting can arguably be evaulated as a face-enhancing act.
This face-enhancing act corresponds to Chen's entitlement displayed in the prior
turn as he compliments Chen on his experience (here glossed as *mianzi*) which
can help resolve the dispute quickly, and therefore also establishes relational connection through implying that this negotiation cannot be resolved without Chen's
assistance. Thus, by implicitly praising Chen's negotiating skills to resolve the dispute and satisfy the two parties in front of the injured party, Luo is thereby, in
passing, implicitly proposing that the injured party agrees to decrease the amount
of compensation or at least opens up space to negotiate this. The moves in the
course of this sequence which Luo appears to employ aim to achieve a particular
interactional goal, that is, to enhance Chen's separation face with the other parties
by ratifying Chen's high entitlement, as well as creating relational connection with
Chen by emphasising the need for his skills in guiding the negotiation. Through
increasing the degree of the relational connection and separation simultaneously
with Chen, the compliment can be interpreted as a negotiation strategy aimed at
persuading the recipient to accommodate the implied request, namely, to allow a
decrease in the proposed amount of compensation, or at least allow greater space
for further negotiation of the amount.

After the backroom discussion amongst those in the at-fault party, all the members returned to the main mediation room, and Lin initiated the negotiation again in turn 29.

(section omitted)

29   Lin: >án-ne hit-lō-ah lah hònn< lán tī   kóng ê   tī hia   khiú lái

                this   that   PRT PRT   we just say PRT ASP there pull CP

                khiú khì ˚hònn˚ ( ) siūnn kóng duì hit-lō-ah

                pull CP   PRT   think CP   for that

                khah bô lé-māu lah

                more N polite PRT

                ˚hònn˚(.) ah lán hit-leh sū-tsú   tsit pinn hònn(.)i ˚mā˚

                PRT   PRT we that   person at fault this side PRT 3sg also

                >mā ài< pang lán kah i   thé-liōng tsìt-ē   ah i   ê

                also need help we CP 3sg considerate a little PRT 3sg ASSC

                ling-lìk (.) hònn %ji-xian% án-ne hònn (.)ah:

                capacity   PRT limit   this PRT   PRT

                sam-ah tshit án-ne

                thirty-seven this

                (.) ah (.) tshiánn lán hònn ho-siong   kah   ˚(thé-liōng)˚

                    PRT   please we PRT each other be-passive considerate

        Well, we think it's not polite towards the deceased while we are bargaining there. I think [the people at the side of victim] need to help show consideration to the person at fault, in terms of his [financial] capacity, his limit. Three million seven hundred thousand [dollars]. Please show consideration to each other

Lin first advises that it is not polite to bargain over the life of the deceased, namely, to negotiate the amount of compensation for the loss of a life. He then starts appealing to the injured party to show their empathy towards Kuo's limited financial capacity. The token of *quá tī siūnn* ('I think') indicates that Kuo's following counter proposal might be actually or potentially projecting a threat to or conflict with the recipient's opinions (Endo 2013), as the subsequent proposal might be inconsistent with the injured party's interactional goal. He subsequently proposes an amount of three million seven hundred thousand dollars for compensation, which is inclusive of Kuo's insurance compensation. Prior to making this proposal, he displays hesitation through pauses and repeated hedges (*hit-lō-ah*; *hit-leh*, 'that'), which indicate that the proposed amount might be unsatisfactory for the injured party and thus could threaten the injured party's perceived entitlement in making their original proposal, and thus project a potential threat to the injured party's separation face with the at-fault party. As Lin is asking for them to show consideration towards Kuo's financial capability, he implicitly claims that the proposed amount of compensation is Kuo's upper limit. At the end of his turn, he explicitly appeals to the emotions of the injured party by saying, *tshiánn lán hònn ho-siong- kah thé-liōng* ('please let's show consideration towards each other'). In this way, Lin, in passing, implies that they have shown due consideration towards the injured party through the modified amount of compensation, which is approaching Kuo's utmost limit, and is therefore asking the same in return. However, the request that they show consideration towards Kuo is markedly softened and is barely audible. In this way, Lin thereby indexes emotive involvement in his hesitant stance, while at the same time requesting that the co-participants accept the proposed amount of compensation. This can be evaluated as occasioning a potential threat to their separation face, namely, the injured party's entitlement in this asymmetrical relationship. However, the formulation of this request is made concomitant with the prosodically heightened token of *thé-liōng* ('consideration'), a display of emotive involvement which is arguably sequentially organised, and thereby implies that emotive reciprocity should be shown by the co-participants (Selting 1994: 380). On the other hand, the sequence is also a counter proposal to that suggested by Lin, who displays the at-fault party's entitlement to negotiate against the injured party's perceived entitlement (Asmuß & Oshima 2012: 83).

After Lin's implicit request for the injured party to take the counter offer, Chen then initiates the following turns, calling for a private discussion outside the mediation room amongst the members of the victim's party.

```
30          (4.0)

31   Chen: sam-   pah-      tshit-tsap-bān

           Three million seven hundred thousand

           Three million seven hundred thousand dollars

32          (8.0)

33   Lin:   sg     kóng i (.)hit-leh pó-hiám   í-guā (.) hònn (.) lán koh

            count CP   3sg  that    insurance accident PRT      we    also

            >koh< pah-         lī

            also  one million two

            It means that apart from the insurance [indemnity] we also pay one
            million two hundred thousand dollars

34          (5.0)

35   Chen: >LÁI LÁI (.) UĀNN  LÁN LÁI  TSIA KÓNG< LÁI kái-kuat khan ē

            come come     change we come here talk CP   resolve  see  able
```

```
                    sing    bô (.) >ka-kī ( ) bô-huat-tōo<=
                    success N       self      N  solution
```
Come. It's our turn to discuss. See if we can close the deal. We are insiders, [how can we have] no solution?

36   Luo:
```
                                          =[HIO   LAH THÉ-LIŎNG
                                            right PRT consider
         TSÌT-SUT-Á LAH (.) I   HEH  TSÒ KANG-Á-LÂNG E: ]
         a little    PRT    3sg that labour          PRT
```
Right, show a little consideration. He is [just a] labourer

37   Wu:
```
                              [                       ] LÍ
                                                        you
         TSHUN-TIÚNN        THÓO-TĪ-KONG    LÍ NEH: HNGH
         head of the village local land lord you PRT PRT
```
You, [as] head of the village, [are like] the local land lord

(Lu, Chiu and Chen stepped outside to discuss among themselves)

At this point, Chen repeats Lin's proposed indemnity again in order to confirm the amount, (which is $NT3,700,000). Lin then takes the repetition as confirmation of understanding, as well as seeking for elaboration after a significant eight-second pause, further explaining, in turn 33, that the total amount of compensation will consist of the indemnity from the insurance company and Kuo's extra civil compensation. This part of the sequence is thus a post expansion that corresponds to the prior turn of renegotiating the at-fault party's degree of entitlement relative to Luo's understanding of their footing (as the representatives of the at-fault party) in this context. It therefore challenges the display of the injured party's entitlement in the initial proposal, as the initial one proposed by the injured party exceeds Kuo's financial capacity (Asmuß & Oshima 2012: 83). A five-second pause occurs at this point where the side of the injured party does not respond to the proposal immediately, which could be interpreted as a dispreferred response and thus potentially implicative of a refusal of the proposed amount. However, rather than confronting or challenging the at-fault party's display of entitlement, Chen neither accepts or rejects the proposal on behalf of Lu and Chiu, but rather calls on members of the injured party and Wu in turn 35 for another backroom negotiation outside the mediation room with regard to the at-fault party's counter proposal. Through the prosodic cues of stress, increased volume and compression along with the use of the imperative mood, Chen signals an emphatic speech style which casts himself as a representative with high entitlement, and thereby projects an authoritative identity (*mianzi*) in this context. By using the word *ka-ki* (Mandarin: *ziji* (*ren*); lit., 'self, insider') in saying *ka-kī*

( ) *bô-huat-tōo*, Chen evokes the relationship of 'same side' with the injured party, claiming that a resolution to the compensation issue can be inevitably sought within the insider relationship through the presupposition embedded in the rhetorical question '[how can we have] no solution?' The epistemic rights displayed in this rhetorical question act to block the possibility of rejecting this claim, as a strong assertive stance is indexed by the negative interrogative question (Heritage 2002; Du Bois & Kärkkäinen 2012: 461), namely, a party who has a relationship (*guanxi*) with him will certainly be able to settle this negotiation, that is to settle on a mutually agreeable sum. On the other hand, the prosodic contour simultaneously plays a significant role in displaying Chen's emotive involvement via an emphatic speech style that indicates his expectations with respect to the degree of emotivity involved in their existing relationship (Selting 1994). Therefore, at this point, Chen explicitly evokes the relational connection with the people on the side of the injured party, concurrently alluding to the obligations implicitly arising for Lu and Chiu from their ongoing relationship (*guanxi*), in particular, to agree to settle the deal.

The call for another backroom negotiation occasions Luo's immediate response in turn 36, where he latches onto Chen's rhetorical question. Luo thus displays a strongly affiliative stance through the paralinguistic cues of latching and increased volume, which corresponds with Chen's evoking of his inside relationship with the injured party, and thereby displays complete agreement with the suggestion to settle on the modified proposal. On the other hand, in speaking on behalf of Kuo and Kong (in particular for Kuo), Luo issues an imperative request to the victim party that they show consideration towards Kuo, who is a labourer. Building on the presumption that labourers do not have good incomes, Luo implicitly asks them to take Kuo's limited financial capacity into account, and thereby increase the likelihood of acceptance of the modified proposal (i.e., reduced indemnity) through evoking an emotive stance. This request, in conjunction with a markedly increased volume, arguably emphasises Luo's emotive involvement in this sequential implicative activity (Selting 1994: 380), namely, soliciting emotive reciprocity from the injured party to accept the modified proposal. On the other hand, with his self-selected speaking turn, Luo positions himself as occupying a legitimate role to solicit emotivity from the injured party on behalf of Kuo (and Kong), on the basis of their ongoing 'insider' relationship.

While Luo is appealing for the victim's party to show consideration towards Kuo who is a labourer, Wu also attempts to persuade Chen (and also Lu and Chiu) to accept the proposed indemnity at the same time in turn 37. Wu's utterance in overlapping with Luo's, is delivered in an emphatic speech style when addressing Chen, whose social position is the head of the village, as a deity, *thóo-tī-kong* (Mandarin: *tudigong,* lit: 'local land lord'). This deity originating from Taoism is commonly known and is the most prevalent spirit in folk belief in Taiwanese society. It is generally believed that *thóo-tī-kong* is the deity whom people pray to for good fortune, wealth, wellbeing and harvest, as it is positioned at the lower level among all the deities in Taoism and so is considered closer to the human world. By equating Chen's position as head of the village with a deity, Wu implies that the authority held in his role as *thóo-tī-kong* will enable them to achieve a mutually agreeable amount of compensation, as the referenced deity has the ability to fulfil people's wishes beyond those possible through the hands of human beings. In the metonymic reference to Chen as the *thóo-tī-kong*, Wu concurrently projects a face-enhancing act (*mianzi*) to Chen, that is, attributing a prestigious identity by qualifying Chen's role as parallel to that of the deity who people pray to, as well as indirectly requesting for them to agree to the proposed amount of indemnity.

Lu, Chiu and Chen then step outside to have a backroom discussion at this point. Wu voluntarily makes a post commentary:

```
38   Wu:   %zhe tiaojie   dai   ganqing      (.) dai   difang renshi
           this mediation carry emotive quality carry local  human matter

           de   qingmian (.) wo shi qien   xianyiyuan-%

           ASSC emotive face I  be   former MLC
```

This mediation involves emotive quality and the emotive face from the local people. I am the former MLC

Wu explicitly claims that the negotiation requires *ganqing* (emotive quality) as well as *qingmian* (emotive face). In other words, the display of an emotive stance, such as showing sympathy, empathy or consideration and face concerns are significant strategies in facilitating negotiations and achieving mutually agreeable resolutions. On the other hand, Wu also explicitly indicates his position as a former MLC, relating his important role in broader society and his connections (*guanxi*) with people who are involved, through which he shows his reflexive awareness of the significant role his face plays in this mediation.

The backroom discussion took around ten minutes while the rest of the participants engaged in small talk with each other during that time. Due to a greater degree of sensitivity in regard to these backroom discussions, I was neither allowed to participate nor make any recordings. Near the end of the backroom discussion, Lin was called to join in the discussion. A few minutes after he was called, the discussion came to an end, and all the participants from the discussion returned to the mediation room. The CM then called a recorder who works in the council to come in and start taking the minutes, including the agreed amount of compensation. At this point, it was evident that the injured party had agreed on the amount of compensation the at-fault party should offer, and there was no further negotiation interaction.

This mediation interaction involved the interactional achievement of a variety of face practices in the course of the sequence, in particular, establishing the participation framework, soliciting emotivity, as well as implying and responding indirectly. Whether they are employed by the advocates or the participants directly involved in the accident, the analysis has shown that their ultimate aim is to achieve an interactional goal, that is, to reach a mutually agreeable amount of excess between the at-fault party and the injured party. Although those face practices are identified individually, they are interlinked to form chains of indirect responses as they attend to their connection face or separation face, or even both, particularly the practices of soliciting emotivity, and implying and responding indirectly. The latter is what has been referred to as 'implicitude', where the participants are 'doing delicacy' and 'off-recordness' (Chang 1999) in order to avoid topicalising any sensitive issues (Bertucelli-Papi 2000). On the other hand, the practice of establishing the participation framework is employed to establish the involved participant's interactional footings, thereby attempting to evoke their speaking authorities and responsibilities at the very beginning of the mediation. All of these face practices, therefore, have illuminated the relationship between the socio-cognitive and interactional basis of interpretings of their connection face and separation face through analysing sequences in which participants orient to face and face practices in interaction.

Demystifying face in Chinese: emerging themes in business interactions

In previous chapters, interactions between insurance agents and their clients or their representatives either in business settings or mediation sessions have been analytically investigated. Through the lens of an interactional pragmatic approach, the analysis has shown how face and face practices are interactionally achieved in Taiwanese business settings by participants who interpret the meanings and actions of the co-participants in the course of the sequences. In this chapter, the key findings of the analysis and the implications for theorising face will be further discussed. The first section will provide a summary of key face practices identified in the analysis of Taiwanese business interactions. In doing so, it will further explicate how those face practices in fact highlight the way in which this series of practices is employed in the Taiwanese business setting in order to achieve particular interactional goals, that is, how face practices constitute a diverse range of negotiation strategies. Since the ultimate purpose of the interactants is to reach the interactional goal, the interactional data has also demonstrated how the interplay between business-oriented benefits and face concerns (i.e., *mianzi*) leads to a diverse range of face practices in the business context. The second section will thus discuss the intersection between interactional goals and face concerns. Third, since the relationship between participants is found to be salient in this series of face practices, the connectedness and the separateness elements of relationality, which are proposed in Face Constituting Theory (FCT), are discussed further. When participants interact with each other, the cultural-general dialectic of connection and separation is found to be realised through the (perceived) long-term relationship (*guanxi*) and the relational entitlement of participants, which thus constitutes the two core socio-cognitive underpinnings of face in Taiwanese business settings. The display of either the (perceived) long-term relationship (*guanxi*) or the relational entitlement in the interactional data has been shown to be congruent with the participants' interpreting and evaluation of face in the course of interactions. Fourthly, after discussing the notion of connection underpinning face in Taiwanese business contexts, the inherent emotivity of face will be subsequently explored, as the (perceived) *guanxi* entails the concept of emotivity which is nurtured over time as the long-term relationship (*guanxi*) develops. The Chinese emic concept of face, *mianzi*, is found to be emotively invested and therefore the folk notions of emotivity, such as *renqing* and *ganqing* which underpin face practices, are also discussed here. Lastly, through examining the socio-cognitive constructs of face, namely, *guanxi* and relational entitlement as the manifestation of connection and separation, the relationship between the interactive and socio-cognitive grounding of face will be addressed. It is argued that face is not only conjointly co-constituted through the sequences of the interactions, but also as constitutive of the interaction, in the sense that it can enter through recipient design as shown in the analysis.

6.1 Face practices arising from business negotiations

Within the analytical approach of interactional pragmatics, naturally occurring business interactions were audio (visually) recorded. In this way, the methodology enabled me to identify a number of key face practices as they arose authentically in the business context. During the process of insurance negotiation, both the insurance agents and clients or representatives appear to employ face practices in order to facilitate their communication and thus ultimately reach their interactional goals. There were five main face practices found in the course of the analysis, namely, the use of strategic embarrassment, soliciting emotivity, implying and responding indirectly, establishing the participation framework and 'evoking formality' through code-switching, all of which have shed light on the relationship between achieving face at the same time as achieving the participants' interactional goals. The following sub-sections will then outline how face practices are prompted by participants while attempting to achieve their interactional goal.

6.1.1 Establishing a participation framework: relational interconnectivity and relational entitlements

Establishing a participation framework was found to constitute one of the face practices in the analysis, particularly in the mediation session involving the participants who were negotiating the amount of compensation over a death in a car accident. According to Goffman (1981), the participation framework is defined as follows:

> [T]he relation of any one such member to this utterance can be called his 'participation status' relative to it, and that of all the persons in the gathering the 'participation framework' for that moment of speech (p.137).

The relationship and positioning of the participants are thus salient to the talk involved in a particular social environment (Goodwin 2000: 178). In other words, different footings of the participants such as production format and participation status can arise in a social interaction. This can, of course, therefore involve issues of face.

As Chapter 5 explained, the data shows that the chair of the committee initiated the mediation session by establishing a participation framework, namely, allocating the participants' speaking authority as well as acknowledging the various responsibilities of the participants involved in the mediation session. By allocating the speaking authority and responsibility at the very beginning of his opening speech, he attempted to evoke the involved participants' awareness of each individual's footing in this particular social environment, that is, the interactional positions, which encompass different roles and responsibilities across the participants (Dynel 2011: 456). There are arguably two underlying purposes for allocating their interactional positions in this way. On the one hand, the participants are acknowledged vis-à-vis the interconnected relationships between all parties, that is, their connection face. For instance, while the chair of the committee initiated the mediation session, he specifically mentioned the people with whom he has familial relationships by using terms of address that indicate family ties. By doing so, the involved participants are therefore reminded of their insider relationships as well as their associations (*guanxi*). Therefore, the emic concepts relating to their connection face, such as *ganqing/renqing* (emotivity) are also evoked simultaneously, and consequently a sense of mutual favour and obligations is thus also implicitly suggested. On the other hand, with the allocation of interactional positions, all the participants are acknowledged vis-à-vis each individual's speaking and proposing rights through this practice, that is, linking the involved people to the participation framework through their relational entitlements in this mediation scenario. Through this practice the committee chair is thus also co-constituting each participant's relational entitlements, namely, their separation face, and therefore highlights the relationality inevitably involved when evoking different interactional positions. However, it is important to note that this relational entitlement only exists in the context of these situated relationships, rather than constituting a component of individual identity. For example, in the analysis presented in the multiparty mediation interaction, the chair of the committee invokes the 'power' to allocate the speaking rights vis-à-vis the involved participants in the mediation context. Moreover, in the same analysis where the chair acknowledged the relationship between Lu and Liu (the deceased victim), Lu was given the speaking authority in the brother-sister relationship with Liu, although the main beneficiary of the compensation is Chiu. Lu then obtained the relational entitlements on behalf of Chiu through the acknowledgment of his contextual footing for the entire session of the mediation.

What can be seen here is that the practice of establishing a participation framework is a means of co-constituting the basic parameters of the participant's connection and separation face, so that the individuals are aware of their interconnectivity as well as their speaking rights and relational entitlement vis-à-vis their respective interactional footings. This constitutes one way in which face concerns can legitimately enter into the interaction through recipient design and interpretation.

6.1.2 'Evoking formality' through code-switching

Code-switching has previously been hypothesised to be related to face practices in Taiwan according to Su (2001, 2009). By investigating face-to-face interactions in business contexts, it has indeed been found that code-switching can be used to manage face-threatening communicative situations. This particular face practice of 'evoking formality' of code-switching was identified in one of the multiparty mediation interactions, when the insurance agent Ying was questioned by the advocate of the injured party, Hsu, about which insurance company he works for. It is evident from the sequence of the interaction that Ying felt potentially face-threatened at this point by Hsu's interrupting interrogative. In other words, when Hsu attempted to get involved in the mediation, that is, to propose possibilities for concluding the negotiations about the amount of compensation, he declined the prior turn by Ying, who refused to pay for the entire medical costs requested by the chair of the committee. At this point, Hsu simultaneously challenges Ying's relational entitlement by challenging Ying's inability to compensate the injured party for the entire medical costs, and so Ying's separation face with the victim and the at-fault parties was potentially threatened. Ying's subsequent response in which he code-switched from the predominant language of Taiwanese in that negotiation to Mandarin Chinese can therefore be seen as an indexical strategy with social import, namely, creating greater relational distance and also evoking a more formal social relationship by re-identifying his social distance from one of being part of the in-group in a Taiwanese-dominated context to one of neutrality given the name of his company (Su 2009: 18). This practice of 'evoking formality' through code-switching involves a shift in Ying's relational footing vis-à-vis the others. Given the shift in his relational footing through code-switching from Taiwanese to Mandarin Chinese, Ying also evokes a formal social relationship with the co-participants by indexing his institutional position, as Mandarin

Chinese is generally considered to be an official language used in formal settings (cf. O'Driscoll 2001 on the relationship between code-switching and face).

This is therefore consonant with Su's (2001, 2009) claim that code-switching can be used to negotiate interpersonal relationships and achieve specific communicative goals, particularly when face is at risk. From the interactional perspective, the findings have shown that code-switching in this study is used as a linguistic resource to define one's social relationship with one's co-participants. By shifting to a non-dominant code within the group, Ying distinguishes himself from most other people in the situated speaking community and evokes a formal social relationship (cf. O'Driscoll 2001: 262). Ying sequentially distances himself from the potentially directed face-threat to his relational entitlement, i.e., his separation face with the victim and at-fault parties by indexing his social status and relationship with the interactants. More specifically, through evoking the relational distance and a formal institutional relationship, Ying indexes his institutional status as a competent insurance agent as well as evoking greater formality. This institutional status and formality are evoked by Ying, who attempts to justify his previous claim that he is not able to compensate the injured party for the entire amount of medical costs and thereby strategically rejects Hsu's previous potential threat to his relational entitlement with both the injured and the at-fault parties. That is to say, the index of institutional footing and formality arising from the relational distance can be prompted by this type of practice. 'Evoking formality' through code-switching thus arguably constitutes a face practice whereby participants can create relational distance in order to manage a potentially face-threatening situation.

6.1.3 Strategic embarrassment: topicalising unmet expectations

Another key face practice identified was strategic embarrassment, as seen in analysis of dyadic business interaction. In the analysis, when the insurance agent Lan visited his client Chen, Lan strategically embarrassed Chen when requesting him to shift other car insurance business to Lan. Interestingly, the same practice also appears in the triadic interaction of analysis 3 but it was occasioned by the representative rather the insurance agent. The representative Hsu also strategically embarrassed the insurance agent Ying while attempting to negotiate for better compensation on behalf of the injured party in the car accident.

This particular face practice (i.e., strategic embarrassment) involves topicalising unmet expectations which simultaneously highlights the participants' perceptions of the relationship. The ongoing relationships of the participants, as well as particular aspects of the context that can be invoked by participants, is necessary in order to more fully explain this practice. In other words, strategic embarrassment is directed at the relationships between the participants first and foremost. Strategic embarrassment is used to evoke awareness of unmet expectations embedded in the ongoing relationships between the participants. While implications for the interpreting of their persons/idenitities (e.g., professional reputation) are likely to have also arisen during the course of these interactions, these interpretings of their persons are only relevant because of the ongoing interactional achievement of their relationships. Without relationships, whether they be close and intimate or only temporary, one's projected claims in relation to one's self-image are largely irrelevant. For this reason, the analysis of strategic embarrassment has highlighted the participants' interpretings of their relationships.

Strategic embarrassment is possible only because business people in Taiwan place great value on their relationships. It is also worth noting that topicalising unmet expectations occasions an opportunity for the addressee to fulfil these expectations, and thereby strengthen their relationship and associated reputations. In other words, by meeting these expectations through his or her response, the recipient may arguably occasion evaluations of face support, subsequent to previously constituting an evaluation of face threat. Therefore, the findings arguably demonstrate that strategic embarrassment primarily threatens the participants' relationship rather than their own personal or relational identity. It is evident that face could be under-theorised or misinterpreted if the analyst were to focus only on the identities when investigating face.

On the other hand, the ultimate purpose of strategic embarrassment via topicalising the unmet expectations is to achieve one's interactional goals. Spencer-Oatey (2005) identifies interactional goals as one of the factors influencing how people perceive face in interactions in her theoretical framework of Rapport Management. She suggests that in some cases the two types of interactional goals might be interdependent, namely, transactional and relational goals, and the management of relational goals is required to achieve a transactional goal (2005: 107). Therefore, the interplay of a transactional goal and a relational goal can impact on how people perceive face in ongoing relationship management. Behaviour orienting to particular interactional goals is open to interactants' perceptions and judgments, with the effect on face depending on the urgency of the transactional goals (Spencer-Oatey 2005). However, in this case, while strategic embarrassment occasioned by an attempt to achieve transactional goals gives rise to face threat, the evoking of the participants' ongoing relationship makes this face threat allowable in this circumstance. Therefore, the interactional goal in this analysis does not only override face concern (O'Driscoll 2011; Spencer-Oatey 2009), but has also highlighted that face is to do with the relationship between the participants. In other words, when a participant attempts to achieve a transactional goal in the interaction, their relationship with others is also evoked at the same time. The way in which strategic embarrassment can constitute a face practice thus illustrates that we need to move beyond the common conceptualis-ation of face as a person-centred notion to one that is rooted in the relationship between participants.

It is also worth briefly mentioning here that there is no emic concept of face-threatening in Chinese. Therefore, strategic embarrassment is a good exam-ple of a significant but neglected face practice which can be found through ana-lysing emic practices rather than being restricted to analysing emic concepts. On the other hand, the importance of relationships in interpersonal interactions has been relatively neglected in the analysis of face threats thus far. The study of emic concepts and practices can shed light on the relative neglect of face practices in Chinese that involve face threats as constitutive of the practice itself rather than something simply to be avoided.

6.1.4 Soliciting emotivity

Soliciting emotivity is another key face practice identified in the findings of the analysis. This practice appeared in Chapter 5, the mediation negotiation in which the setting of the scenario was a triadic negotiation session among the insurance agent, the injured party, the at-fault party and the other representatives, who were negotiating a mutually agreeable amount of compensation for a car accident. In the course of the negotiation, the participants who were taking the main nego-tiating roles were found to repeatedly implicitly request the other party to show 'consideration', thereby invoking emotivity, especially between the advocate of the at-fault party and the advocate of the injured party.

As mentioned earlier, emotive discourse can become an important dimen-sion of face in social interaction, as showing feelings can be used strategically to achieve interactional goals (Işık-Güler and Ruhi 2010: 633; Ruhi 2009c: 107). This face practice of soliciting emotivity is thus consonant with what has been claimed in regard to the fundamentally emotive nature of face. To solicit emotivity is to appeal to the other to take up another perspective and share the same emotive stance (Ruhi 2009b). The advocates for the injured party and the at-fault party in the analysis are both evoking emotion through the strategies of story-telling and explicit requests to show consideration or sympathy. As evident from the prosodic cues, the verbal tokens that the solicitor uses arguably display emotive involvement in an attempt to evoke the co-participant's emotive stance (Selting 1994). In other words, the display of emotive involvement in conjunction with the request to show consideration is therefore an attempt to solicit a display of emotive reciprocity from the co-participants.

The display of emotional concern thus becomes significant here. As discussed previously in Chapter 2, emotivity, relationships and face are tightly intercon-nected in Chinese relational practices from an emic perspective. That is to say, showing emotional support is an important part of face practice in Chinese relational work (cf. Chang & Holt 1994). Through appealing to the other to show an emotive stance, the solicitor at the same time alludes to face concern, namely, the separation face as well as the connection face between the participants. Separation face in this context encompasses the solicitor's relational entitlement vis-à-vis the co-participants in requesting better compensation via the story-telling sequence. When the advocate of the injured party, Lu, initiates the negotiation session, he first attempts to evoke an emotive stance of sympathy from the at fault-party by the strategy of story-telling. The advocate for the at-fault party, Lin, also attempts to invoke the same practice in order to solicit emotivity from the injured party by alluding to the financial pressure on Kuo, the at-fault party. In this way, Lin also implicitly invokes his entitlement to demand a decrease in the extra amount of compensation. On the other hand, connection face is also involved as, while negotiating their relational entitlements on behalf of each party, the solicitor concurrently asks the recipient(s) to show emotivity, that is, by requesting the other grant a favour through reciprocally displaying emotion. In other words, soliciting emotivity involves an appeal to *renqing*, which is conceptualised as a sense of mutual aid in social conduct that is constructed through social relationships (Yang 1994). According to Chang and Holt (1994), showing an appropriate amount of human emotion is an important way of maintaining the relationships in Chinese communication. Soliciting emotivity by showing one's own emotions first is thus a means of establishing the connection face with the recipient(s), namely to build an emotive relationship, or what is termed *renqing*, that encompasses mutual aid and reciprocity.

Hence, by soliciting emotivity between the participants during the negotiation, the (potential) threats to face arising from making direct requests with regard to the amount of compensation can be minimised, since the display and acknowledgment of emotivity allude to mutual face concerns. This practice ostensibly requests the co-participant to show emotivity, sympathy or consideration, but implicitly occasions a particular evaluation of face support. Therefore, soliciting emotivity is arguably not only a means to negotiate or mitigate their relational entitlement in the course of the mediation, but is also a means of establishing their connection face with the co-participants at the same time, that is, to co-construct their *guanxi*.

An important finding here is that, in contrast to the common treatment of emotion as an outcome of facework (Brown & Levison 1978, 1987; Goffman 1967: 6; Schlenker & Pontari 2000; Spencer-Oatey 2005, 2007; Terkourafi 2007: 325, 355), emotivity is not only the outcome of face practices in social interaction, but is also inherently in itself part of face practices. To put it another way, emotivity is not only occasioned by threats to support face, but is also, at times, constitutive of face itself. According to the traditional view, emotion arises when the perceptions of one's behaviour are not in line with one's expectations in regard to face. However, the display or acknowledgment of emotivity prior to making any such evaluations can also significantly impact on the interpretation of face. In other words, orienting to emotions/emotivity is not just a product of interaction, but is constitutive of interaction, as it can be seen to enter into recipient design in the case of soliciting emotivity (cf. Spencer-Oatey 2005; Langlotz & Locher 2013). It is thus argued here that face and face practices are both inherently emotively invested.

6.1.5 'Doing delicacy' and responding indirectly

There are a number of exchange turns of implying in the course of the business interaction, particularly in the multiparty mediation interaction. What could be broadly termed 'implying' actually encompasses two separate face practices that are interlinked, namely, 'doing delicacy' and responding indirectly (Jefferson, Sacks & Schegloff 1987; Lerner 2013, Walker, Drew & Local 2011). Face practice is thus similar to the social action of 'doing delicacy' where 'the speakers and their recipients pay special attention to what can and cannot be properly said in conversation – and to when one is overstepping the limits of propriety' (Lerner 2013: 95). In this case, the 'delicacy' involved is that the compensation is for the loss of someone's life. The potential impropriety to be avoided is thus haggling over the amount of compensation in lieu of this life. By implying such a request, the participants treat the purpose of the compensation as something that should be left unsaid. In other words, by avoiding saying something explicitly, the speaker orients to the unsaid as an impropriety, and therefore 'doing delicacy' can be achieved through implying (Haugh 2013). This 'doing delicacy' thus orients to the participants' connection face as a face practice.

Subsequent indirect responses by the participants are sequentially occasioned by the action of 'doing delicacy' through an implied request. In other words, while the participants attempt to negotiate or mitigate their separation face and connection face through implicature ('doing delicacy'), the practice of responding indirectly is also used by the co-participants at this point. This is consistent with what has been argued by Walker, Drew & Local (2011) that, 'responding indirectly is used to display a speaker's analysis of the action of the prior turn' (p. 2450). These indirect responses thus shed light on the evaluations of the co-participants who are the recipients of the original implicature with regard to the prior requests. More specifically, on one hand, by responding indirectly, the speaker treats the prior turn through an implied refusal as inapposite (Walker, Drew & Local 2011: 2441). In this way, the speaker attempts to claim one's relational entitlement vis-à-vis the recipient in the negotiation. On the other hand, the implied refusal is simultaneously 'doing delicacy', mitigating the effect on their *guanxi*, that is, avoiding impropriety, thereby allowing them to maintain their relational connection.

Interestingly, these two practices link to form interlinked chains of implicatures and indirect responses. This is what Bertucelli-Papi (2000) calls 'implicitude', which is 'based on the assumption that a common background of shared knowledge is reciprocally accessible for referent identification' (p. 149). In other words, 'implicitude' involves discussing or negotiating something over the course of a sequence without actually making the topic or target of the negotiation explicit. She also further claims that the invitation to implicitude is 'an implicit agreement on what can remain unsaid and on recognition and acceptance of the intention to leave it unsaid as a mutually shared premise for the construction of what is meant' (Bertucelli-Papi 2000: 153). The concept of implicitude is thus arguably consonant with the chains of implicatures and indirect responses observed here, which encompass both 'doing delicacy' and treating the prior turn as inapposite through indirectly responding. In other words, implicitude involves an 'off-record' negotiation framework, in the context of which the participants carry on negotiations through chains of 'indirect responses' that allow for 'off-recordness'. This type of face practice is employed particularly to avoid going on record through topicalising sensitive issues, namely, as a practice of face-threat avoidance to their separation face as well as maintenance of their connection face. That is to say, if the advocate on behalf of the at-fault party had initiated the request to reduce the amount of compensation without 'doing delicacy', such as an explicit request could be framed or interpreted as a face-threat to the injured party's separation face vis-à-vis the at-fault party. Also, if the recipient of the implied request were to respond to the previous request directly with no delicacy, he/she might have ostensibly refused the action of 'doing delicacy', that is, rejected the mitigation of the threat to their connection face. Therefore, the chains of indirect responses, i.e., the implicitude as a negotiation framework, are arguably interactionally co-constituted by the participants in this mediation context as a means of not only mitigating the projected (potential) face-threatening acts to their separation face that going on record might entail, but also of 'doing delicacy' to maintain their connection face.

The above-mentioned face practices in this data set of business interactions that have been identified through empirical analysis include some that have not been previously acknowledged (i.e., strategic embarrassment of face threat, soliciting emotivity, establishing a participation framework) or have remained not well understood in the field (i.e., responding indirectly, evoking formality through code-switching). The discovery of these practices has shed light on the underlying trajectory of business interactions, which involves attending to and claiming face as well as strategically deflecting potential face threats, through evoking either their interpersonal relationship (*guanxi*) or their relational entitlement in order to ultimately achieve their interactional goals. Through employing the methodologies of interactional pragmatics and ethnographic interviews, a variety of face practices from an emic perspective were teased out, rather than limiting the analysis of face practices to ones involving either face-support or face-threat avoidance. A significant implication of the analysis of the face practices used in the business settings is that face and face practices involve a rich and complex tapestry of emic notions relating to face. These will be discussed further in the following sections, and their importance for better understanding the practices identified in this analysis will be demonstrated.

6.2 Interplay of *lizi* and *mianzi*

Two key themes that have arisen in the analysis of the various face practices identified in this study involve the interplay of face and interactional goals, on the one hand, and the emic conceptualisation of face as a person-centred concept, on the other. One overall finding has been that face practices are occasioned by different negotiation strategies in the business context in order to ultimately achieve the interactional goals of those negotiations (see Spencer-Oatey 2009). Across the data set, the interactional goals in the business setting were found to be primarily related to either obtaining insurance business in dyadic case negotiations, or reaching a mutually agreeable amount of compensation in the multiparty mediation sessions. In other words, the interactional goal in the business context can be understood as relating to concrete benefits such as obtaining a monetary transaction or receiving a satisfactory amount of indemnity. There is thus an interesting implication arising from this series of face practices, namely, that all the face practices occasioned in the course of achieving interactional goals are used by the participants to attend to either their *guanxi* (relationship) or relational entitlements, that is, their connection or separation face. The interplay of the interactional goals and face in this study is therefore worth discussing further in order to gain a better understanding of the significance of face practices in business settings.

From an emic perspective, interactional goals and face arise through the interplay of *lizi* and *mianzi*. One of the key claims made by informants in the ethnographic interviews was the idea that the emic conceptualisation of face, *mianzi*, is closely linked in dynamic tension with issues of profit or gain (*lizi*), the latter of which arise as a matter of course in business negotiations. *Lizi* was used as a euphemism in the ethnographic interviews for tangible profits or gains, such as obtaining insurance business or a satisfactory amount of compensation. The emic conceptualisation of face as *mianzi* was also understood by informants as 'possession' of either individuals or groups that can be quantified in a way analogous to money, i.e., one can have more and the other can have less (Arundale 2013: 13). Face practices attending to either connection or separation face in business contexts can thus be seen to appeal to complex emic conceptualisations involving economic metaphors that associate face with substantial money or profits (Arundale 2010a: 2094; Haugh 2007a: 664; O'Driscoll 2011: 13). In other words, participants may conceptualise these negotiations in terms of loss and gain of both *lizi* and *mianzi*. However, while various practices of co-constituting face are observable in the Taiwanese business context, participants are not necessarily consciously aware of doing these practices themselves. Such practices are found through closely analysing the naturally occurring interactions to tease out how the participants achieve social actions and meanings within their cultural group in everyday talk and conduct. When such practices involve an orientation to face, they are termed first-order or emic face practices (Arundale 2013: 10). Crucially, such face practices are not necessarily synonymous with emic conceptualisations of face. As Arundale argues, emic conceptualisations are 'concepts and terms regarding face, which members employ at times in describing face as a phenomenon implicated in their own and other's action … a set of understandings and descriptive practices by which they index aspects of what they are doing in terms of face. These understandings and practices comprise the cultural group's first order or emic conceptualisation of face' (2013: 10). The notion of 'respectability face' proposed by Spencer-Oatey (2005) is arguably one example of an emic conceptualisation of face derived largely from the Chinese notion of *mianzi*. Most notably, respectability face is also conceptualised as a kind of 'possession' which an individual (or group of individuals) can have more or less of. In this way, then, emic conceptualisations of face have entered into theories of face.

One potentially fruitful way of exploring the intersection between emic conceptualisations and emic practices is proposed by Arundale, when he argues that 'face is constituted not only in direct interaction with others, but also in observing others apart from interacting with them, as well as in envisioning potential interaction, all at different levels of "distance" from the person who is interpreting the interaction' (Arundale 2013: 13). It is in 'observing others apart from interacting with them' and in 'envisioning potential interaction' that emic conceptualisations of face can arise and, in the case of Chinese, clearly have arisen. In other words, while face practices are always rooted in actual interaction and so are always locally situated for contingent purposes, emic concepts form largely apart from interaction over time within a particular society or culture. Another way of putting this is that emic conceptualisations are 'framed by the members of the cultural group and explained within their cultural milieu, and hence are central to member's description of face', whereas emic practices are 'framed by the analyst and explained within a cultural-general theoretical conceptualisation ideally sensitive to cultural-specific construals of those general phenomena, and hence are central to the observer's explanations of face' (Arundale 2013: 11). It is thus perhaps not surprising that not all emic practices are congruent with emic conceptualisations, and that not all emic conceptualisations have counterparts in emic practices (see Chapter 4).

From the interview and interactional data, then, through which these emic conceptualisations and emic practices can be teased out, it is argued that there is always inevitably a dynamic tension arising in business negotiations, in that the participants need to find a balance between *mianzi* and *lizi* in order to achieve their interactional goals. However, it is worth noting that interactional goals can override face concerns if there is a considerable amount of money involved according to one of the interview informants (cf. Brown & Levinson 1987: 94–98; Spencer-Oatey 2009: 28). That is to say, since face practices are a reflection of the interplay of *lizi* and *mianzi*, functioning as tactful ways of negotiating the participants' connection face and separation face in the course of achieving their interactional goals, it is apparent that interactional goals therefore lie at the core of those face practices in business settings.

6.3 Face, relationality and relationships

Face has long been theorised as a claimed or desirable self-image, building on Goffman's (1967) seminal work. The grounding of face in notions of identity (Locher 2008; Spencer-Oatey 2007, 2009) is thus a logical development of the original formulation of face by Goffman. Indeed, it is also consistent with the emic concept of *mianzi* on which Goffman's claims about face were arguably largely derived (Haugh 2005, 2013; Terkourafi 2007). However, the examination of face practices undertaken here indicates that problems may arise if face is treated only as a personal belonging without taking interpersonal relationships into account. For instance, He and Zhang (2011) in examining face reduced the notion of relationship to relational identities which emphasise individual attributes in relating to others. However, such an analysis highlights only one's social attributes within a relational or social network but neglects the level of the actual *relationship* between the persons, thereby arguably overly constraining the analysis of emic practices in Chinese (Haugh 2013: 11–12). That is to say, face can involve not only an awareness of one's position within a network of relationships with others, but also those relationships in themselves (Chang & Haugh 2011b, 2013). At least from an emic perspective, it has been shown that face is not limited to the social attributes of individuals (Haugh 2013: 12). Face is more than just identity or even relational identity, as these are both person-centred attributes. Face ultimately resides in relationships, and so is socially centred instead. In other words, as relationships are constructed by persons in interaction, face can be understood as both interpretation of persons-in-relationships and interpretation of those relationships themselves.

Face Constituting Theory (FCT) can be used to explore this point further. In FCT, it is argued that persons should be conceptualised as dialectically related to relationships (Arundale 2006, 2009, 2010a, 2010b). As mentioned earlier in Chapter 2, persons are defined as socially constructed individuals in a particular social/relational network. In Arundale's work (2009, 2010a, 2010b), persons and relationships are defined as interdependently related through the individual–social dialectic.

> A relationship is a phenomenon conceptualised in terms of a social system, whereas identity is a phenomenon conceptualised in terms of an individual system, that framing privileging the individual pole of the individual/social dialectic. Identity remains a person-centered attribute regardless of whether the aspect of identity involved is one's identity as singular self, one's identity as member of a collective, or one's identity as a participant in a relationship (Arundale 2010a: 2091).

On this view, 'persons' include various kinds of identities, including relational identities, e.g., an insurance agent vis-à-vis clients or the ongoing relationship between the insurance agent and his clients. In FCT, it is argued, however, that persons are constituted through relationships, while relationships are necessarily constituted by persons in interaction.

Face can thus be framed, on the other hand, as persons-in-relationships, which involves those aspects of face pertaining to relational separation. For example, face (*mianzi*) in Taiwanese business interactions is argued to be associated with a particular social status and its accompanying entitlement within particular situated relationships. This reflects the fact that the emic concept of *mianzi* is a largely person-centred attribute. However, separation face always arises as persons as constituted in relationships, not persons in isolation as autonomous monads. In other words, such status and entitlement are only recognisable in the context of particular relationships. In the case of well-known public figures, this can naturally extend to a lot more people than is normally the case for ordinary persons. These different relational entitlements are thus constituted by different individuals as relational distinction in interpersonal interactions in Taiwan. From the findings of the analysis, here it is also argued that the display of entitlement occasions attempts to invoke relationality by participants. In other words, the display of entitlement is a reflection of the asymmetric nature of relationships, such as the situated positions of the injured and at-fault parties in the mediation sessions, showing the participants' interpreting of their separation face in the context of their relationships. More specifically, the displays of and responses to entitlement are employed by participants in a way that is congruent with the participants' understanding of relationality in those situated interactions.

On the other hand, face can be conceptualised as relationship constituted in interaction by persons, which involves those aspects of face pertaining to relational connection. In the case of face (*mianzi*) in Taiwanese business interactions, this is argued to encompass *guanxi*, which involves emotively invested and mutually reciprocal relationships. Through their *guanxi*, persons can constitute themselves as relationally connected in interpersonal interactions in Taiwan (Chang & Haugh 2011b). *Guanxi*, from the perspective of emic analysis, is defined as long-term relationships through which emotivity is nurtured over time (cf. Arundale 2010a), and so also encompasses *gangqing* and *renqing*, as suggested in Chapter 2. These two types of emotivity are the core elements constituting human emotions in Chinese interpersonal communication. Acknowledging or showing emotivity (*ganqing/renqing*), which entails mutual obligations and rights within a reciprocal relationship (*guanxi*), displays an individual's socio-cognitive awareness of his or her relational connection with others, as well as being a means for an individual to dialectically display his or her emotivity (Chang & Holt 1994; Hsiang 1974). The analysis of the face practice of strategic embarrassment is a good example of the importance of emotivity for relationships, as it involves participants topicalising unmet expectations arising from their *guanxi*, which has been infused over long periods with emotivity. This particular face practice is thus possible and allowable only when a reciprocal relationship is perceived to exist between participants.

In FCT, Arundale (2010b) argues that persons should be conceptualised as individuals in a social environment, that is, individuals as constructed by others with whom they are linked in social interaction, while face is inherently relational. Based on close examination of face practices in Chinese, the claim that face should be treated as relational has been supported, both in the sense of it being understood as interpretation of persons-in-relationships and also in the sense of it being analysed as interpretations of relationships as constructed by persons in themselves. More attention should thus be paid to the dialectic interplay between the relational connection and separation, since face is not merely a personal possession but also an inherently relational phenomenon (Arundale 2006; 2009: 38, 43).

It is further argued here that the face and face practices involve a dialectic interplay of *guanxi* and relational entitlement in the Taiwanese business context (see the model in Figure 6.1).

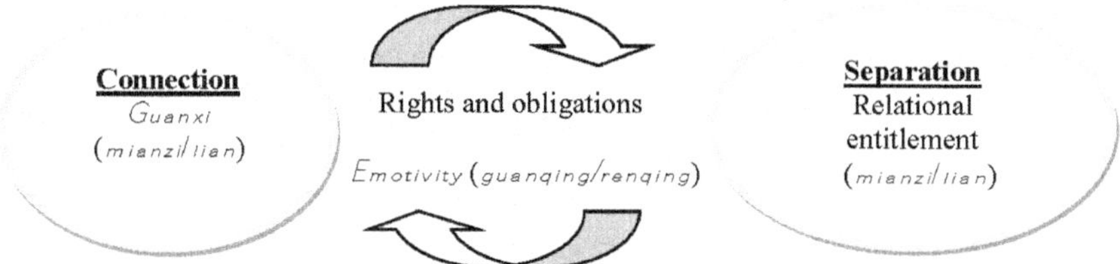

Figure 6.1: The model of relational connection and separation in Taiwanese business communication

The model in Figure 6.1 is proposed to theorise the relational connection and separation in Taiwanese business communication. *Guanxi* and relational entitlement have been found through the analysis of the interactional data to be the two most significant cultural construals of the relational dialectic of separation face and connection face in Taiwanese business interactions. Importantly, in this model relational entitlements vis-à-vis other persons are more emphasised than the individual's own image or identity, and so it illuminates the *relationality* of face as persons-in-relationships based on the model of FCT. The elements of *ganqing/renqing* (emotivity) involved in an existing relationship also impact on the dynamic interplay between the dialectical connectedness and separateness. When emotivity is evoked in interaction, the embedded concepts of rights and obligations also inevitably arise in such contexts. On the other hand, the dialectical interplay of connection face and separation face also drives the cultivation of *ganqing/renqing*, whether in an existing relationship or in a newly established relationship. For instance, the practice of soliciting emotivity illustrates this dynamic interplay of connection and separation. This practice involves the solicitor displaying and acknowledging emotivity in order to make a request, yet also at the same time alluding to a concern for both connection face and separation face. The solicitor thus not only negotiates or mitigates their relational entitlement, but also attempts to co-construct their *guanxi* with the other participants through this face practice.

6.4 Emotivity

Following up one of the findings that soliciting emotivity is also a face practice in Taiwanese business interactions, *mianzi* has been argued to be emotively invested as a socio-cognitive construct embedded within the relational connection, and thus emotivity has not been restricted to the status of being only an outcome of facework (cf. Spencer-Oatey 2005; Langlotz & Locher 2013). In other words, it has been suggested that orienting to emotions/emotivity does not merely emerge as a product of interaction, but is also constitutive of the interaction itself. The aspect of emotivity and its relationship to facework/face practices is thus worth discussing further. Since the notion of face originates from Chinese emic concepts, it should come as no surprise that it is a fundamentally emotively invested construct, as, when we trace back to the emic perspective on face, we find it involves key folk notions of emotivity in Chinese, such as *ganqing/renqing* (emotive quality/human emotion) and *chengyi* (sincerity).

The emic concept of face in Chinese, *mianzi*, according to Chang and Holt (1994) is defined as showing emotional concern. By "'[g]iving" and "claiming" *mianzi*, relational participants acknowledge the mutual bond between them, thereby showing emotional support' (p. 109). On the other hand, acknowledging emotivity (*ganqing/renqing*) entails mutual obligations within a reciprocal relation (*guanxi*), and so face (*mianzi*) can thus be employed as a relational resource thereby enabling face practices (Chang & Holt 1994; Hsiang 1974). In other words, these face practices originate from emic collocations that carry the concepts of emotivity, meaning that *mianzi* is thus inherently emotively invested. Interestingly, from the findings of this study, it was found that evoking either *ganqing/renqing* (emotive quality/human emotion), *chengyi* (sincerity) or *tiliang* (consideration) can be understood as a euphemism for tangible benefits in the Taiwanese business context (such as favours, profits, discounts on costs, money, satisfactory amount of compensation, etc.), which are also a significant aspect in relational practices in Taiwanese interpersonal communication. That is to say, by acknowledging or offering such tangible benefits, one is claimed to show or display one's emotivity towards the other, and thus, in passing, show one's concern for, *mianzi*, of the other. Since these folk notions of emotivity in Chinese lie at the core of the socio-cognitive construct of face, they are more than simply the outcome of face practices, but are also elements driving face practices in the interaction.

In Spencer-Oatey's proposed theory of Rapport Management (2000, 2007, 2008), it is claimed that emotivity arises naturally when there is an expectation associated with social behaviours, and thus emotivity is the product of interactions when face is involved. If one's perceptions of others' behaviour are not in conformity with one's expectations, some emotional reactions might arise (Spencer-Oatey 2007: 644). However, according to the findings of this analysis of face practices in Taiwanese business interactions, this is perhaps an overly constrained theorisation of emotions, namely, as a response or outcome of interaction. Emotivity can also be constitutive of the interaction when face is involved, either for claiming or offering face, and so always enters into the recipient design of turns in interactional sequences. This finding thus lends support to Ruhi's (2009b, 2009c) work on conceptualising face and relational work by taking the emotion perspective, where affect is argued to be the grounding of face and relational work. According to Ruhi, the display of emotion can be used strategically to achieve interactional goals (Işık-Güler & Ruhi 2010: 633; Ruhi 2009c: 107) such as empathy, with which one does the 'affect sharing' and 'perspective-taking' that underpin the socio-cognitive component drawn up in attending to the other's face. Similarly, what has been found here is also that the display of emotivity in Chinese, which involves complex folk notions that underpin a Chinese speaker's mental or socio-cognitive state, can also be an important strategy for achieving interactional goals in Taiwanese business settings.

In the diagram in Figure 6.2, Ruhi (2009b) treats empathy as a core emotion in situating face and relational work. Face and relational work are framed as an emotion script which involves a variety of components. The emotion relating to the interactional goals in Ruhi's theorisation of face and relational work is most relevant to the findings of this research, including the practice of soliciting emotivity. When participants display or acknowledge emotivity, they attempt to achieve their transactional and interpersonal goals by attending to the co-participant's separation face and connection face (see also the previous section). On the other hand, the co-participants then inevitably interactionally co-construct their interpretation of meanings and actions occasioned by this display or acknowledgment of emotivity, and in this way face emerges, namely, the connection face and sep-

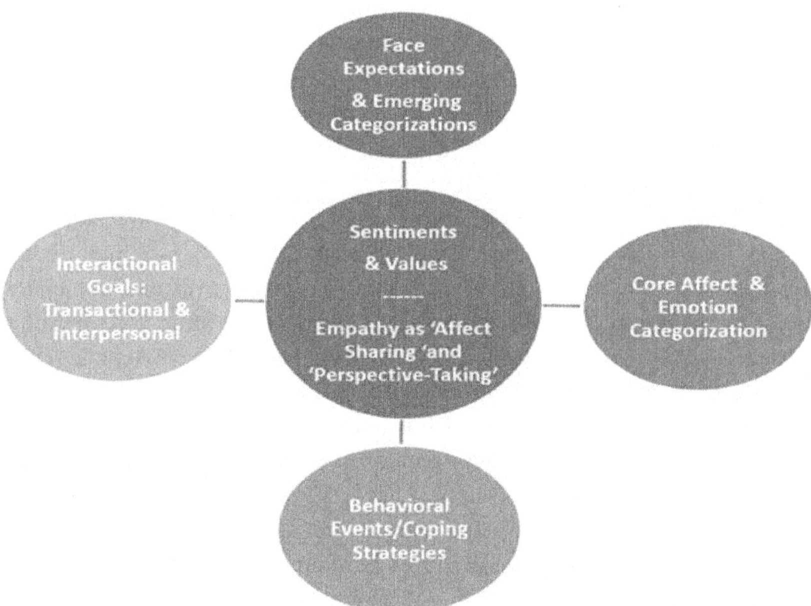

Figure 6.2: Ruhi's (2009b) proposal of theorising emotions in face and relational work

aration face between the participants. Therefore, building on the theorisation of emotion/emotivity (Ruhi 2009b), it has been reiterated that the relationship between emotions/emotivity and face as well as relational work is complex and therefore that we need to extend the traditional view of face to include emotivity/emotion at its core.

6.5 Socio-cognitive and interactive grounding of face

The analysis of business interactions has highlighted the interconnectivity between the socio-cognitive and interactive dimensions of face. We have seen that face is co-constituted through interaction in the analysis of face practices in Taiwanese business interactions. On the other hand, the socio-cognitive construct of face (*mianzi*) is also constitutive of interaction in that it influences the recipient design which is what occasions face practices in interactions in the first place. It is suggested here that the cognitive-interactive grounding of face lies in the cultural construals of connectedness and separateness found in this study, namely, *guanxi* and relational entitlement, as it is these socio-cognitive constructs that underpin the manifestation of face in interaction. That is to say, face is both co-constituted in and constitutive of interaction. Or put differently, face can be a cause of behaviour but also emerge as an effect, since if 'a mental representation of face was employed when formulating an utterance, then face is a cause of some sort' (Hatfield & Hahn 2011: 1305). The former refers to a person's interpretings of relational connection and separation which is conjointly co-constituted through the sequences of the interaction with others (Arundale 2010a), while the latter refers to expectations in regard to face entering into interaction through recipient design (Haugh 2009a, 2010a).

According to FCT, although the 'interpretation of face is perforce always an interpretation formed by an individual' (Arundale 2013: 18), face interpretings are themselves conjointly co-constituted. Participants, however, can (conjointly) co-constitute interpretings of face at three different levels: direct face interpreting, displaced face interpreting and reflexive face interpreting (Arundale 2010a: 2090). A direct face interpreting is defined as a participant's own provisional or operative interpreting of face which is interactionally achieved or conjointly co-constituted in talk with another participant, while a displaced face interpreting refers to a participant's interpreting of another participant's direct face interpreting. A reflexive face interpreting involves one participant forming an interpreting of the other participant's interpreting of the first participant's direct face interpreting (Arundale 2010a: 2090). Moreover, in Arundale's recent work, he has further explicated the three levels of face interpreting by describing them as 'my interpreting of our-connection-and-separation-at-this-moment' (direct interpreting), 'my interpreting of your interpreting of our-connection-and-separation-at-this-moment' (displaced interpreting) and 'my interpreting of your interpreting of my interpreting of our-connection-and-separation-at-this-moment' (reflexive interpreting) (2013: 18).

In applying FCT to face in Chinese, this study has found that the participants oriented to all of those three levels of interpreting. Through the analysis of the two core elements of connection face and separation face, which are *guanxi* and relational entitlement respectively, it was found that the interpreting of face by participants could be direct, displaced and reflexive. First, direct interpretings of face, i.e., the interpreting of either the *guanxi* and/or relational entitlement with the other participant(s) were observed through examining their uptake in interaction. It was found that an interpreting of either *guanxi* and/or relational entitlement can underpin inferences about the other participant's prior turn in the interaction, since through the sequential interpreting of either *guanxi* or relational entitlement, together with one's uptake in the interaction, the current speaker holds the other speaker accountable for that prior face interpreting. Socio-cognitive interpreting of *guanxi* or relational entitlement thus enters through the recipient design which occasions or influences the uptake of the other participant's interpreting of a direct interpreting of *guanxi* or relational entitlement. For example, in multiparty mediation interaction, the chair of the committee initiates the mediation session with the face practice of establishing the participation framework by referring to the relative titles:

> This time we have a few representatives. Me, he called me granduncle (maternal) ((pointing to the Kuo and Kong)) and you [call me] granduncle (paternal) ((pointing to Chen)). But [we] don't mix [the relationship between Chen and me] here. I, as a senior, come to help care about this matter.

This is clear evidence of his direct interpreting of their connection face and separation face with the involved participants.

Second, a displaced face interpreting involves one participant's interpreting of another participant's interpreting of their *guanxi* and/or relational entitlement. One of the extracts taken from the ethnographic interviews, when the native informants were asked to reflect on their interpreting of their connection face and separation face with their clients throughout their experience in doing business, serves as a good example to illustrate this point. This informant gave an example where she helped her client to obtain an amount of compensation higher than her client expected, and she interpreted her client's interpreting of her conduct as positive. She commented as follows: '[S]ome clients are very nice, [because] they treat you as a very professional consultant. Sometimes if you help him deal with indemnification and he is indemnified more money than he expected, he will be very happy and very respectful towards us.' Here she had not only formed her own direct interpreting of their connection face and separation face, namely, as an insurance agent vis-à-vis the client, but she also had formed her own displaced interpreting of her client's positive interpreting of their connection face and separation face.

Finally, a reflexive face interpreting involves one participant's interpreting of the other's interpreting of that participant's interpreting of their *guanxi* or relational entitlement. A post-recording commentary from one of the insurance agents illustrates an example of a reflexive face interpreting, that is, 'my interpreting of your interpreting of my interpreting on-our-connection-and-separation face' (see Chapter 5). Ying commented on the mediation interaction where Hsu, one of the advocates on behalf of the victim party strategically embarrassed him during the mediation. He reflected on the interaction and commented that his evaluation of Hsu's (negative) evaluation of his interpretation of their connection-and-separation-face was negative, when he commented on Hsu's deployment of strategic embarrassment as follows:

> Then what they normally do, they will firstly suppress the insurance company
> on the basis of [his]position, saying 'the insurance is terrible', 'the insurance
> company is disappointing', 'very unyielding', 'bad indemnity'. Otherwise, they
> say, 'don't insure with them next time' [PI-Y1: 1: 05].

Through this, we can see the insurance agent's uptake of Hsu's negative assessment of Ying's previous interpreting of their connection face and separation face, that is, their *guanxi* and relational entitlement are inadequate for achieving the desired interactional goal.

It has been suggested here that a dialectical relationship exists between social-cognitive and interactional aspects of face. In other words, they coexist at the same time, although the one or the other can nevertheless be foregrounded depending on the interactional scenarios. All three levels of interpreting of *guanxi* or relational entitlement can thus be (conjointly) co-constituted in the business setting that has been examined in this study. The cognitive and interactional aspect of face should therefore both be taken into account when analysing face, as it is evident from the analysis of face practices in business interactions that face is both sequentially and interactionally co-constituted, as well as being constitutive of interaction. Even though face interpretings are always an interpretation formed by an individual, the question remains as to how those interpretations are formed in the first place, either non-sequentially or sequentially as an interactional achievement. Through using the methodology of ethnographic and post-recording interviews to complement interactional analysis, participants' metapragmatic comments were elicited and provided insight into their interpretings of their own and others' interactional moves. Although such comments do not present the cognitive status itself, since conducting post-recording interviews can be regarded as creating a whole new interaction, they nevertheless provided strong evidence that participants orient to face beyond the confines of a particular interactional moment. For this reason, face must be theorised as both socio-cognitive and interactional in nature. Thus, as participants orient to the other participants' interactional moves, face can be treated as a socio-cognitive property in their design of responses in the sequential turn, yet is also simultaneously co-created as the interaction develops. That is to say, both socio-cognitive and interactional aspects of face (*mianzi*) need to be addressed by researchers in both synchronic (in the moment) and diachronic (over time) interactions when analysing face.

CHAPTER 7

Conclusion

As the series of face practices were identified in this analysis, the cultural-specific construals of *guanxi* and relational entitlement – which represent the connection face and separation face respectively, according to the theoretical framework of FCT that has been drawn upon in this study – were found to be key to understanding face in Taiwanese business settings. The dynamic interplay of the interactional goals of participants and their connection face and/or separation face arising from those face practices reflects that the main foci of business negotiations is not on the individual attributes or identities (that have long been theorised as face in previous research), but rather is on the negotiation of their *guanxi* and relational entitlements in the context of ongoing relationships between the participants in Taiwanese business settings. The participants draw on their *guanxi* and relational entitlement in order to help achieve their transactional goal (e.g., selling insurance, gaining higher indemnity etc.) and simultaneously carefully manage their *guanxi* so they can preserve it for the future.

In other words, face is inherently relational, both in the sense of it being understood as an interpretation of persons-in-relationships and also in the sense of it being analysed as interpretations of relationships as construed by those persons themselves. Nevertheless, it is important to note here that cognitive constructs of interpreting *guanxi* and relational entitlement between persons are not static, as they emerge through interlinked interactions over time; that is to say, *guanxi* and relational entitlement exist as cognitive constructs inherent to, *not* separate to, interactions. The examination of interlinked interactions is therefore necessary in order to provide a more comprehensive picture of participant's subjective understandings, that is, through longitudinal interactions as well as ethnographic and follow-up interviews, as the cognitive constructs underpinning the interpreting of *guanxi* and relational entitlement are conjointly co-constituted across a diverse range of interactions.

Therefore, face cannot be fully understood if it is theorised as individual attributes or identities without taking the relationships of these individuals into account. The finding is that *guanxi* and relational entitlement are able to elucidate the underpinnings of face practices in Taiwanese business interactions and thus make the analysis of the emic practices more explanatory in being grounded in the understandings of participants themselves (cf. Su & Huang 2002). The dialectic interplay of connection and separation, namely, *guanxi* and relational entitlement in interaction, arguably lies at the core of these face practices. The interpreting of *guanxi* and/or relational entitlement is thus both sequentially and interactionally co-constituted, as well as being constitutive of interaction. Face in Taiwanese business settings, namely, both *guanxi* and relational entitlement, is thus not only conjointly co-constituted through the sequences of the interactions, but are also constitutive of such interactions, in the sense that they can enter as cognitive constructs to which participants orient in recipient design.

7.1 Implications for theorising face

The distinction between emic conceptualisations and emic practices, as well as the importance of relationships, has important implications for theorising face. In this section, the implications of this analysis for theorising face in the analysis of discourse and social phenomena more generally, and for future research on face in Chinese in particular, are outlined.

One key finding of this research is that an investigation drawing on both the perspectives of emic conceptualisations and emic practices is necessary when theorising face. The concept of face can hardly be demystified if research on face in Chinese simply relies on emic conceptualisations that draw on folk collocations or expressions. Through the lens of interactional pragmatics, this research has revealed the underpinnings of face and faces practices in naturally occurring interactions, and has thereby shed light on actual face practices, particularly in relation to business people. In doing business in the Chinese context, it has been argued that participants are negotiating their *guanxi* and relational entitlements through those dynamic face practices in order to achieve their interactional goals with co-participants. The analysis has demonstrated that participants strategically and delicately manage their connection face and separation face through these practices. However, notably, those practices go beyond what has been theorised as the stereotypical Chinese indirect forms of communication. For instance, the practice of 'doing delicacy' and responding indirectly involves strategically negotiating and managing their *guanxi* and relational entitlements back and forth with their co-participants, but in a way that avoids topicalising any possible sensitivities, such as threats to either their connection face or separation face. Business people can be informed that awareness of the dialectic interplay of connection face and separation face lies at the core of achieving their interactional goals in business contexts. By strategically evoking *guanxi* and utilising relational entitlements, business people can ultimately reach their interactional goals and also co-construct ongoing positive interpersonal *guanxi*.

On the other hand, while it is clear that face in Chinese cannot always be used to ground studies of im/politeness in Chinese (see also Hinze 2012), face in Brown and Levinson's sense (1978, 1987), which focuses on individual attributes or identities, is also clearly inadequate to theorise face in Chinese. Thus, although face and im/politeness are inextricably linked, from an emic perspective, the inherent relationality of face should be given more attention, particularly when studying face and face practices in interpersonal interactions. Face practices, as identified in this analysis, are only rather indirectly associated with im/politeness work, but instead are strongly associated with negotiating relationships (i.e., relational connection and separation) between the participants. Hence, face should thus be treated and examined in its own right, so as to avoid neglecting the core of relationality that underpins face in Chinese.

7.2 Prospects for future research

This book contributes to the fields of pragmatics and business and communication studies. However, this book on face can be further extended to other fields, including intercultural and cross-cultural studies. Future research, for instance, could further examine interactions in intercultural business settings where both similar as well as distinctive face practices may arise. From the example of a study of the intercultural apology between Taiwanese and Australians (Chang & Haugh 2011a), for instance, there is clearly a lot of scope for diverging understandings and evaluations of im/politeness arising in intercultural interactions. It would be worthwhile investigating whether diverging face and face practices also arise in intercultural business settings. An investigation of how face and face practices arise in intercultural interactions is therefore an important area for future research (cf. Stadler & Spencer-Oatey 2009; Spencer-Oatey & Stadler 2009; Spencer-Oatey, Ng & Dong 2008).

As this book pays particular attention to communication in Chinese, specifically amongst business people in negotiation contexts, it is suggested that research in relation to face and face practices could also be extended by investigating interactions in interpersonal or non-institutional settings in Chinese. How participants interpret face in those contexts and how face and face practices are interactionally achieved are both issues worthy of further study. On the other hand, there has not been much attention paid to mediation and negotiation studies in the field of pragmatics (although cf. Firth 1995; Jenks, Firth & Trinder 2012; Trinder, Firth & Jenks 2010), let alone research which focuses on mediation and business negotiations in Chinese to date (cf. Shen 2006; Yang 2008). In other words, mediation and negotiation in Chinese contexts should receive more attention in order to develop a more comprehensive theoretical framework for analysing face in different Chinese business contexts. Furthermore, as Taiwan is not the only Chinese-speaking community, it is also worth investigating face and face practices in other Chinese-speaking communities, such as Mainland China, Hong Kong, Singapore and so on. Future research should examine whether face and face practice in Chinese arise in the same way as they do in Taiwan. From the findings of the analysis, it is hypothesised that distinctive emic concepts of face and folk notions in relation to face might conceivably arise across these different cultural contexts. Further research on face and face practices in different Chinese-speaking communities is therefore required.

In conclusion, this book has identified how face and face practices are interactionally achieved in Taiwanese business interactions. It has provided evidence that participants interpret connection face and separation face as *guanxi* and relational entitlements respectively, as well as outlining various face practices through which participants orient to face in the course of furthering their own agendas or accomplishing particular interactional goals. The significance of applying both emic and etic perspectives in examining face has also been highlighted. This significance applies particularly to studying face in a specific cultural context where numerous folk notions related to face can be relevant to an analysis. By taking an emic perspective, an important implication for business people is that *relationality* in either dyadic or multiparty business negotiations should be taken into account. To be able to achieve interactional goals, business people must pay attention to the interplay of their *guanxi* and relational entitlements and enact their relational roles by evoking emotivity accordingly in business negotiations.

References

Arundale, R. (1999). An alternative model and ideology of communication for an alternative to politeness theory. *Pragmatics*, *9*(1), 119–153. http: //dx.doi.org/10.1075/prag.9.1.07aru

Arundale, R. (2004). Co-constituting face in conversation: An alternative to Brown and Levinson's politeness theory. 90th Annual National Communication Association Conference, Chicago, Illinois.

Arundale, R. (2005). Pragmatics, conversational implicature and conversation. In K. Fitch & R. Sanders (Eds.), *Hanbook of language and social interaction* (pp. 41–63). Mahwah, NJ: Lawrence Erlbaum.

Arundale, R. (2006). Face as relational and interactional: A communication framework for research on face, facework, and politeness. *Journal of Politeness Research*, *2*(2), 193–216. http: //dx.doi.org/10.1515/PR.2006.011

Arundale, R. (2008). Relating Japanese emic face concepts and face constituting theory. (Unpublished manuscript). University of Alaska Fairbanks.

Arundale, R. (2009). Face as emergent in interpersonal communication: An alternative to Goffman. In F. Bargiela-Chiappini & M. Haugh (Eds.), *Face, communication and social interaction* (pp. 33–54). London: Equinox.

Arundale, R. (2010a). Constituting face in conversation: Face, facework and interactional achievement. *Journal of Pragmatics*, *42*(8), 2078–2105. http: //dx.doi.org/10.1016/j.pragma.2009.12.021

Arundale, R. (2010b). Relating. In M. A. Locher & S. L. Graham (Eds.), *Interpersonal pragmatics* (pp. 137–166). Berlin: Mouton de Gruyter.

Arundale, R. (2013). Conceptualising 'interaction' in interpersonal pragmatics: Implications for understanding and research. *Journal of Pragmatics*, *58*, 12–26. http: //dx.doi.org/10.1016/j.pragma.2013.02.009

Arundale, R., & Good, D. (2002). Boundaries and sequences in studying conversation. In A. Fetzer & C. Meierkord (Eds.), *Rethinking sequenciality: Linguistics meets conversational interaction* (pp. 121–150). Amsterdam: John Benjamins. http: //dx.doi.org/10.1075/pbns.103.06aru

Asmuß, B., & Oshima, S. (2012). Negotiation of entitlement in proposal sequences. *Discourse Studies*, *14*(1), 67–86. http: //dx.doi.org/10.1177/1461445611427215

Auer, P. (2005). A postscript: Code-switching and social identity. *Journal of Pragmatics, 37*(3), 403–410. http: //dx.doi.org/10.1016/j.pragma.2004.10.010

Bargiela-Chiappini, F. (2003). Face and politeness: New (insights) for (old) concepts. *Journal of Pragmatics, 35*(10–11), 1453–1469. http: //dx.doi.org/10.1016/S0378-2166(02)00173-X

Bargiela-Chiappini, F. (2006). Face. In K. Brown (Ed.), *Encyclopedia of languages and linguistics.* (Vol. 4, pp. 421–423. Amsterdam: Elsevier. http: //dx.doi.org/10.1016/B0-08-044854-2/00337-0

Bargiela-Chiappini, F., Chakorn, O.-O., Chew Chye Lay, G., Jung, Y., Kong, K. C. C., Nair-Venugopal, S., & Tanaka, H. (2007). Eastern voices: Enriching research on communication in business: A forum. *Discourse & Communication, 1*(2), 131–152. http: //dx.doi.org/10.1177/1750481307071983

Baxter, L. A., & Montgomery, B. M. (1996). *Relating: Dialogues and dialectics.* New York, NY: Guilford.

Bertucelli-Papi, M. (2000). *Implicitness in text and discourse.* Pisa: Edizioni ETS.

Bo, Y. (1992). *The ugly chairman and the crisis of Chinese culture.* J. Qing & T. D. J. Cohn (Eds.). Sydney: Allen and Unwin.

Bradford, L., & Petronio, S. (1998). Strategic embarrassment: The culprit of emotion. In P. Andersen & L. Guerrero (Eds.), *Handbook of communication and emotion* (pp. 99–121). San Diego, CA: Academic Press.

Brown, P., & Levinson, S. (1978). Universals in language usage: Politeness phenomena. In E. Goody (Ed.), *Questions and politeness* (pp. 56–311). Cambridge: Cambridge University Press.

Brown, P., & Levinson, S. (1987). *Politeness. Some universals in language usage.* Cambridge: Cambridge University Press.

Chafe, W. L. (2002). Prosody and emotion in a sample of real speech. In P. Fries., M. Cummings., D. Lockwood & W. Sprueill (Eds.), *Relations and functions within and around language* (pp. 277–315). London: Continuum.

Chan, A. M. (2006). The Chinese concepts of guanxi, mianzi, renzing and bao: Their interrelationships and implications for international business. Australian and New Zealand Marketing Academy Conference, Queensland University of Technology.

Chang, H.-C. (1999). The 'well-defined' is 'ambiguous' – indeterminacy in Chinese conversation. *Journal of Pragmatics, 31*(4), 535–556. http: //dx.doi.org/10.1016/S0378-2166(98)00088-5

Chang, H.-C., & Holt, R. (1994). A Chinese perspective on face as inter-relation concern. In S. Ting-Toomey (Ed.), *The challenge of facework* (pp. 95–132). Albany, NY: State University of New York Press.

Chang, W.-L. M. (2008). The interactional achievement of face in Taiwanese business interactions (Unpublished honours thesis). Griffith University, Nathan, Queensland, Australia.

Chang, W.-L. M., & Haugh, M. (2011a). Evaluations of im/politeness of an intercultural apology. *Intercultural Pragmatics*, *8*(3), 411–442. http: //dx.doi.org/10.1515/iprg.2011.019

Chang, W.-L. M., & Haugh, M. (2011b). The strategic embarrassment and face threatening in business interactions. *Journal of Pragmatics*, *43*(12), 2948–2963. http: //dx.doi.org/10.1016/j.pragma.2011.05.009

Chang, W.-L. M & Haugh, M. (2013). Face in Taiwanese business interactions: From emic concepts to emic practices. In Y. Pan & D. Z. Kádár (Eds.), *Chinese discourse and interaction: Theory and practice* (pp. 126–150). London: Equinox.

Chen, V. (1990). *Mien tze* at the Chinese dinner table: A study of the interactional accomplishment of face. *Research on Language and Social Interaction*, *24*(1–4), 109–140. http: //dx.doi.org/10.1080/08351819009389334

Cheng, C.-Y. (1986). The concept of face and its Confucian roots. *Journal of Chinese Philosophy*, *13*(3), 329–348. http: //dx.doi.org/10.1111/j.1540-6253.1986.tb00102.x

Choi, S.-C., & Lee, S.-J. (2002). Two-component model of chemyon-oriented behaviors in Korea: Constructive and defensive chemyon. *Journal of Cross-Cultural Psychology*, *33*(3), 332–345. http: //dx.doi.org/10.1177/0022022102033003008

Clark, H. (1996). *Using language*. Cambridge: Cambridge University Press. http: //dx.doi.org/10.1017/CBO9780511620539

Clift, R. (1999). Irony in conversation. *Language in Society*, *28*(4), 523–553. http: //dx.doi.org/10.1017/S0047404599004029

Couper-Kuhlen, E. (2012). On affectivity and preference in responses to rejection. *Text & Talk*, *32*(4), 453–475.

Craven, A., & Potter, J. (2010). Directives: Entitlement and contingency in action. *Discourse Studies*, *12*(4), 419–442. http: //dx.doi.org/10.1177/1461445610370126

Curl, T. S., & Drew, P. (2008). Contingency and action: A comparison of two forms of requesting. *Research on Language and Social Interaction*, *41*(2), 129–153. http: //dx.doi.org/10.1080/08351810802028613

Deppermann, A., & Schütte, W. (2008). Data and transcription. In G. Antos, E. Ventola & T. Weber (Eds.), *Handbook of interpersonal communication* (pp. 179–213). Berlin: De Gruyter.

Domenici, K., & Littlejohn, S. (2006). *Facework: Bridging theory and practice*. Thousand Oaks, CA: Sage.

Drew, P. (1998). Complaints about transgressions and misconduct. *Research on Language and Social Interaction*, *31*(3–4), 295–325. http: //dx.doi.org/10.1080/08351813.1998.9683595

Drew, P., & Holt, E. (1988). Complainable matters: The use of idiomatic expressions in making complaints. *Social Problems*, *35*(4), 398–417. http: //dx.doi.org/10.2307/800594

Drew, P., & Walker, T. (2009). Going too far: Complaining, escalating and dissafiliation. *Journal of Pragmatics*, *41*(12), 2400–2414. http: //dx.doi.org/10.1016/j.pragma.2008.09.046

Du Bois, J. W. D., & Kärkkäinen, E. (2012). Taking a stance on emotion: Affect, sequence, and intersubjectivity in dialogic interaction. *Text & Talk, 32*(4), 433–451.

Dynel, M. (2011). Revisiting Goffman's postulates on participant statuses in verbal interaction. *Language and Linguistics Compass. Sociolinguistics, 5*(7), 454–465.

Endo, T. (2013). Epistemic stance in Mandarin conversation: The positions and functions of *wo juede* (I feel/think). In Y. Pan & D. Z. Kádár (Eds.), *Chinese discourse and interaction: Theory and practice* (pp. 12–34). London: Equinox.

Firth, A. (Ed.). (1995). *The discourse of negotiation: Studies of language in workplace.* Oxford: Pergamon.

Gang, X. & Hua Z. (1965) *Cihai.* Hong Kong: Ci hai bian Ji Wei Yuan Hui.

Gabrenya, W. K. J., & Hwang, K.-K. (1996). Chinese social interaction: Harmony and hierachy on the good earth. In M. H. Bond (Ed.), *Chinese Psychology* (pp. 309–321). New York, NY: Oxford University Press.

Gao, G. (1996). Self and other: A Chinese perspective on interpersonal relationships. In W. Gudykunst, S. Ting-Toomey & T. Nishida (Eds.), *Communication in personal relationships across cultures* (pp. 81–101). Thousand Oaks, CA: Sage.

Gao, G. (1998). An initial analysis of the effects of face and concern for other in Chinese interpersonal communication. *International Journal of Intercultural Relations, 22*(4), 467–482. http: //dx.doi.org/10.1016/S0147-1767(98)00019-4

Gao, G. (2009). Face and self in Chinese communication. In F. Bargiela-Chiappini & M. Haugh (Eds.), *Face, communication and social interaction* (pp. 175–191). London: Equinox.

Gao, G., & Ting-Toomey, S. (1998). *Communicating effectively with the Chinese.* Thousand Oaks, CA: Sage.

Gao, G., Ting-Toomey, S., & Gudykunst, W. B. (1996). Chinese communication processes. In M. H. Bond (Ed.), *Chinese Psychology* (pp. 280–293). New York: Oxford University Press.

Gardner, R. (1997). The listener and minimal responses in conversational interaction. *Prospects, 12,* 2–31.

Glenn, P. (2003). *Laughter in interaction.* Cambridge: Cambridge University Press. http: //dx.doi.org/10.1017/CBO9780511519888

Goddard, C. (2006). 'Lift your game, Martina!' – Deadpan jocular irony and the ethnopragmatics of Australian English. In C. Goddard (Ed.), *Ethnopragmatics: Understanding discourse in cultural context* (pp. 65–97). Berlin: Mouton de Gruyter.

Goffman, E. (1955). On face-work: An analysis of ritual elements in social interaction. *Psychiatry, 18*(3), 213–231.

Goffman, E. (1956). Embarrassment and social organization. *American Journal of Sociology, 62*(3), 264–271. http: //dx.doi.org/10.1086/222003

Goffman, E. (1967). *Interaction ritual: Essays on face-to-face behavior.* New York: Pantheon Books.

Goffman, E. (1981). *Forms of talk*. Philadelphia: University of Pennsylvania Press.

Good, D. (1995). Where does foresight end and hindsight begin? In E. Goody (Ed.), *Social Intelligence and Interaction* (pp. 139–49). Cambridge: Cambridge University Press. http://dx.doi.org/10.1017/CBO9780511621710.009

Goodwin, C. (2000). Action and embodiment within situated human interaction. *Journal of Pragmatics, 32*(10), 1489–1522. http://dx.doi.org/10.1016/S0378-2166(99)00096-X

Goodwin, C., & Goodwin, M. (2000). Emotion within situated activity. In A. Duranti (Ed.), *Linguistic anthropology: A reader* (pp. 239–257). Sussex: Blackwell.

Goodwin, C., & Tang, C. S.-K. (1996). Chinese personal relationships. In M. H. Bond (Ed.), *Chinese Psychology* (pp. 294–308). New York: Oxford University Press.

Gross, E., & Stone, G. (1964). Embarrassment and the analysis of role requirements. *American Journal of Sociology, 70*(1), 1–15. http://dx.doi.org/10.1086/223733

Gu, Y. (1990). Politeness phenomena in modern Chinese. *Journal of Pragmatics, 14*(2), 237–257. http://dx.doi.org/10.1016/0378-2166(90)90082-O

Gu, Y. (2011). Modern Chinese politeness revisited. In F. Bargiela-Chiappini & D. Z. Kádár (Eds.), *Politeness across Cultures* (pp. 128–148). London: Palgrave Macmillan.

Gumperz, J. J. (Ed.). (1982). *Language and social identity*. Cambridge: Cambridge University Press.

Gumperz, J. J. (1992). Contextualization and understanding. In A. Duranti & C. Goodwin (Eds.), *Rethinking context* (pp. 229–252). Cambridge: Cambridge University Press.

Hahn, J., & Hatfield, H. (2011). Group face in Korea and the United States: Taking responsibility for the individual and the group. *Multilingua, 30*(1), 25–70. http://dx.doi.org/10.1515/mult.2011.003

Harris, M. (1968). *The rise of anthropological theory*. New York: Walker and Company.

Harris, M. (1990). Emics and etics revised. In T. Headland, K. Pike & M. Harris (Eds.), *Emics and etics: The insider/outsider debate* (pp. 48–61). Newbury Park: Sage.

Hatfield, H., & Hahn, J.-W. (2011). What Korean apologies require of politeness theory. *Journal of Pragmatics, 43*(5), 1303–1317. http://dx.doi.org/10.1016/j.pragma.2010.10.028

Haugh, M. (2005). What does 'face' mean to the Japanese? Understanding the import of 'face' in Japanese business interaction. In F. Bargiela-Chiappini & M. Gotti (Eds.), *Asian Business Discourse(s)* (pp. 211–239). Berlin: Peter Lang.

Haugh, M. (2006). Emic perspectives on the positive–negative politeness distinction. *Culture. Language and Representation, 3*, 17–26.

Haugh, M. (2007a). Emic conceptualisations of (im)politeness and face in Japanese: Implications for the discursive negotiation of second language learner identities. *Journal of Pragmatics, 39*(4), 657–680. http://dx.doi.org/10.1016/j.pragma.2006.12.005

Haugh, M. (2007b). The discursive challenge to politeness research: An interactional alternative. *Journal of Politeness Research, 3*(2), 295–317. http://dx.doi.org/10.1515/PR.2007.013

Haugh, M. (2009a). Face and interaction. In F. Bargiela-Chiappini & M. Haugh (Eds.), *Face, Communication and Social Interaction* (pp. 1–30). London: Equinox.

Haugh, M. (2009b). Intention(ality) and the conceptualisation of communication in pragmatics. *Australian Journal of Linguistics, 29*(1), 91–113. http: //dx.doi.org/10.1080/07268600802516301

Haugh, M. (2010a). Jocular mockery, (dis)affiliation, and face. *Journal of Pragmatics, 42*(8), 2106–2119. http: //dx.doi.org/10.1016/j.pragma.2009.12.018

Haugh, M. (2013). Disentangling face, facework and im/politeness. *Sociocultural Pragmatics, 1*, 46–73.

Haugh, M., Chang, W.-L. M., & Kádár, D. (2015). 'Doing deference': Identities and relational practices in Chinese online discussion boards. *Pragmatics, 25*(1), 73–97

Haugh, M., & Hinze, C. (2003). A metalinguistic approach to deconstructing the concepts of 'face' and 'politeness' in Chinese, English and Japanese. *Journal of Pragmatics, 35*(10–11), 1581–1611. http: //dx.doi.org/10.1016/S0378-2166(03)00049-3

Haugh, M., & Watanabe, Y. (2009). Analysing Japanese 'face-in-interaction': Insights from intercultural business meetings. In F. Bargiela-Chiappini & M. Haugh (Eds.), *Face, communication and social interaction* (pp. 78–95). London: Equinox.

He, M., & Zhang, S. (2011). Re-conceptualizing the Chinese concept of face from a face-sensitive perspective: A case study of a modern Chinese TV drama. *Journal of Pragmatics, 43*(9), 2360–2372. http: //dx.doi.org/10.1016/j.pragma.2011.03.004

Headland, T. N. (1990). Introduction: A dialogue between Kenneth Pike and Marvin Harris on emics and etics. In T. N. Headland, K. L. Pike & M. Harris (Eds.), *Emics and etics: The insider/outsider debate* (pp. 13–17). London: Sage.

Heath, C. (1988). Embarrassment and interactional organization. In P. Drew & A. Wootton (Eds.), *Erving Goffman: Exploring the interaction order* (pp. 136–160). Cambridge: Polity Press.

Heritage, J. (2002). The limits of questioning: Negative interrogatives and hostile question content. *Journal of Pragmatics, 34*(10–11), 1427–1446. http: //dx.doi.org/10.1016/ S0378-2166(02)00072-3

Heritage, J., & Raymond, G. (2012). Navigating epistemic landscapes: Acquiescence, agency and resistance in responses to polar questions. In J-P. D. Ruiter (Ed.), *Questions* (pp. 179–192). Cambridge: Cambridge University Press.

Hinze, C. (2002). *Re-thinking 'face': Pursuing an emic–etic understanding of Chinese mian and lian and English face.* (Unpublished PhD thesis). University of Queensland, Brisbane, Australia.

Hinze, C. (2005). Looking into 'face': The importance of Chinese *mian* and *lian* as emic categories. In F. Bargiela-Chiappini & M. Gotti (Eds.), *Asian Business Discourse(s)* (pp. 169–210). Berlin: Peter Lang.

Hinze, C. (2012). Chinese politeness is not about 'face': Evidence from the business world. *Journal of Politeness Research, 8*(1), 11–27. http: //dx.doi.org/10.1515/JPLR.2012.002

Ho, D. Y.-F. (1976). On the concept of face. *American Journal of Sociology, 81*(4), 867–884. http://dx.doi.org/10.1086/226145

Ho, D. Y.-F. (1994). Face dynamics: From conceptualization to measurement. In S. Ting-Toomey (Ed.), *The Challenge of Facework* (pp. 269–85). New York: State University of New York Press.

Hsiang, T. C. (1974). *Research on Chinese characteristics.* Taipei: Shang-wu Publishing Company.

Hu, X. (1944). The Chinese concept of face. *American Anthropologist, 46*(1), 45–64. http://dx.doi.org/10.1525/aa.1944.46.1.02a00040

Hua, Z., Wei, L., & Yuan, Q. (2000). The sequential organisation of gift offering and acceptance in Chinese. *Journal of Pragmatics, 32*(1), 81–103. http://dx.doi.org/10.1016/S0378-2166(99)00039-9

Hwang, K.-K. (1987). Face and favour: The Chinese power game. *American Journal of Sociology, 92*(4), 944–974. http://dx.doi.org/10.1086/228588

Hwang, K.-K. (2006). Moral face and social face: Contingent self-esteem in Confucian society. *International Journal of Psychology, 41*(4), 276–281. http://dx.doi.org/10.1080/00207590544000040

Işık-Güler, H., & Ruhi, Ş. (2010). Face and impoliteness at the intersection with emotions: A corpus based study in Turkish. *Intercultural Pragmatics, 7*(4), 625–660. http://dx.doi.org/10.1515/iprg.2010.028

Jefferson, G. (2004). Glossary of transcript symbols with an introduction. In G. Lerner (Ed.), *Conversation analysis: Studies from the first generation* (pp. 13–23). Amsterdam: John Benjamins. http://dx.doi.org/10.1075/pbns.125.02jef

Jefferson, G., Sacks, H., & Schegloff, E. (1987). Notes on laughter in the pursuit of intimacy. In G. Button & J. R. E. Lee (Eds.), *Talk and social organisation* (pp. 152–205). Clevedon: Multilingual Matters.

Jenks, C., Firth, A., & Trinder, L. (2012). When disputants dispute: Interactional aspects of arguments in family mediation sessions. *Text & Talk, 32*(3), 307–327.

Kádár, D., & Mills, S. (Eds.) (2011). *Politeness in Asia.* Cambridge: Cambridge University Press. http://dx.doi.org/10.1017/CBO9780511977886

Keevallik, L. (2010). Minimal answers to yes/no questions in the service of sequence organization. *Discourse Studies, 12*(3), 283–309. http://dx.doi.org/10.1177/1461445610363951

Krone, K., Garrett, M., & Chen, L. (1992). Managerial communication practices in Chinese factories: A preliminary investigation. *Journal of Business Communication, 29*(3), 229–252. http://dx.doi.org/10.1177/002194369202900303

Langlotz, A. (2010). Social cognition. In M. A. Locher & S. L. Graham (Eds.), *Interpersonal Pragmatics* (pp. 167–204). Berlin: Mouton de Gruyter.

Langlotz, A., & Locher, M. (2013). The role of emotions in relational work. *Journal of Pragmatics, 58*, 87–107. http://dx.doi.org/10.1016/j.pragma.2013.05.014

Lerner, G. (2013). On the place of hesitating in delicate formulations: A turn-constructional infrastructure for collaborative indiscretion. In M. Hayashi, G. Raymond & J. Sidnell (Eds.), *Conversational Repair and Human Understanding* (pp. 95–134). Cambridge: Cambridge University Press.

Lerner, G. H. (1996). Finding 'face' in the preference structures in talk-in-interaction. *Social Psychology Quarterly, 59*(4), 303–321.

Lett, J. (1990). Emics and etics: Notes on the epistemology of anthropology. In T. Headland, K. Pike & M. Harris (Eds.), *Emics and etics: The insider/outsider debate* (pp. 127–142). Newbury Park: Sage.

Leung, T. K. P., & Chan, R. Y.-K. (2003). Face, favour and positioning – a Chinese power game. *European Journal of Marketing, 37*(11/12), 1575–1598. http: //dx.doi. org/10.1108/03090560310495366

Lewis, M. (1993). Self-conscious emotions: Embarrassment, pride, shame, and guilt. In M. Lewis & J. Haviland (Eds.), *Handbook of Emotions* (pp. 563–573). New York: The Guilford Press.

Lim, T.-S., & Choi, S.-H. (1996). Interpersonal relationships in Korea. In W. Gudykunst, S. Ting-Toomey & T. Nishida (Eds.), *Communication in personal relationships across cultures* (pp. 122–136). Thousand Oaks, CA: Sage.

Lin, C., & Yamaguchi, S. (2007). Japanese folk concept of mentsu: An indigenous approach from psychological perspectives. In G. Zheng., K. Leung & J. G. Adair (Eds.), *Perspectives and progress in contemporary cross-cultural psychology* (pp. 343–357). Beijing: The International Association of Cross-Cultural Psychology.

Locher, M. A. (2008). Relational work, politeness, and identity construction. In G. Antos & E. Ventola (Eds.), *Handbook of interpersonal communication* (pp. 509–540). Berlin: Mouton de Gruyter.

Locher, M. A. (2011). Situated impoliteness: The interface between identity work and relational construction. In B. Davies, M. Haugh & A. Merrison (Eds.), *Situated politeness* (pp. 187–208). London: Continuum.

Mao, L. (1994). Beyond politeness theory: 'Face' revisited and renewed. *Journal of Pragmatics, 21*(5), 451–486. http: //dx.doi.org/10.1016/0378-2166(94)90025-6

Matsumoto, Y. (1988). Reexamination of the universality of face: Politeness phenomena in Japanese. *Journal of Pragmatics, 12*(4), 403–426. http: //dx.doi.org/10.1016/0378-2166(88)90003-3

Maynard, D. W. (2010). Demur, defer, and deter: Concrete, actual practices for negotiation in interaction. *Negotiation Journal, 26*(2), 125–143. http: //dx.doi.org/10.1111/j.1571-9979.2010.00261.x

Myers-Scotton, C. (1998). A theoretical introduction to the markedness model. In C. Myers-Scotton (Ed.), *Codes and consequences* (pp. 18–38). New York: Oxford University Press.

Myers-Scotton, C. (2006). *Multiple voices: An introduction to bilingualism*. Oxford: Blackwell Publishing.

O'Driscoll, J. (1996). About face: A defence and elaboration of universal dualism. *Journal of Pragmatics, 25*(1), 1–32. http: //dx.doi.org/10.1016/0378-2166(94)00069-X

O'Driscoll, J. (2001). A face model of language choice. *Multilingua, 20*(3), 245–268. http: //dx.doi.org/10.1515/mult.2001.002

O'Driscoll, J. (2011). Some issues with the concept of face: When, what, how and how much? In F. Bargiela-Chiappini & D. Z. Kádár (Eds.), *Politeness across Cultures* (pp. 17–41). Basingstoke: Palgrave Macmillan.

Pan, Y. (2000). *Politeness in Chinese face-to-face interaction.* Stanford, CA: Ablex.

Pan, Y. (2008). Cross-cultural communication norms and survey interviews. In H. Sun & D. Z. Kádár (Eds.), *It's the dragon's turn: Chinese institutional discourses* (pp. 17–76). Bern: Peter Lang.

Pan, Y. (2011). Methodological issues in East Asian politeness research. In D. Z. Kádár & S. Mills (Eds.), *Politeness in East Asia* (pp. 71–97). Cambridge: Cambridge University Press. http: //dx.doi.org/10.1017/CBO9780511977886.006

Pan, Y., & Kádár, D. Z. (2011). *Politeness in historical and contemporary Chinese.* London: Continuum.

Perakyla, A. (2004). Reliability and validity in research based on naturally occurring social interaction. In D. Silverman (Ed.), *Qualitative research: Theory, method and practice* (pp. 283–304). London: Sage.

Pike K. (1990). On the emics and etics of Pike and Harris. In T. N. Headland, K. L. Pike & M. Harris (Eds.), *Emics and etics: The insider/outsider debate* (pp. 28–47).London: Sage.

Pomerantz, A. (1984). Agreeing and disagreeing with assessments: Some features of preferred/dispreferred turn shapes. In J. M. Atkinson & J. Heritage (Eds.), *Structures of social action: Studies in conversation analysis* (pp. 57–101). Cambridge: Cambridge University Press.

Potter, J., & Hepburn, A. (2005). Qualitative interviews in psychology: Problems and possibilities. *Qualitative Research in Psychology, 2*(4), 281–307. http: //dx.doi.org/10.1191/1478088705qp045oa

Raymond, G. (2003). Grammar and social organization: Yes/no interrogatives and the structure of responding. *American Sociological Review, 68*(6), 939–967. http: //dx.doi.org/10.2307/1519752

Retzinger, S. (1991). *Violent emotions shame and rage in marital quarrels.* Newbury Park: Sage. http: //dx.doi.org/10.4135/9781483325927

Rue, Y.-J., & Zhang, G. Q. (2008). *Request strategies: A comparative study in Mandarin Chinese and Korean.* Amsterdam: John Benjamins. http: //dx.doi.org/10.1075/pbns.177

Ruhi, Ş. (2007). Higher-order intentions and self-politeness in evaluations of (im)politeness: The relevance of compliment responses. *Australian Journal of Linguistics, 27*(2), 107–145. http: //dx.doi.org/10.1080/07268600701522756

Ruhi, Ş. (2009a). A place for emotions in conceptualizing face and relational work. Paper presented at the International Symposium on Face and Politeness, Griffith University, Brisbane, 10 July 2009.

Ruhi, Ş. (2009b). Evoking face in self and other-presentation in Turkish. In F. Bargiela-Chiappini & M. Haugh (Eds.), *Face, Communication and Social Interaction* (pp. 155–174). London: Equinox.

Ruhi, Ş., & Işık-Güler, H. (2007). Conceptualizing face and relational work in (im)politeness: Revelations from politeness lexemes and idioms in Turkish. *Journal of Pragmatics*, *39*(4), 681–711. http://dx.doi.org/10.1016/j.pragma.2006.11.013

Sandlund, E. (2004). *Feeling by doing: The social organisation of everyday emotions in academic talk-in-interaction* (Unpublished PhD thesis). Karlstad University, Sweden.

Schegloff, E. (1991). Reflections on talk and social structure. In D. Boden & D. H. Zimmerman (Eds.), *Talk and social structure: Studies in ethonomethodology and conversation analysis* (pp. 44–70). Cambridge: Polity Press.

Schegloff, E. (2005). On complainability. *Social Problems*, *52*(4), 449–476. http://dx.doi.org/10.1525/sp.2005.52.4.449

Schlenker, B., & Pontari, B. (2000). The strategic control of information: Impression management and self-presentation in daily life. In A. Tesser, R. Felson & J. Suls (Eds.), *Psychological Perspectives on Self and Identity* (pp. 199–232). Washington, DC: American Psychological Association. http://dx.doi.org/10.1037/10357-008

Schneider, M. J. (1985). Verbal and nonverbal indices of the communicative performance and acculturation of Chinese immigrants. *International Journal of Intercultural Relations*, *9*(3), 271–283. http://dx.doi.org/10.1016/0147-1767(85)90029-X

Scollon, R., & Wong-Scollen, S. (1991). Topic confusion in English–Asian discourse. *World Englishes*, *10*(2), 113–125. http://dx.doi.org/10.1111/j.1467-971X.1991.tb00145.x

Scollon, R., & Wong-Scollen, S. (1994). Face parameters in East–West discourse. In S. Ting-Toomey (Ed.), *The challenge of facework: Cross-cultural and interpersonal issues* (pp. 133–157). New York, NY: State University of New York Press.

Selting, M. (1994). Emphatic speech style with special focus on the prosodic signalling of heightened emotive involvement in conversation. *Journal of Pragmatics*, *22*(3–4), 375–408. http://dx.doi.org/10.1016/0378-2166(94)90116-3

Selting, M. (1996). Prosody as an activity-type distinctive cue in conversation: The case of so-called 'astonished' questions in repair initiation. In E. Couper-Kuhlen & M. Selting (Eds.), *Prosody in conversation: Interactional studies* (pp. 231–270). Cambridge: Cambridge University Press. http://dx.doi.org/10.1017/CBO9780511597862.008

Sharkey, W. (1992). Uses and responses to intentional embarrassment. *Communication Studies*, *43*(4), 257–275. http://dx.doi.org/10.1080/10510979209368377

Sharkey, W. (1997). Why would anyone want to intentionally embarrass me? In R. M. Kowalski (Ed.), *Aversive Interpersonal Behaviours* (pp. 57–90). New York: Plenum. http://dx.doi.org/10.1007/978-1-4757-9354-3_4

Shen, L. (2006). *A discourse analysis of Chinese disagreement management strategies in business negotiation settings* (Unpublished PhD dissertation). The University of Arizona, Tucson.

Spencer-Oatey, H. (2000). Rapport management: A framework for analysis. In H. Spencer-Oatey (Ed.), *Culturally speaking: Managing rapport through talk across cultures* (pp. 11–46). London: Continuum.

Spencer-Oatey, H. (2005). (Im)politeness, face and perceptions of rapport: Unpackaging their bases and interrelationships. *Journal of Politeness Research, 1*(1), 95–120. http: // dx.doi.org/10.1515/jplr.2005.1.1.95

Spencer-Oatey, H. (2007). Theories of identity and the analysis of face. *Journal of Pragmatics, 39*(4), 639–656. http: //dx.doi.org/10.1016/j.pragma.2006.12.004

Spencer-Oatey, H. (2008). *Face, (im)politeness and rapport.* In H. Spencer-Oatey (Ed.), *Culturally speaking: Culture, communication and politeness theory* (pp. 11–47). London: Continuum.

Spencer-Oatey, H. (2009). Face, identity and interactional goals. In F. Bargiela-Chiappini & M. Haugh (Eds.), *Face, communication and social interaction* (pp. 137–154). London: Equinox.

Spencer-Oatey, H., Ng, P., & Dong, L. (2008). British and Chinese reactions to compliment responses. In H. Spencer-Oatey (Ed.), *Culturally speaking: Culture, communication and politeness theory* (pp. 95–117). London: Continuum.

Spencer-Oatey, H., & Stadler, S. (2009). The global people competency framework: Competences for effective intercultural interaction. *Warwick Occasional Papers in Applied Linguistics* 3: 1–39.

Stadler, S., & Spencer-Oatey, H. (2009) Sino-British interaction in professional contexts. *Warwick Occasional Papers in Applied Linguistics* 6: 1–20.

Stewart, J. (1995). Philosophical features of social approaches to interpersonal communication. In W. Leeds-Hurwitz (Ed.), *Social approaches to communication* (pp. 23–45). New York: Guilford.

Stivers, T. (2011). Morality and question design: 'Of course' as contesting a presupposition of askability. In T. Stivers & M. Steensig (Eds.), *The morality of knowledge in conversation* (pp. 82–106). Cambridge: Cambridge University Press. http: //dx.doi.org/10.1017/CBO9780511921674.005

Stivers, T., & Enfield, N. J. (2010). A coding scheme for question-response sequences in conversation. *Journal of Pragmatics, 42*(10), 2620–2626. http: //dx.doi.org/10.1016/j.pragma.2010.04.002

Stivers, T., & Hayashi, M. (2010). Transformative answers: One way to resist a question's constraints. *Language in Society, 39*(1), 1–25. http: //dx.doi.org/10.1017/S0047404509990637

Stivers, T., Mondada, L., & Steensig, J. (2011). Knowledge, morality and affiliation in social interaction. In T. Stivers & M. Steensig (Eds.), *The morality of knowledge in conver-*

sation (pp. 1–3). Cambridge: Cambridge University Press. http: //dx.doi.org/10.1017/ CBO9780511921674.002

Su, H.-Y. (2001). Code-switching between Mandarin and Taiwanese in three telephone conversations: The negotiation of interpersonal relationships among bilingual speakers in Taiwan. *The Eighth Annual Symposium about Language and Society* (pp. 430–446). Austin, Texas.

Su, H.-Y. (2009). Code-switching in managing a face-threatening communicative task: Footing and ambiguity in conversational interaction in Taiwan. *Journal of Pragmatics, 41*(2), 372–392. http: //dx.doi.org/10.1016/j.pragma.2008.10.007

Su, L. I.-W., & Huang, S.-P. (2002). Harmonious face threatening acts and politeness: A special consideration. *National Taiwan Working Papers in Linguistics* 5: 175–202.

Sung, K. (2001). Elder respect: Exploration of ideals and forms in East Asia. *Journal of Aging Studies, 15*(1), 13–26. http: //dx.doi.org/10.1016/S0890-4065(00)00014-1

Sung, K., & Kim, B. (2009). *Respect for the elderly: Implications for human service providers.* Lanham, MD: University Press of America.

Tannen, D. (1984). *Conversational style: Analyzing talk among friends.* Norwood, NJ: Ablex.

Terkourafi, M. (2007). Toward a universal notion of face for a universal notion of cooperation. In I. Kecskes & L. Horn (Eds.), *Explorations in pragmatics: Linguistic, cognitive and intercultural aspects* (pp. 313–344). Berlin: Mouton de Gruyter.

Ting-Toomey, S. (1999). *Communicating across cultures.* New York, NY: Guilford Press.

Ting-Toomey, S. (2005). Identity negotiation theory: Crossing cultural boundaries. In W. Gudykunst (Ed.), *Theorizing about intercultural communication* (pp. 211–233). Thousand Oaks, CA: Sage.

Trinder, L., Firth, A., & Jenks, C. (2010). So presumably things have moved on since then? The interactional management of risk allegations in child contact dispute resolution. *International Journal of Law, Policy and the Family, 24*(1), 29–53. http: //dx.doi. org/10.1093/lawfam/ebp010

Walker, T., Drew, P., & Local, J. (2011). Responding indirectly. *Journal of Pragmatics, 43*(9), 2434–2451. http: //dx.doi.org/10.1016/j.pragma.2011.02.012

Watanabe, Y. (2009). *Face and power in intercultural business communication: The case of a Japanese company in Australia* (Unpublished PhD dissertation). Griffith University, Nathan, Queensland, Australia.

Watts, R. (2003). *Politeness.* Cambridge: Cambridge University Press. http: //dx.doi. org/10.1017/CBO9780511615184

Wierzbicka, A. (1996). Contrastive sociolinguistics and the theory of 'cultural scripts': Chinese vs. English. In M. Hellinger & U. Ammon (Eds.), *Contrasive Sociolinguistics* (pp. 313–344). Berlin: Mouton de Gruyter. http: //dx.doi.org/10.1515/9783110811551.313

Wu, R.-J. R. (2004). *Stance-in-talk: A conversation analysis of Mandarin final particles.* Amsterdam: John Benjamins. http: //dx.doi.org/10.1075/pbns.117

Yabuuchi, A. (2004). Face in Chinese, Japanese and U.S. American Cultures. *Journal of Asian Pacific Communication, 14*(2), 261–299. http: //dx.doi.org/10.1075/japc.14.2.05yab

Yang, K. S. (1992). Do traditional and modern values coexist in a modern Chinese society? Conference on Chinese Perspectives on Values. Taipei: Centre for Sinological Studies.

Yang, M. M.-H. (1994). *Gifts, favors and banquets: The art of social relationships in China.* Ithaca, NY: Cornell University Press.

Yang, P. (2007). Nonverbal affiliative phenomena in Mandarin Chinese conversation. *Journal of Intercultural Communication, 15*, 1–41.

Yang, P. (2010). Managing mianzi in Mandarin Chinese talk-in-interaction: A nonverbal perspective. *Semiotica, 181*, 179–223.

Yang, W. (2008). *A discourse analysis of trade negotiations* (Unpublished PhD dissertation). Hong Kong Baptist University.

Ye, Z.-D. (2004). Chinese categorization of interpersonal relationships and cultural logic of Chinese interaction: An indigenous perspective. *Intercultural Pragmatics, 1–2*, 211–230.

Yu, M.-C. (2003). On the universality of face: Evidence from Chinese compliment response behaviour. *Journal of Pragmatics, 35*(10–11), 1679–1710. http: //dx.doi.org/10.1016/S0378-2166(03)00074-2

Index

CPSIA information can be obtained at www.ICGtesting.com
Printed in the USA
BVOW06*0442110116

432011BV00003B/8/P